50¢

THE VENTURE OF PRAYER

THE VENTURE
OF PRAYER

by

HUBERT NORTHCOTT

Priest of the Community of the Resurrection

LONDON

S · P · C · K

1954

First published in 1950 by S.P.C.K.,
Reprinted 1951, 1954
Northumberland Avenue, London, W.C.2
Printed in Great Britain by
Billing and Sons Limited, Guildford and London

CONTENTS

ACKNOWLEDGEMENTS

EVEN a book on prayer has a way of shaping itself and forcing the author's hand. Nevertheless three convictions at the back of my mind decided the main outlines. The first was that a book on prayer should start with God and His Church. Obvious though that is, yet both in writing and in practice it tends to slip into the background, so that the emphasis falls on the individual and his own thoughts or feelings about God; or that the Church is introduced only as an aid in his journey instead of as the home and setting of his whole life, however solitary that may be. This involved covering ground which, many may think, might have been taken for granted, and which has certainly been better covered by others.

Secondly, it seemed to me important to stress the continuity of contemplative, or "mystical", prayer, with the more ordinary forms of prayer. The best way of doing that, I thought, was to begin at the beginning of the spiritual life and go on to the final stages. A book that either began or stopped short on the threshold of contemplation would fail to make that clear.

Thirdly, as my object was to encourage others in their prayer rather than to discuss theories, I decided I must, so far as possible, write from my own experience both as an individual, still learning to pray himself, and as a priest who has had to deal intimately with other souls. That experience includes the reading and re-reading of most of the great Catholic masters of the spiritual life during the past thirty years. Other writers have already set forth the essence of their teaching far more competently than I could hope to do.

My thanks are particularly due to the Lord Bishop of Ely for so kindly consenting to write the Preface.

My unexpected dispatch to South Africa prevented me from dealing with the business of revision and of preparing the book for publication. Therefore I owe a deeper debt of gratitude than I can ever express to my brother in Religion, Fr. Geoffrey Curtis, C.R., not only for his invaluable counsel, but still more for the trouble he has taken in seeing the book through the press. Fr. Mark Tweedy, Fr. Dominic Whitnall, Fr. George Sidebotham,

7

and Brother Barnabas Dugdale, all likewise of the Community of the Resurrection, have also been of great assistance and put me in their debt.

The book partly owes its existence to our greatly beloved and deeply revered father in Religion, Fr. Keble Talbot, C.R. As my Superior some years ago he urged me more than once to write on the subject of prayer, and later encouraged the beginnings of this book. I take this opportunity to express in regard to him above all my abiding and thankful indebtedness which has far older and deeper roots.

Acknowledgements for permission to quote are due to the following: the Cambridge University Press for quotations from Gibb and Montgomery's edition of *The Confessions of St. Augustine;* the Oxford University Press for a quotation from *Invitation to Pilgrimage*, by John Baillie; Macmillan & Co. Ltd. for a quotation from Bergson's *Two Sources;* the Lutterworth Press for a quotation from *The Mediator*, by Emil Brunner; Geoffrey Bles Ltd., Centenary Press, for a quotation from Maritain's *Redeeming the Time;* Burns, Oates, and Washbourne for quotations from *The Mistress of Vision*, by Francis Thompson, and from *My Solitude*, by Alice Meynell; the Talbot Press for the verse beginning "I see His Blood", by J. Plunkett; Jonathan Cape Limited and the Trustees of the T. E. Lawrence Estate for the quotation from *Seven Pillars of Wisdom*, by T. E. Lawrence; J. M. Dent & Sons for the quotation from *Jacopone da Todi*, by Evelyn Underhill.

St. Francis' Priory, HUBERT NORTHCOTT, C.R.
Sekukuniland.

PREFACE

In 1919, when a Chaplain in the Army of Occupation in Germany, I noticed a private who was a regular attendant at the daily Eucharist in the Church Army Hut. It was a surprise to discover that this private was Father Northcott of the Community of the Resurrection, who had enlisted in an infantry regiment. Shortly after I was demobilized; but some years later I had the privilege of attending a Retreat conducted by him. When I was asked to write a Preface to this book, I readily consented, not only because I have the honour of being Visitor to the Community of the Resurrection, but because it was a happy reminder of a meeting nearly thirty years ago.

But there is another reason. I believe that this is a book that is much needed. There are many books on prayer, and some of them valuable, but no apology is needed for this. Much is being said and written nowadays about Evangelism; and very rightly. But it is possible, amid the activity which is the popular expression of our lives in these days, that we may forget to make our foundations sure. The foundation of the evangelistic work of the Church is prayer. If, to change the metaphor, that is not the mainspring of our activity, we shall be spending our money on that which satisfieth not.

This is not only, or chiefly, a book for the clergy. Some of the greatest teachers of prayer have been lay people, men and women, and this book has the needs of the laity as well as those of the clergy in mind. It is strange that in a country like ours, which has always been suspicious of clericalism, the laity have too frequently not realized (perhaps because they have not been taught) that the life of prayer is open to them, and that God asks them to practise it.

But, as I have said, it is for the clergy also. We clergy are tempted to forget that one of our primary pastoral duties is the instruction of our people in the life of prayer. This duty is often neglected, sometimes because, as the days go on, we ourselves have become slack and neglectful; and we are painfully conscious

that we are not worthy to teach others about things of which we
are sadly ignorant.

Those who read this book, clergy and laity alike, will find in
it instructions for all. The real beginner, just realizing the un-
explored country of communion with God, will be gently led from
the elementary stages; those who have been, maybe for many
years, trying to follow the way of prayer, will find help, instruction and encouragement. The life of prayer may be described as
a pilgrimage; but no pilgrimage is easy. We do not go on pil-
grimages in luxury liners. Fr. Northcott never allows us to forget
that at every stage there are difficulties to be faced and overcome.
Everyone can make the journey, but it is a journey uphill: as we
travel, the views of the surrounding country open out before us;
but beyond the ridge we see above us, there are others still to be
surmounted. At times we are out of breath; at other times the
mists and the clouds come down. But the sun shines now and
then, and much beauty and grandeur are revealed. It may be that
the latter part of the book will not be for everyone: there are
many who can practise contemplation, but who do not, either
because they know nothing about it, or because they are too
humble to attempt it. Fr. Northcott will help these; and those
who are not called to this method of prayer will nevertheless profit
by knowing something about it.

A book which embodies the experience of men and women of
prayer through the centuries and from all parts of the Church
must of necessity deal with theological and technical terms. Fr.
Northcott does not shirk theological problems: it is impossible to
speak about God without being theological. One of our temptations to-day is to forget in our sermons and instructions this very
obvious truth. Fr. Northcott has a special gift, as it seems to me,
of explaining these theological terms by reference to the ordinary
things of life within the experience of all: but in so doing, he does
not empty them of their meaning.

Prayer is essentially individual; it is the soul's communion
with God; but this individuality must be preserved from eccen-
tricity. Throughout this book we are shown the background of
the Bible and of the teaching and worship of the Church.

But there is, I dare to say, yet more in this book. In our
reading we discover that the writer, as he leads us along the road,
knows every inch of it himself. A good teacher must not only
have sound academic knowledge of his subject; he must know

· how his knowledge fits in to everyday experience—of others as well as his own. I believe many will be helped by Fr. Northcott for this reason.

Let me add a warning: prayer cannot be learnt in five minutes, nor just by reading a book once. This book must be pondered over and read again and again; and the only way to learn how to pray is to pray, remembering that God wants us to pray and is waiting to help us.

It is not an easy book to read. No book on prayer can be easy: but all can understand. May God use this for the deepening and strengthening of the life of His Church and of His people.

Ely   EDWARD ELY

INTRODUCTION

THIS book is not a systematic or exhaustive treatise on prayer, though it traverses the whole course of the prayer life and sketches out its background. Its object is pastoral and devotional, practical rather than theoretical, and it is intended to supplement other books on prayer. It gives separate chapters to certain subjects which seemed to need such treatment, e.g. Love, the Will of God, the Dark Night, even at the risk of some repetition. It is written for all those who, whatever their stage of spiritual progress, desire to pray more and better.

The book begins with the background of the prayer life, God's purpose for the soul, and some main facts of the Christian revelation about God. God is the creator and sustainer of all, revealing Himself in nature, history, and the individual soul; a Trinity not a monad.

The Church is the home of prayer. It is the Body of Christ, the redeemed Society with its corporate life, worship, and sacraments. Certain privileges and obligations follow from our membership (Chapter III). But each member as a child of God has within the Church his own private life of prayer and discipline. Mental prayer and meditation are considered in Chapter IV.

The next two chapters treat the obstacles which confront the individual—the world, the flesh, and the devil—and the need of an adequate training (ascesis) to deal with them, and of the principles which should govern it (Chapters V and VI).

The value of modern psychology and the question of how far it modifies or reaffirms the old teaching, and especially its insistence on the need of self-knowledge, of a full personality, and of a "master-sentiment", are treated in Chapter VII. Chapter VIII is on the prayer of Intercession.

The meaning of Christian love with its relation to sexual passion (cf. Soloviev), and the loving of self for God's sake and of one's neighbour as oneself, comprises Chapter IX.

This leads up to a chapter on the theory of contemplative prayer.

The next four chapters deal with the beginnings of the Prayer of Contemplation and its development, its marks, and some counsels for contemplatives (Chapters X–XIII). As this prayer leads to a more complete surrender to the Will of God, a further chapter concerns the Will of God (Chapter XIV).

Some of the essential features of the Dark Night, which forms a large part of contemplation, are studied in Chapter XV. The last two chapters deal with Reparation and the final flowering of Contemplative Prayer, the Spiritual Marriage and five of its characteristics.

PART I

Regnum coelorum violenza pate
   da caldo amore e da viva speranza
   che vince la divina volontate;
Non a guisa che l'uomo all'uom sopranza,
   ma vince lei perchè vuole esser vinta,
   e vinta vince con sua beninanza.

              Dante. *Paradiso* xx, 94-99.

          ... Fervent love,
And lively hope, with violence assail
The Kingdom of the Heavens, and overcome
The will of the most High; not in such sort
As man prevails o'er man; but conquers it,
Because 'tis willing to be conquered; still,
Though conquered, by its mercy conquering.

              trans. H. F. Cary.

CHAPTER I

THE PEOPLE AND THE COVENANT

"WHAT is man," cried the psalmist, "that thou art mindful of him?" (Ps. 8. 4.) Throughout the ages men have puzzled over the question of man's origin and destiny. A deep pessimism has marked the majority of their answers. The Emperor Marcus Aurelius declared: "The time of a man's life is a point, the substance of it ever flowing, the sense obscure, and the whole composition of the body tending to corruption. His soul is restless, fortune uncertain, and fame doubtful; to be brief, as a stream so are all things belonging to the body; as a dream, or as a smoke, so are all that belong unto the soul. Our life is a warfare, and a mere pilgrimage" (*Meditations* 2. 15). Therefore the only refuge for man lay in philosophy, which would enable him to bear everything contentedly, and "above all things to expect death". We are, it may be, still more familiar with a similar estimate of man, couched in far more moving terms by the author of the Book of Wisdom (Ch. 2), summing up the views of the "ungodly men". But if their estimate of man was much the same as the Emperor's, they proposed a very different remedy from philosophy.

Other men, intoxicated with the development of scientific knowledge and an awakened interest in man himself, dreamed of mankind carried forward by some law of inevitable progress, though they did not stop to ask themselves whither progress would take them. The events of the present century have shattered all such dreams. Men realize that the increase of knowledge has created monsters which they can only partially control, modern robots which threaten to exterminate their inventors.

R. L. Stevenson in his essay *Pulvis et Umbra* perhaps sums up the world's attitude towards the psalmist's question. He represents man as a strange incomprehensible creature, battling against enormous obstacles, clinging for no clear reason to the thought of duty as the one guiding light. There seems no prospect of success

B   17

or final happiness in all this, yet the author ends with a faint hope that surely it will not be wholly in vain.

Contrasted with all such speculations about man, the psalmist's cry is full of light. It reveals that he had realized man's true significance. Man's worth lies not in the possession of any particular virtues or knowledge, but in the fact that God is mindful of him. The psalmist is as aware as Marcus Aurelius of man's limitations and transitoriness, but in spite of it all man has infinite value because he is precious in the eyes of God. His cry is a cry of amazed and adoring thankfulness.

The psalmist believed in common with every other member of his race that God had a purpose of infinite love and mercy towards man, and that He had chosen out the people of Israel and established a covenant with them for the accomplishment of that purpose. The Bible contains the story of that covenant relationship. (It would be more accurate to speak of the Old Covenant and the New Covenant instead of the Old Testament and the New Testament. The word "testament" suggests a legacy or the making of a will rather than a solemn agreement or covenant between two parties. All through the Bible story we are concerned with such a covenant.)

However, at first the covenant was a peculiar one. For it did not take the form of an agreement between two contracting parties, in which each party pledges itself to fulfil certain conditions provided that the other party fulfils its side of the contract. The first mention of the covenant is given in Genesis 9. 9. It occurs after man's fall from grace. Noah, we are told, was a " righteous man and perfect in his generations. Noah walked with God " (Gen. 6. 9). Therefore God to save him and his from destruction gave him certain commands, which he fulfilled. God then " established " His covenant with him and with every living creature. No conditions were attached, but only a promise that never again should there be a flood to destroy the earth. It proclaimed God's care for man and the sacredness of human life.

Later on God renewed the covenant with Abraham. As before, it followed an act of obedience on man's side. At God's bidding Abraham had left his home and kindred. Then one awe-ful night, after the patriarch had prepared materials for a sacrifice, " behold, a smoking furnace, and a flaming torch that passed between the pieces " (Gen. 15. 17). And there " the Lord made a covenant with Abram ". But again no conditions were made. It contained simply a divine promise: " Unto thy seed have I given this land." But subsequently conditions were attached. They were two: (1) " Walk before me, and be thou perfect." (2) Every male must be circumcised as a token of the covenant (Gen. 17). This covenant meant that God took Abraham and his seed under his particular providence and promised to be their God. They for their part must accept Him as their God and dedicate themselves wholly to Him.

Once again God renewed His covenant with Israel, this time to Moses on Mount Sinai (Exod. 19). Through Moses for the first time it assumes the form of a true covenant, i.e. of a contract between two parties, solemnized by a religious ceremony. Moses ordered an altar to be built and sacrifice to be offered. Then he read to the people God's conditions, which they accepted. Moses thereupon sprinkled them with the blood of the sacrifice, saying, " Behold the blood of the covenant which the Lord hath made with you " (Exod. 24).

In these three accounts of God's covenant with man, four lessons stand out clearly:

. (1) God maintains an unalterable purpose of love for man whom He has created. It is essentially redemptive and it includes the whole of mankind in its embrace. The promise made to Noah was quite general in its terms: it applied to " all flesh ". The promise to Abraham concerned in the first place only Abraham himself and his descendants. But these would be multitudinous in number, and furthermore " all the nations of the earth shall be blessed in him " (Gen. 18. 18).

(2) Although the covenant is with the nation, and the blessings promised are for the nation and ultimately for the whole world, yet God acts through individuals. In each case the individual seems to be chosen not because he represents his people, but rather because he differs so much from them. Again, in the fulfilling of the covenant, the rite of circumcision and the demand for moral

uprightness lay a special emphasis on the individual. There is no
salvation by proxy or *en masse*. The world is to be saved through
an elect race, but each member has his own part to play and his
own value in the sight of God.

(3) The covenant is the reward of heroic ventures of faith and
obedience on the part of individuals. At a moment when all
seemed well on the earth, when people were " eating and drinking,
marrying and giving in marriage ", Noah was bidden to prepare
the ark; and he obeyed. " By faith Abraham, when he was called,
obeyed to go out unto a place which he was to receive for an
inheritance; and he went out, not knowing whither he went "
(Heb. 11. 8). " By faith Moses . . . refused to be called the son of
Pharaoh's daughter, choosing rather to be evil entreated with the
people of God . . . By faith he forsook Egypt, not fearing the
wrath of the king: for he endured, as seeing him who is invisible."
(Ibid, vv. 24, 27.)

(4) God's promise to Abraham looked down through the ages.
It envisaged a long process. At the moment there was nothing.
Abraham was old and he had no heir to carry on his name and
raise up seed after him. Again at the ratification of the covenant
with Moses there was no prospect of an immediate fulfilment of
the divine promises. The possession of the promised land seemed
more hopeless than ever. Moses and his people could but accept
God's word and go forward in faith.

The rest of the Bible contains the story of God's unvarying
faithfulness to His covenant (this is partly what is meant by His
" righteousness "), and of the Israelites' continual failure to observe
it. Israel beyond all possibility of return forfeited whatever claims
they had on God's goodness and forbearance. Then came the
crowning act of His love in sending His only Son to redeem
mankind and form the New Israel. Still, as before, the divine
purpose embraces the whole human race. Jesus Christ is the new
Adam. But still, as before, God's mercy is mediated to the world
through an elect people, His Church. As before, each member
must submit to a rite of initiation. Still, as before, and even more
urgently than before, there is the demand made upon each for
holiness and moral perfection. But this time, through the rite,
grace is given and the indwelling of God Himself to enable each to

reach that perfection and keep the covenant. The true promised land, the Kingdom of Heaven, has taken the place of Canaan, " an inheritance incorruptible, and undefiled, and that fadeth not away, reserved in heaven for you " (1 Pet. 1. 4); reserved in heaven for the full enjoyment thereof, but nevertheless entered already here and now.

Thus the covenant relation between God and His people is deeply embedded in the Christian Faith. When our Lord on the eve of His Passion gathered up His whole work of redemption in one symbolic and representative act at the Last Supper, He spoke of it expressly as the " New Covenant " But this new covenant was the fulfilment, not the abrogation, of the old. The old covenant was the shadow, here was the substance. In Jesus Christ is the realization of the promises which God had made to Israel, and through Israel to the whole world. We have to a large extent lost sight to-day of this covenant relationship and its continuity in the gospel. Centuries of individualism have concentrated attention on God's dealings with each single soul. It is imperative to see the individual in the wider setting. God's redemptive purpose embraces the whole world and it is mediated through the Church, which is the Body of Christ. The Old Testament is occupied mainly with God's relations with the chosen people as a unit, and the people as a unit stand or fall together. Nevertheless the individual even here has his place. All the way through God deals also with individual souls, and through them He teaches and leads His people. Abraham and Moses were real persons, not national symbols, and the Bible describes an amazing intimacy and individuality in their relations with God. If at first the individual often seems identified with the nation, from the time of Jeremiah onwards the sense of individual responsibility to the claims of God grows increasingly prominent. Jeremiah showed himself acutely conscious of his apartness from his fellow-countrymen, and of his own life with God, even though at the same time he is identified with them both in their spiritual inheritance and in their temporal misfortunes.

A book on prayer must perforce deal mainly with the individual and his response to God's call. It is all the more necessary, therefore, at the beginning to insist on this universal character of the divine purpose. The individual's life of prayer can only grow safely provided that he realizes this wider context and sees himself as but one of a multitude that no man can number, as but one of the elect people of God, the Body of Christ, as but part of God's instrument for the gathering of the whole world into the Kingdom of Heaven.

The process of salvation is still a long one as it was for the patriarchs. They indeed could only greet the promises from afar, whilst for us they have been fulfilled in Christ Jesus. Nevertheless each member of Christ has to " work out his own salvation with fear and trembling " in Christ. St. Paul sums up the process in one sentence: " Whom he foreknew, he also fore-ordained to be conformed to the image of his son . . . and whom he fore-ordained, them also he called; and whom he called, them also he justified: and whom he justified, them also he glorified." (Rom. 8. 29 f.) It is the process of " sanctification ", only to be completed in the life beyond, and for most people the way is a long and painful one. So St. Paul himself found it (cf. Rom. 7: Phil. 3: 2 Tim. 4).

The question arises: if we are the people of the covenant, if in Christ we inherit the promises of God to His people, what does this special relationship with God mean? God promised Abraham " to be a God unto thee " (Gen. 17. 7). The Mosaic covenant expands that promise: " I will walk among you and will be your God, and ye shall be my people." (Lev. 26. 12.) In the darkest days of Israel's history the prophets held it forth repeatedly as a beacon light to cheer and guide the nation (cf. Jer. 31. 33: Ezek. 11. 20: Zech. 8. 8). The New Covenant has made that promise both a realized fact and a hope for the future. Our Lord told His disciples, " If a man love me, he will keep my word: and my Father will love him, and we will come unto him and make our abode with him." (Jn. 14. 23.) St. Paul reminds the Corinthians that that has become an accomplished fact for the Christian: " We are a temple of the living God; even as God said, I will dwell in them, and walk in them; and I will be their God, and they shall be my people." (2 Cor. 6. 16.) The author of the Apocalypse sees the holy city coming down out of heaven and hears a great voice saying, " Behold the tabernacle of God is with men and he shall dwell with them, and they shall be his people and God himself shall be with them, and be their God." (Rev. 21. 3.)

Clearly then the essence of the covenant lies in God's action in choosing the people of Israel as His own and in pledging Himself to dwell with them and be their God. God is ever faithful, and it is His eternal purpose that His people should enjoy this fellowship with Him. For that they were created. Sin ruined their capacity to respond. Therefore He redeems them " with a mighty hand and outstretched arm ", and purges each soul that it may be capable of this mysterious intimacy with its Creator. The Bible gives us adumbrations of what is involved in the indwelling of God in His people, of the requirements it lays upon them, and of the privileges which it brings to them in some measure now, to be enjoyed fully in the next world. The first requirement is summed up in the demand for holiness: " Be ye holy even as I am holy." Holy, first because the people are God's chosen, set apart for His habitation: holy again, because only the sinless can thus dwell with God. But something further is involved.

(1) To dwell with God means to love God. Fear of the deity is common to all religions. When did Israel learn that love must have the first place? We cannot say. It goes far back in their history and appears in the Mosaic covenant: " Hear O Israel: the Lord thy God is one Lord: and thou shalt love the Lord thy God with all thine heart, and with all thy soul, and with all thy might." (Deut. 6. 4 f.) But the Old Testament does not harp much on this theme. It occurs sporadically, e.g. in the psalms, " I will love thee, O Lord my strength " (Ps. 18. 1), and the psalmist speaks frequently of love for the law of God, e.g. " My delight shall be in thy commandments which I have loved "; " Lord, what love have I unto thy law "; " I love thy commandments above gold and precious stone." (Ps. 119. 47, 97, 127.) The writers preferred to enlarge upon God's love for Israel, and of that some never tire of speaking. One of the most striking developments in the New Testament lies in the prominence given by our Lord to man's love for God in Christ. He takes up the first and great commandment, " Thou shalt love the Lord thy God ", etc. (making one significant addition, " with all thy mind "). Further, He gives special prominence to the commandment, " Thou shalt love thy neighbour as thyself ", which He says is " like unto the first ". To love God entails trying to please Him, to do His will, to love what He loves. God loves our neighbour as He loves us. That is why the second commandment is " like unto the first ", not as an alternative to it,

but as part of its fulfilment.   But we shall return to this subject later in the book.

(2) To dwell with God means also to know Him in some measure at least, not merely to know about Him, but to know Him with that mutual knowledge which can only exist between persons. The prophet Jeremiah proclaimed it in words of inspiring beauty: " This is the covenant that I will make with the house of Israel after those days, saïth the Lord; I will put my law in their inward parts, and in their heart will I write it; and I will be their God, and they shall be my people; and they shall teach no more every man his neighbour and every man his brother, saying, Know the Lord: for they shall all know me, from the least unto the greatest of them, saith the Lord: for I will forgive their iniquity and their sin will I remember no more." (Jer. 31. 33, 34.)   Something of the possibilities of that knowledge of God had been vouchsafed to Moses.   His relation with God was the nearest approach man had known to the days of innocence when God had walked and talked with Adam in the garden of Eden.   Through the ages the Israelites looked back to it with awe and longing.   " The Lord spake unto Moses face to face as a man speaketh unto his friend." (Exod. 33. 11.)   Only under the New Covenant would such intimacy again become possible.   Our Lord heralds it in His words to His disciples, " Ye are my friends, if ye do the things which I command you. No longer do I call you servants; for the servant knoweth not what his Lord doeth: but I have called you friends" (Jn. 15. 14, 15), and that intimacy with God, He declared, is vital: " This is life eternal, that they should know thee the only true God, and him whom thou hast sent, even Jesus Christ." (Jn. 17. 3.)

(3) To dwell with God means (eventually) to see God face to face.   It is strange how the thought of the vision of God haunted men through the centuries.   Moses talked with God " face to face ".   Yet even Moses longed for a still clearer vision: " Shew me, I pray thee, thy glory."   The answer came, " Thou canst not see my face: for man shall not see me and live " (Exod. 33. 18, 20). Men came to recognize in the vision of God the fullest realization of their covenant relationship with God.   " My soul is athirst for God, yea even for the living God.   When shall I come to appear before the presence of God? " (Ps. 42. 2.)   " Thus have I looked for thee in holiness: that I might behold thy power and glory."

(Ps. 63. 3.) The desire persisted although men believed that to see God brought death to sinful man. The note of fear bursts from the lips of Isaiah in the moment of his vision: "Woe is me for I am undone, because I am a man of unclean lips and dwell in the midst of a people of unclean lips: for mine eyes have seen the king, the Lord of hosts." (Isa. 6. 5.) Nevertheless the hope lifted men above the miseries of their actual state and helped them to look beyond them, even beyond death itself, to the moment when they would see God face to face. It comforted Job in the midst of his misfortunes. His tortured soul looked beyond them all, beyond the apparent hopelessness of his lot, to that vision of God, which was the crown of human happiness. "Yet from my flesh shall I see God: whom I shall see for myself, and mine eyes shall behold" (Job 19. 26, 27).

Even so it remained the dim distant dream of the few. Our Lord's coming brought its realization within the range of all, some vision of God here in this world, the unclouded vision in the world beyond. "He that hath seen me hath seen the Father" (Jn. 14. 9). "Blessed are the pure in heart for they shall see God." (Matt. 5. 8.) For His disciples a glad certainty takes the place of the old tremulous yearning: "Now we see in a mirror darkly; but then face to face" (1 Cor. 13. 12). "We know that . . . we shall be like him, for we shall see him as he is." (1 Jn. 3. 2.) "His servants shall do him service, and they shall see his face and his name shall be on their foreheads." (Rev. 22. 3, 4.)

Thus the Bible's answer and the Church's answer to the psalmist's question, "What is man?" stands out with bracing clarity amid all pagan philosophies. Man is a creature made by God and dependent upon Him, created for union with God Himself. In becoming a member of the chosen people, the new Israel, the Church, he is drawn into a covenant relation with God of a peculiar intimacy, with a part to play in the divine purpose for the world. The whole meaning of his life and his complete happiness lies in this union with God, in this sharing in the beloved community's vision of God. It involves knowing, loving, serving, and seeing God.

If the goal of human life is this vision of God, knowing and loving God, if this be God's gracious purpose for man, then prayer must occupy a considerable place in his life. For prayer is in essence just personal communion with God. But like the patriarchs of the old covenant the beginner must make the venture of faith, launching out into the unknown country of prayer, though at first it seems to offer nothing at all commensurate with the sacrifices demanded.

As his prayer grows, he realizes a little better the inestimable richness of his lot, of his inheritance with the saints, of his call to this amazing friendship with God. Further still, he becomes conscious of the rhythm of the divine will, that will of perfect love, embracing the whole universe, and working for the happiness of each single creature. If this teaches him his own insignificance, at the same time it fills him with an overmastering desire, as he feels himself caught in the stream of God's love. He yearns both to give himself as completely as he can to play his part in this cosmic plan, and also to pierce through the veils that still hide God from him and see Him face to face.

But who is God? What has He revealed to us about Himself?

CHAPTER II

CONCERNING GOD

A BOOK on prayer rightly begins with God. God the Almighty, the All-Wise, the All-Loving, the Eternal, Life Himself, has made us for union with Himself. A very natural desire exists in many people, and it is more than mere curiosity, to have known some of the great characters in history, e.g. Julius Caesar, Shakespeare, Napoleon or, it may be, some living person who figures largely in the world to-day. But what must it be to know Him, who made them all, who held their destiny in His hand, and who is still the same to-day! Or again, we know persons whom we love greatly for their characters, their charm, their wit, their goodness. But what must it be to know God who created them, and to find that their lovableness is but the palest of pale reflections of the divine beauty!

The prospect of seeing God does not greatly attract men in this present age, not even many of those who believe in Him and wish to serve Him. They do not look beyond the service of their fellows, with a hope of everlasting life in the perfected society of heaven. They might appreciate the first half of St. Irenaeus's well-known epigram, "The glory of God is a living man", but the second half, "and the life of man is the vision of God", would leave them bewildered. Is it not because the idea of God conveys so little to them? In earlier days men seem to have been wiser. Even if their own lives showed small respect for God's command-ments, at least they knew that to know and love God and at last to see Him was the supreme aim of life. The men and women they prized most highly were those who seemed to have advanced furthest towards this. Then, they flocked to see a saint or venerate his relics in the same way as people to-day flock to see a film-star or collect souvenirs. The difference is significant and disturbing.

To attempt to set forth in these pages the attractiveness of God would be a hopeless task, more hopeless than that of the lover trying to describe the charms of his beloved. But there is a difference. The lover may easily be mistaken in his beloved, as his friends may well know. But God is *ex hypothesi* all and more than all we could say or think. It is not that we are at fault, but that the reality so far outsoars both imagination and words. St. Paul declares that in his moment of clearest vision he heard " unspeakable words " (2 Cor. 12. 4). So St. Thomas Aquinas is said to have left his *Summa* unfinished owing to the vision he had seen, which made all attempts to write seem useless. So Dante tried to understand the vision vouchsafed to him, but " the flight was not for my wing ". The unknown author of the *Mirror of Simple Souls* also gave up the attempt in despair: " All that may be said of God or written, or in the heart may be thought, that to which the greatest sayings attain, it is more gabbings than it is true sayings." (Div. 15.) Nevertheless we may at least set down certain facts about God which form the basis for such experiences. It is of the highest importance to meditate often on the Being of God and His attributes. To those far advanced in prayer it becomes their one absorbing occupation. But long before such a stage is reached there is need for some consideration of it. We must have some knowledge of a person before we can love him, and even though, as friendship grows, love penetrates where knowledge cannot come, it is knowledge which must lead to the threshold. Knowledge and love indeed go hand in hand, each playing its part and enriching one another in that mysterious work of the union of soul with soul. That is equally true of the still more mysterious business of the union of the soul with God. It must suffice for our purpose here to call attention to four facts about God, of which the great masters of prayer never weary of telling.

(1) God is the Creator of all that is made, and He created it out of nothing. All things, therefore, are in Him, depend on Him, and owe to Him whatever reality they have. Some of the mystics say daring things about this, that God *is* all things, but even their most daring statements must be sharply distinguished from similar utterances of the pantheist. Their emphasis is on God the Creator, the transcendent One, immanent indeed in His creation but in no way part of it. The Bible opens with the story of creation, content to take over largely current accounts of the beginning of the world, but revolutionizing them by the emphasis laid on the fact that it was God who brought it all into being out

of nothing. Each subsequent revelation, whether it be to Moses, or to the prophets, or to the psalmists, stresses His otherness, His completeness, and His mysteriousness: " All the nations are as nothing before him: they are counted to him less than nothing and vanity. To whom then will ye liken God? It is he that sitteth upon the circle of the earth, and the inhabitants thereof are as grasshoppers; that stretcheth out the heavens as a curtain, and spreadeth them out as a tent to dwell in: that bringeth princes to nothing; he maketh the judges of the earth as vanity. . . . Lift up your eyes on high, and see who hath created these, that bringeth out their hosts by number: he calleth them all by name; by the greatness of his might, and for that he is strong in power, not one is lacking." (Isa. 40.) In the last book of the Bible St. John the Divine records a veiled vision of One seated on a throne set in heaven, only to be described in symbols, whilst around Him all creation gathers in worship—not only the living creatures and the elders and angels, " ten thousand times ten thousand and thousands of thousands ", but " every created thing which is in the heaven and on the earth and under the earth, and on the sea and all things that are in them" (Rev. 5). The message is the same—the All-Great, utterly transcendent God, Creator of all, and all creation acknowledges His lordship. " All things were made by Him, and without Him was not anything made that hath been made." (Jn. 1. 3.)

Throughout the ages the saints take up the theme, each trying to express in his own way the wonder of God. Their writings make clear that they are not merely repeating a theory which satisfies their intellect, but that they are dealing with a vivid personal experience. It comes ever fresh to them, satisfies their whole being, yet passes utterly their comprehension, let alone their powers of description, though attempt to describe it they must. Take, for instance, perhaps the most familiar of such attempts, and that by a master of self-expression, St. Augustine of Hippo. He utters a string of staccato sentences, superlatives, antitheses, and paradoxes, rendered most impressive by their very incompleteness, and adumbrating a reality as fascinating as it is tremendous: " What, therefore, is my God? What, I ask, except the Lord God? For who is Lord except the Lord? Or who is God except our God? Highest, best, most mighty, most all-mighty, most merciful yet most just, most hidden yet most present, most beautiful yet most strong, stable yet incomprehensible, unchangeable yet changing all, never new, never old, making all new, yet making the proud decay and they know it not; ever toiling, ever at rest, gathering though lacking not, supporting, filling, shielding, creating, nourishing, and bringing to perfection, seeking though in want of nothing. . . . And what have I now said, my God, my life, my holy delight, or what does anyone say when he speaks of Thee? Yet woe to them that say nothing of Thee, since those who say most are no better than dumb."[1]

The student may find in such passages traces of the Neoplatonist, Plotinus; still more in those where the saint speaks of the beauty of God. But they all bear witness to a more vivid personal experience of God and a richer knowledge of Him than ever was granted to the pagan. Indeed, where the resemblance in form to the ideas or language of the Neoplatonists is closest, just there the spiritual content differs most strikingly. St. Augustine probably learnt from them to think of the beauty of God, for the Greeks worshipped Beauty as they worshipped nothing else. But with him it has become a spiritual reality—God Himself revealed to him, not merely as the " Form " of all visible things nor guessed at as the author of so much created beauty, but as the living Personal God, with whom he has loving communion. Throughout the Church's history the saints are enthralled by that beauty of God, and, as they try to speak of it, their faltering words bear witness again to the freshness and reality of their own experience. Whatever may have caused their conversions at first, what holds them is not God's greatness nor His awfulness but His marvellous attractiveness, His beauty. " They asked the Lover ", wrote Ramon Lull, " where his love first began. And he replied: ' It began in the glory of my Beloved; and from that beginning I was led to love my neighbour even as myself and to cease to care for deception and falsehood.' "[2] St. Augustine's well-known cry in the Confessions loses nothing of its freshness and intensity through being quoted so often: " Too late have I loved Thee, O Beauty, so ancient yet ever new, too late have I loved Thee! Lo! Thou wast within and I without, and there I misshapen was rushing in search of Thee amidst those lovely shapes which Thou hadst formed. Thou wast with me and I was not with Thee. . . . Thou didst call,

---

[1] *Confessions*, I. 4. From Gibb and Montgomery's edition. (Cambridge, 1908.)
[2] *Book of the Lover and the Beloved*, trans. by Allison Peers, sec. 61.

shout, shatter my deafness: Thou didst flash, shine, scatter my
blindness. And I drew in my breath and I pant for Thee, I tasted
thee and I hunger and thirst. Thou didst touch me, and I burned
for Thy peace."[1] It is a far cry from St. Augustine to the Blessed
Angela of Foligno, but she too stands in the line of saints with
their perception of God as the All-Beautiful. She attempts to
describe a vision, but she can only stammer out vague phrases
about seeing a " fulness " and a beauty which satisfied her whole
being, though she cannot describe it: " I saw nothing bodily, but
there was, just as it is in heaven, such beauty that I cannot say
anything else except that I saw Supreme Beauty, containing all
good. And all the saints stood praising that glorious Beauty."[2]
We can leap the centuries again and find such a saint as St. John
of the Cross also trying to speak his praise of that glorious beauty.
Something of the intensity of his own experience breaks through
even the carefully weighed phrases of the theologian: " All the
beauty of the creatures, compared with the infinite beauty of God,
is the height of deformity. . . . Thus the soul that is affectioned
to the beauty of any creature is as the height of deformity in the
eyes of God . . . and all the grace and beauty of the creatures,
compared with the grace of God, is the height of misery and of
unattractiveness. Wherefore the soul that is ravished by the graces
and beauties of the creatures has only supreme misery and
unattractiveness in the eyes of God; and thus it cannot be capable
of the infinite grace and loveliness of God."[3] Those words of
St. John of the Cross have a special importance. They express
the considered judgement of one who was himself a great poet.
It may be true that all mystics are in some measure poets, but not
many of them have won so high a place amongst poets as he.
He therefore could and did appreciate to the full the appeal of
sensuous beauty. His poems and his life bear ample witness to
this. It was in the woods and in the moonlight that he seemed
to find a special delight in praying. So far created beauty was
to him an avenue to God. This makes all the more impressive
his apparent depreciation of the " beauty of the creatures ". Yet
he is far from denying that beauty. He only says that " compared
with the infinite beauty of God it is the height of deformity ". It
is the argument from the less to the greater. If created beauty, as

[1] *Confessions*, X. 27.
[2] *Visiones*, Ch. XXI.
[3] *Ascent of Mount Carmel*, I, 4.

we know it, is so enthralling, what must the beauty of God who created it be like? And he speaks as one who has had some glimpses of it vouchsafed to him. He once asked one of his penitents: "Wherein does your prayer consist?" The answer came: "In considering the Beauty of God, and in rejoicing that He has such beauty."[1]

Again, St. John's words mark the almost infinite chasm that separates the Christian mystic from what is called "Nature-mysticism". When Keats cried:

"Beauty is truth, truth beauty—that is all
Ye know on earth, and all ye need to know,"

he meant that sensuous beauty was for him ultimate Reality, and that there was no need to seek further. St. John of the Cross could have said the same words, but he would have meant just the opposite. He would rather have said Truth is beauty: the ultimate Reality, God Himself, is perfect Beauty and to know God is all that one need know. But, until one has found Him, one does not begin to know what beauty really is. The only way to catch the vision of the Truth is to learn complete detachment from sensuous beauty.

Indeed, the weakness of the nature-mystic lies precisely in the fact that he is content to take the beauty of Nature at its face value, and not to look further. Wordsworth was aware of a spirit "subtly interfused" with it all. He found his satisfaction in a kind of merging of self with that spirit. Even his teaching has a pantheistic strain, though he had a deeper belief in God than many of his fellow-poets. St. John of the Cross, on the other hand, with a sense of beauty equal to Wordsworth's, stresses the utter transcendence of God. God is the wholly Other, the alone perfect Beauty. St. John speaks for all the great Catholic mystics.

(2) The second fact about God is that He wills to reveal Himself to man. The cry of the saint, so often repeated through the ages, "Verily, Thou art a God that hidest Thyself", does not contradict this. The saint himself would be the first to say that it is the very fulness of the divine self-revelation that causes the cry.

[1] Quoted E. Underhill, *Worship*, p. 5. (London, Nisbet, 1937.)

He is blinded by excess of light, as the natural eye is blinded by the midday sun. Old writers loved to speak of the "ladder" of creation by which man could ascend to God. We need not try to climb that ladder here, rung by rung, but we may call attention to the three main channels through which God has revealed Himself.

(a) There is Nature, the created world, all bearing the impress of its Creator, eloquent of God for those who are touched with His grace. Yet how strangely baffling it can be. Never does God, even through the most perfect of His creatures or the most wonderful of His works, make His self-revelation here unmistakable. And even where faith has pierced the veil and found God, the soul becomes still more acutely aware of depths and depths beyond. "Verily, Thou art a God that hidest Thyself." Yet all that does not excuse man for failing to find God in His creation. As St. Paul said: "For the invisible things of him since the creation of the world are clearly seen, being perceived through the things that are made, even his everlasting power and divinity; that they may be without excuse: because that, knowing God, they glorified him not as God, neither gave thanks" (Rom. 1. 20).

(b) God reveals Himself through history—the story of His dealings with men and nations. Here the revelation at first sight seems more baffling still. Men continually ask whether there is any purpose in history at all. It is interesting that the most important attempt in recent years to answer that question emanates from a Jew, Karl Marx, in his theory of dialectics; although he entirely failed to see the true principle of the dialectic of history. For the Jews stand forth as God's chosen people to be the home of His self-revelation and witness to the world of His might. They learnt to see that revelation in the working out of their national destiny. Yet even so they misread the message, although a long line of prophets tried to interpret it to them. The Old Testament spells out the story through the ages, shows God's shepherding of His people in spite of their unfaithfulness, preparing them for His final revelation in Jesus Christ. It is in the story of the Jewish people that His methods of revelation must be studied. Two main principles seem to emerge, which here we can only mention. One is the principle of election—the selection of one particular race to be the focus of His revelation and the means

c

for the propagation of His truth throughout the ages. No other race can take from the Jews the honour of being entrusted with this, though their function has now passed to the Holy Catholic Church. And still God selects groups and individuals through whom to reveal Himself and His will.

The second principle is that the divine judgements work themselves out in some sense automatically. It remains true for nations as for individuals that "whatsoever a man soweth, that shall he reap". "Penalty", Professor Maritain has said, "is—in the moral order itself—the fruit of the wound inflicted on a being through his own freedom voluntarily at fault, and this natural fruit *is* the satisfaction of the law. The penalty is the working out of the fault; our punishment is our choice. It is terrible to fall into the hands of the living God, for those hands give to each man what his will has settled on."[1] According to the Marxian dialectic, history reveals mankind staggering through the centuries like a drunken man, plunging first on one side of the road then on the other. Truth lies in the middle and man in his efforts to reach it stumbles into some excess. That leads to reaction. But the reaction is too violent and there is excess in the other direction. Other political theorists have pointed out how nations seem to run through a cycle of government—monarchy degraded into despotism leads to reaction. An aristocracy, it may be, takes the place of the sovereign. That again causes reaction and democracy takes its place, leading to some still more communistic form. Chaos comes, and once again the strong hand returns in the shape of a military dictator, who sets up a dynasty. Karl Marx, however, saw something more in this than a never-ending cycle. The reactions become closer approximations to the truth and at last the true government will triumph—the reign of the proletariat. It is the old Jewish theocracy—the reign of the people of God, only he has left out God.

We are not concerned with an estimate of Marxism. But at least it shows history's judgement on human error and wilfulness. They bring their own reward. God does not need to manifest His decisions by special providences. Yet, on the other hand, the Old Testament shows His patience and graciousness towards His people in spite of their unfaithfulness.

[1] *Redeeming the Time*, p. 133. (G. Bles, Centenary Press, 1943.)

Nevertheless the picture remains a puzzling one, even as we look at it through the ages and in the light of the prophets' vision. What are we to say of the state of the world to-day? Who will read its riddle? Doubtless God still sends His prophets to interpret the meaning of His providence, but do we recognize or understand His messengers?

From one point of view the work of prophets is no longer so necessary, for in Jesus Christ God has made His final and complete revelation of Himself. In Him God revealed both His own character, that of His only begotten Son, " full of grace and truth ", and also the ultimate meaning of history and of man's blindness.

(c) Finally, God by His Holy Spirit reveals Himself to the individual soul. It is the special gift of our Lord to His Church, though the Holy Spirit is at work throughout the world and is not limited in His action. The subject of inspirations will be dealt with later in this book.[1] The methods of such revelation are manifold; some of them, such as visions and locutions, belong to the realm of the extraordinary. But to all who seek Him is given grace to recognize His presence and to know those things which are congruous to Him, the things which they must do if they would know Him better and understand His other self-revelations. What is important to remember is that this revelation of God within the soul cannot be isolated from those other revelations of which we have been thinking. Throughout the ages men and women have imagined that the individual soul can depend solely on its own interpretation of the divine action within itself—apart from its action within the Church or the world at large. Such isolation leads inevitably to disaster. For God does not contradict Himself. In the seventeenth century George Fox, convinced of the Holy Spirit's presence within him, gave himself wholly and generously to follow what he believed to be His guidance, irrespective of the Church's voice. It led him to reject God's revelation through His Church and to found a sect of his own. The third Person of the Blessed Trinity occupied an almost exclusive position in his theology. His own single-minded devotion saved him from the aberrations into which many of his disciples fell, but his teaching caused a grievous and lasting breach in the Church. Similarly, in the early days of the Church's history, the Montanists attempted to

[1] See p. 236.

establish a religion of the Spirit, relying wholly on individual inspiration. Ever since then such individualism has been a recurring menace to the stability of souls and the unity of the Catholic Church.

However, any revelation of the Eternal God to mortal man must be fraught with danger. It must come to him as a challenge to rise beyond the limits of the created world to union with God Himself. The unknown author of the *Mirror of Simple Souls* speaks truly, if quaintly, when he says that the soul drawn to contemplation is then " dangerous, noble, and delicious " (p. 255). Belief in a God who has revealed, and is continually revealing Himself, keeps the soul throbbing with life and expectation. It is condemned to no static condition, contemplating a past fact or a motionless monad. If God is *semper quietus* he is also *semper agens*, and His people must be always watchful for His coming, ready to respond. Our Lord's message contains a note of urgency, almost of strain: " Watch, for ye know not on what day your Lord cometh." " Therefore be ye also ready" (Matt. 24. 42, 44). That message is much more than an admonition to prepare for the Day of Judgement. It teaches the right attitude of the Christian towards God who reveals Himself. He must be watchful to read the signs of the times, watchful to find God in His creatures, watchful in gazing at Jesus Christ the perfect revelation, watchful to obey the Holy Spirit speaking in his soul. All that, if it constitutes a challenge, at the same time brings an immense comfort and inspiration. For it means that God is ever around and within His people, upholding them, guiding them, ordering all things according to His will.

(3) Jesus Christ, the Son of God, " God of God, Light of lights ", is not only the supreme revelation of God to man, His final and unique revelation, but He is alone " the Way, the Truth, and the Life ". No man cometh to the Father but by Him. His sacrifice upon the Cross and His whole redeeming work has broken down the barrier of sin and made possible for man the union with God which is his very life. Through incorporation into Christ in His Church that union is effected here and now. In this all centres. Without it God's revelation of Himself would only add to man's despair—so beautiful, so wonderful a God for ever infinitely separated from man by man's own wilful sin.

There is no need to enlarge upon this here. But it would be impossible to speak of God and not to mention this one all-important truth. Men have sometimes accused such Christian mystics as the pseudo-Dionysius and even St. John of the Cross of belittling the work of Christ, or at least of leaving little room for Him in their theory of the soul's journey to God. Nothing could be further from the truth. If they do not expatiate on Christ's love and work on earth, it is only because that forms the basis of their teaching. They start as members of Christ's Body owing all to Him, and they are writing for their fellow-members, who are equally conscious of their debt to Christ and who have no need that anyone should teach them again " the rudiments of the oracles of God ", the " first principles of Christ ". And any careful study of their works makes their own faith in Christ abundantly clear. It is true that Christ Himself as God is the goal and the perfect satisfaction of the soul. Yet He Himself said that He was the " door " through which man went in to the Father to find pasture. The author of the Epistle to the Hebrews expands this saying: " Having therefore, brethren, boldness to enter into the holy place by the blood of Jesus, by the way which he dedicated for us, a new and living way, through the veil, that is to say, his flesh; and having a great priest over the house of God, let us draw near with a true heart in fulness of faith " (10. 19). These writers are only being strictly scriptural in taking our Lord at His word, in passing in Him and through Him to the Father. What has happened is that in the Incarnate Christ they have met with God who is spirit, communicating Himself to them in hidden ways, and they are constrained to attempt to tell others of so rich an experience. They strike the same note as the early Fathers. That shows itself in an interesting way in St. Augustine's *Confessions*. The book owes its existence to the saint's faith in Jesus Christ and His redeeming work, and he makes quite clear his debt to Christ. Yet he addresses himself to, and his gaze is turned always towards, God the Blessed Trinity. It was the eternal invisible God Himself whom he sought. Creation convinced him of that God's existence. There was, he tells us, one moment when he had " reached that which is with the flash of one trembling glance ". But that only revealed to him his own incapacity to approach nearer. " So I sought a way of gaining the strength needful for enjoying Him, but found none except by embracing the mediator of God and man, the man Christ Jesus, God above all blessed for ever, who was calling me and saying: 'I am the way of truth and the life.'"[1]

It may not, however, be amiss to add one fact about God revealed by the Incarnation. Christ became Man: He took upon Himself our common humanity, and He died for all men. God is "common to all". Meister Eckhart was fond of insisting on this characteristic of God—that He was like the sun—and here he was only developing our Lord's own words about the Father who made the sun to shine on all, good and bad alike. It was a tremendous contrast and comfort to St. Augustine to come from the abstractions of Neoplatonism to the simplicity of the gospel. As with the Manichaeans, the Neoplatonist deity remained the privilege of the few—a God of the intelligentsia alone, or of the mystic. The rank and file of mankind had little chance of reaching Him. But Christ is for all men, and equally for all. The gospel story is hedged about with mystery, the mystery of the eternal infinite God. No philosopher or mystic will ever get to the bottom of that mystery. Yet the way to it is simple, and "wayfaring men, though fools shall not err therein". The story is one of facts, palpable to all. A village maiden becomes the Mother of God; His birth is first made known to shepherds, and the friends He chooses to spread the gospel are plain fishermen. He Himself says very little about the mystery of redemption which He came to accomplish: certainly He expounded no elaborate theory, but He worked it out in hard concrete facts before the eyes of all. Only in ecstasy after long *ascesis* could the Neoplatonist achieve union with God—an experience limited to the few—but the most matter-of-fact Christian is granted union with God at the outset through means which he can see and handle and hear, "by water and the Word" in Baptism. Again, Mithraism had no message for women; polytheism disgusted the intellectual; but Jesus Christ meets and satisfies all, each on his own level, and lifts them up to God. Moreover, in Christ God gives Himself wholly to each, and, despite a wonderful diversity as to degrees and modes of intimacy, each has full share in Him. So Christ can be named the Spouse of each, yet there is no exclusiveness and no jealousy.

(4) God is a Trinity, three Persons in one God, Father, Son, and Holy Spirit. That is a Christian dogma. The Catholic Faith lays

[1] *Confessions*, VII. 18. Gibb and Montgomery's ed. (Cambridge, 1908.)

it down categorically, for God has revealed it. The trinity of
Plotinus has no resemblance to it, though it does bear pathetic
witness to the failure of a monad to satisfy man's deepest longings.
What is significant is that the experience of the great Catholic
masters of prayer leads them to concentrate their gaze more and
more exclusively on the mystery of the Blessed Trinity. That is
so whether they start, like St. Bernard or St. Francis, from a
passionate devotion to the Incarnate Christ, or whether, like
Dionysius, they seek God through the *Via Negativa*. We are not
concerned now with definitions of the doctrine, but we may well
pause to ask why this truth of the Blessed Trinity, so often left
on one side by preachers and their flocks as too subtle and elaborate
for ordinary people or for everyday religion, should loom so large
in the lives of the saints. The reason is that it meets and satisfies
three great needs of the human soul: the need of a transcendent
God, the need of unity, and the need of a society. God made
man in His own image and made him for Himself, and only the
triune God can satisfy such a creature. But we must remember
that the truth of the Blessed Trinity is part of the divine revelation.
It has not been reached by man's reasoning powers, as something
which seems to satisfy the complexities of the human soul. On
the contrary, men have believed the truth first, and then in
attempting to draw near and worship this triune God they have
found an unexpected richness, satisfying vague deep needs, of which
they were scarcely aware. Nowhere is this better illustrated than
in the life of St. Augustine, for in his Neoplatonist days he had
experience of that natural intellectual contemplation of the One
Absolute, and it had left him unsatisfied. But once convinced
that God was the Blessed Trinity, three Persons in one God, he
found there a fulness and joy which made his Neoplatonic conception of God seem absurdly thin and insubstantial.

The mystery of the Trinity is closely linked with another
revealed mystery of the Faith—God is Love. The two help to
explain one another, and in doing so help to explain in some
measure man to himself, especially with regard to his three needs,
just mentioned, which we will now consider.

(i) Man seeks a transcendent God—one who stands clear from
His creation, loving it indeed, preserving it, yet not enmeshed in
it. The highest human aspirations cannot finally be satisfied by a

God who is a part of creation, involved in its fate, or by a God who needs creation if only as a means of self-contemplation. There is something almost repellent in the idea of a monad god occupied in eternal self-contemplation. It is an interesting fact that a mystic such as Meister Eckhart who, though believing in the Blessed Trinity, went beyond the limits of orthodoxy in seeking as it were to reach behind the three Persons to a single divine essence, should also transgress in insisting on God's need of man, as though He were not really independent of His creation. " God ", he declared, " can no more do without us than we can without Him."[1] And it was Eckhart who exalted knowledge above love. Now love consists in endless self-giving for the sake of the beloved, as well as in the ever-growing delight in, and knowledge of, his perfections. The more perfect the likeness and tl e greater the equality between lover and beloved, the more perfect is the love. For perfect love demands perfect response. There must be reciprocity. Only an equal or greater being can fully satisfy another being's desire. If God were only a monad He could not be Love and transcendent, for He would have no one either to love or to return His love. Even if He were not transcendent and needed His creature, love would be thwarted and imperfect, for there is no equality between creature and creator. But because He is three Persons in one God He can perfectly fulfil in Himself all the demands of love, yet be transcendent, wholly independent of the creation.

(ii) Man at his highest demands unity. Not only does love seek union with the beloved, but the intellect too is ever seeking to find some unity amid all the multiplicity of creation. The philosopher aims at discovering the principle of unity behind all the innumerable facts of life; the scientist seeks to classify the manifold data of his study in some ordered system. Contemplatives repeatedly declare that, as all creatures issued forth from the simplicity of God into the multiplicity of created things, so they are irresistibly impelled to return to that simplicity—to God—drawn by that Love who is God. Medieval writers sometimes even called by the name of love the force which draws the stone cast into the air back to earth. We have seen that if God is Love, He must be more than one Person. But if He were not one, but three separate Gods, that desire for unity would be thwarted of its goal. It

[1] *Works*, I. 44. (John Watkins, London, 1924.)

would leave man with a strange sense of frustration. He might avoid the dualism of the Manichees, but that sense of frustration would have a disruptive effect on his whole outlook and activity. But God is one—three Persons in one God, and that is why man is conscious of this urge to unity. Nicholas of Cusa in his meditations on the Vision of God plays continually with deep satisfaction on the thought of the divine unity lying at the heart of creation, and he sums it up in one short sentence: " Thou art God Almighty, because Thou art absolute simplicity, which is absolute infinity."[1]

A subconscious desire for unity has driven some devout Christians to concentrate their worship almost exclusively on the second Person of the Trinity. This " Jesus cult ", as it has been named, has its dangers, as it is apt to lead to a narrowing of outlook, a tendency to be preoccupied with our Lord's humanity, and to lose sight of the eternal transcendent God. On the other hand, the unity of God tends ever to keep the door open to wider views, for the whole Godhead dwells in each Person of the Trinity. No one can worship the Lord Jesus without also worshipping the other Persons, however inadequately.

(iii) Yet man also belongs to multiplicity. He is one of the myriad created things born into the midst of a society, and needing other human beings like himself. For him as for his Maker, love is of his very essence, and on his own level he needs other beings to love and be loved by. And the Christian knows that in this he is reflecting his Creator, who, like himself, is a social being—a family of three Persons (though He possesses a unity which human persons cannot have). So the Christian's approach to God is never, like the Neoplatonists, merely a " a flight of the alone to the Alone ". An old song says: " One is one and all alone, and evermore shall be so." It opens up a terrifying view—the transcendence of the monad. But the unity of the Blessed Trinity contains a social life of infinite fulness and joy—needing nothing f om without for its absolute perfection. Yet of His bounty has He admitted His creatures to share in that life, and there with the angels and saints the individual soul can be at home, engaged with them in contemplation of the Eternal One in Three. Even to be aware of the mutual love within the Blessed Trinity brings comfort to the soul in distress and draws it out of itself to rejoice therein. Our Lord persistently taught His disciples to look to

[1] *Vision of God*, Ch. XIV.

Heaven as their home. God is their Father who cares for them and knows their necessities before they ask. The sinner is one who has wandered from *home*, and when he turns back penitent his father is waiting to receive him with open arms. The Good Shepherd goes to seek the lost sheep, and when He has found it He brings it *home* rejoicing.

Communion with such a God must give a vastly different outlook upon life from that of the nature-mystic or pantheist contemplative. It shows itself particularly in an outgoing love for others—specially for fellow-members of the divine society. As a recent writer has expressed it: "The life of God is a life in which love is common to the Persons who share it. Of this common life of love we partake through the gift of the spirit. Thus the whole of the divine *koinonia* is present in each disciple and in the community to which he belongs. The Church is the community in which the interchanges of love belonging to the divine life are reproduced in human form."[1] That realization of the common life, of being at home with God as with one's fellow human-beings, finds noble expression in the life and writings of a saint such as St. Mechthild of Magdeburg. As she looked upward to God in prayer she was intensely aware of sharing in this common life. Saints and angels stand around the Blessed Trinity. As she looked out upon those around her still in the world she saw God in every soul, and gave herself to their service in generous love.

[1] Thornton, *Common Life in the Body of Christ*, p. 419. (Dacre Press, Westminster.)

CHAPTER III

THE CHURCH AND WORSHIP

THE *Tripartite Life* of St. Patrick tells the story of two princesses, daughters of King Loegaire; how they came upon St. Patrick seated with his clergy beside a well. Filled with curiosity they asked him who he was. The saint answered by speaking to them of God. Eagerly then they questioned him further: " Tell us about him, how he is seen, how he is loved, how he is found? If he is in youth, or if he is in age? If he is everliving; if he is beautiful? If many have fostered his son? If his daughters are dear and beautiful to the men of the world?" Very briefly and very movingly St. Patrick put before them the truth of the Blessed Trinity. " And the maidens said as it were with one mouth and with one heart: ' How shall we be able to believe in that King? Teach us most diligently that we may see the Lord face to face. Teach us the way and we will do whatsoever thou shalt say unto us.' " The saint gave them some further instruction and then baptized them. But even that did not satisfy them. They asked to see Christ face to face. " And Patrick said to them, ' Ye cannot see Christ unless ye first taste of death, and unless ye receive Christ's Body and His Blood '. And the girls answered: ' Give us the sacrifice that we may be able to see the Spouse.' Then they received the sacrifice, and fell asleep in death."[1]

" Brethren, what shall we do? " was the question put by those who heard St. Peter's sermon on the day of Pentecost. " And Peter said unto them, Repent ye, and be baptized every one of you in the name of Jesus Christ unto the remission of your sins; and ye shall receive the gift of the Holy Ghost." (Acts 2. 37 f.) That is an epitome of the gospel in a sentence. But the gospel is good news, or God's story, only to those who have felt the need of Him, whether they have been " pricked to the heart " by the

[1] *Tripartite Life*, I, 99.

43

sense of their sin like the Jews, or enthralled by the vision of His beauty, like the princesses. All alike must pass through Holy Baptism into the new life within the fellowship of the Church, the Body of Christ. Neither St. Peter nor St. Patrick had any doubt about that, and they had the same answer for Jew and pagan.

It is worth while stressing this fact here, because inevitably a book of this kind must deal largely with the individual and his spiritual life. But that life can only exist and grow within the family life of the Church. We shall be speaking much of contemplative prayer, and the contemplative perhaps most of all needs to be reminded of this truth. The desire for solitude and his deep sense of the immediacy of God sometimes blind him to its importance, make him forget that he owes all to his membership in the Body. And it is an immense comfort and inspiration to realize it. John Bunyan's Christian had to leave home and kindred and set out on a lonely path. Here and there a companion joined him, but his pilgrimage remained a terribly solitary affair till he got to its end beyond the river. Now it is quite true that a certain loneliness awaits everyone in his journey to God. God only knows the deeps of the human soul, and " one deep calleth to another ". But it makes all the difference to undergo that trial supported by the fellowship of His saints. The old maxim, *extra ecclesiam nulla salus* (no salvation outside the Church) sounds a hard saying to many. But it is no piece of religious intolerance: it follows inevitably from the divine economy of redemption. Christ by His incarnate life and passion broke through the bonds of sin and death. He redeemed the whole world, not merely a few chosen souls, but it is only as each soul is caught up into Him that it can share in that salvation. The organ through which that is accomplished is His mystical Body, the Church, and entrance into it is by Holy Baptism. That is the only covenanted way made known to us. That does not prevent God numbering amongst His chosen ones those who through no fault of their own have lived beyond the range of the Church's ministry. His sacraments are sure means of grace and never fail, but they do not limit the scope of God's mercies. God remains free to act without them. So we can declare with complete conviction that Baptism and the Blessed Sacrament are " necessary to salvation ", and yet thankfully admit that Christ's mystical Body includes many who have never been baptized or approached His altar.

Our first necessity as members of that Body, baptized and communicant, if we are to grow in the spiritual life, is to realize something of the implications of membership. By nature we are dependent on others from the moment of our birth, not only for our material needs but for the development of our personalities. Indeed it is only through intercourse with others that we become ourselves. We owe the food we eat, the clothes we wear, the houses we live in, to the labour of our fellow-beings. Association with them and their works gives us ideals, widens our horizon, enlarges our sympathies. Our affections and interests are too closely bound up with our friends and relations to be easily plucked asunder. They become part of ourselves. Entrance into the Family of God, the Church, does not destroy this natural process: it perfects it. Still we need the society of others, and Christ supplies it to us in the communion of saints. Many find a difficulty in realizing their fellowship with the members of the Church in their neighbourhood. The imperfections of these stand out too crudely and they seem to have little devotion to God. The temptation comes then to them to draw apart and live in isolation, or to dream of a past golden age of the Church, when all were saints. But they get something of a shock when they turn to the New Testament and discover that even in the beginnings no such golden age existed. The world got into the Church long before the reign of Constantine. The authors of the New Testament make that painfully clear. They tell us of Ananias and Sapphira, of the murmuring Grecian Jews, of Diotrephes who " loveth to have the pre-eminence ", of Hymenaeus and Alexander undermining the Faith, of others who had " lost their first love "—all these rubbing shoulders with the apostles and great servants of Christ, partaking too of the one loaf. Yet none the less did the Church remain the Family of God, the holy city, the nursery of saints. Even so did the Christian find comfort and strength and inspiration within its fellowship. To-day there is urgent need to recover this sense of fellowship within the Church militant. Too often people try to live in spiritual isolation, meeting at the Eucharist week by week, yet remaining ever strangers.

But the Communion of Saints offers a much wider fellowship than this. It stretches far beyond the confines of a parish, or of a country, or indeed of this world. It includes the souls at rest, and still further the saints in glory. Here another clamant need of the human soul is met and satisfied. All through history men have craved for some assurance of a life beyond the grave, and of a life that still has contacts with their fellows. Such pagan customs as the worship of ancestors, or the provision of food for the departed, or the interment of weapons or other personal possessions in the grave, all bear witness to the dim hope that some kind of social life might be found, however thin and ghostly it might be. Existence in isolation was unthinkable. The Catholic Church supplies through the Communion of Saints the only satisfying answer to that need. Where this truth has been suppressed or minimized men have sought satisfaction in strange unhealthy ways, through mediums and planchettes and table-rapping. And in time of war or pestilence when the need grows more urgent they throng the séances of the spiritualists.

The prejudice in this country against communion with the saints in glory is as unnatural as it is uncatholic. The suppression of so natural a desire has created a complex which shows itself in a certain restlessness, sometimes in some such practices as we have just mentioned. How are we to regain the truth? First of all we must realize the effect of Holy Baptism in making us "members of Christ and inheritors of the kingdom of Heaven". It lifts us into the heavenly society and makes us already partakers of eternal life. Already in some degree this-world barriers are transcended. And what an immeasurable strength it is to know ourselves members of that great multitude which no man can number! There are times when the seeming apathy and irreligion in the world fill us with a sense of impotence. Doubts creep into our minds about the Faith. Can it really be the one and only saving message for the world if so large a proportion of people, and so many good ones among them, reject it? "Lord, are there few that be saved?" Then we remember that we are one with that countless host of saints, with one heart and one mind worshipping before the throne. After all it is the unbelievers who are the few and the scattered, stumbling along in darkness.

We can also accustom ourselves to the presence of the saints, ask them for their prayers, study their lives. The lives of the great saints provide one of the most profitable forms of spiritual reading. Asking for their prayers not only brings us their help but it gives us just that sense of their vitality and their nearness to us which makes real to us our communion with them. Supreme amongst them reigns our Lady, the Blessed Virgin Mary, Mother of God. A deeper note marks our devotion to her, " the sad world's aspirations' one success ", as Coventry Patmore termed her. Little by little we come to realize what we owe to her, both for what she has done in the past and what she does for us now. The mother of our Blessed Lord, she is also the mother of His mystical Body, the Church and all its members—and it is fitting that in our Father's House we should find a mother awaiting us.

What should emerge from all this is a strong purpose to share as fully as possible in this heavenly fellowship. As the Body of Christ it not only teaches, but is, the way to salvation; it not only holds, but is, the Truth. So also is it Life. Therefore its range is universal, the whole truth for the whole world. The Russian Orthodox lay immense stress on this inner wholeness of the Church and this desire to keep within the full stream of its life. They call it *sobornost*—a word which signifies both unity and a common mind. It involves a firm faith in the Holy Catholic Church, a realization that here lies the truth, and a humble seeking of its mind. Heresy is to be abhorred not merely because it contradicts some dogmatic statement, but because it disrupts this unity of heart and mind. Such an outlook gives a greater intellectual freedom than the insistence on .conformity to detailed formulæ. A man who is imbued with the spirit of *sobornost* may safely be allowed to express his views as freely as he will. His reverence for the mind of the Church will save him from separating himself from it. He will also adapt himself to its way of life, both in worship and in the sphere of morals, for he knows that so he will best keep within the stream, instead of drifting alone into some backwater of spiritual experience. Tradition to him is no dead weight of antiquated custom but the living voice of the Church, handed down indeed from the beginning, old but ever new, for each succeeding generation bears witness to its truth and lives in its light. It guards the mystery of Christ Jesus, and only to those who are faithful to it is that mystery revealed. St. Ignatius Loyola was well aware of this, and he added to his *Spiritual Exercises* a number of rules to develop in the individual the spirit of loyalty to the Church and its living tradition—" to have the right sentiments (almost the right attitude) (*para el sentido verdadero*) in the Church militant ". They include such practices as prompt obedience to " the true spouse of Christ our Lord, which is our holy mother,

the Hierarchical Church" (as against the tendency to appeal to the
unwritten laws of an invisible Church), as praising the sacraments,
the precepts, and the evangelical counsels, and refraining from
unnecessary criticism.

I

The first thing to realize within the Church is that it is the
sphere of divine grace, and that that grace is mediated sacra-
mentally. God has taken the initiative in revelation and redemption. "Blessed be the Lord God of Israel, for He hath visited and
redeemed His people, and hath raised up a mighty salvation for
us." And He retains the initiative in coming to them in the
sacraments of His Church. Every crisis and every need of His
people He meets with the appropriate means of grace—Holy
Baptism to cleanse the individual from original sin, and to re-
generate him, making him a member of the Body of Christ;
Holy Confirmation to complete his membersh p and to bestow upon
him the special gifts of the Holy Spirit to fit him for service; the
Eucharist to be food for his pilgrimage; the Sacrament of Penance
to cleanse the soiled baptismal robe; Holy Matrimony to sanctify his
family life; Holy Unction to restore him to health in sickness or
assist him through the gate of death. And by the Sacrament of Holy
Order God sets apart, commissions, and empowers men for the
ministry.

Only gradually do most of us come to understand, and never
fully here, how richly and completely the sacramental life renews
and supernaturalizes our whole being. Grace revolutionizes the
natural man, but it does not destroy his human nature. When
Christ said, "Except a man be born anew, he cannot see the
kingdom of God" (Jn. 3. 3), or when St. Paul wrote, "If any man
is in Christ Jesus he is a new creature" (2 Cor. 5. 17), they did not
mean that his nature must be supplanted by something else. For
grace redeems it. If we say grace supernaturalizes it, we must
understand what the expression signifies. The natural man is
capax Dei, that is, God has given him a nature made in the image
of God and capable of union with Him—able to become supernatural. Christian writers, following the ancient Greek philosophers,
have taught that there are four natural virtues—prudence, justice,
fortitude, temperance. They are qualities which man specially
requires in his relations with his fellow-men, as well as in the
development of his own personality. Now grace does not wash

away those virtues in Holy Baptism to give him something different. It supernaturalizes them and strengthens him to use them aright, for God. For instance, the natural virtue of temperance enables a man to practise self-control in order to achieve success in athletics or war or some other worldly end. But grace enables him to be temperate in a more excellent and comprehensive way, and to practise self-control simply for God's sake. Similarly, by natural fortitude a man will endure great hardships, even death itself, to gain a fortune or serve his country. But supernatural fortitude will inspire him to go through bitter sufferings and death for the glory of God, as it has inspired His martyrs in every age.

Besides the four natural virtues thus supernaturalized there are the three theological virtues of faith, hope, and charity—so called because they are concerned more directly with God, though they too have their counterpart in natural virtues.

Moreover, the Holy Spirit bestows His sevenfold gifts upon each member of Christ's Church. These gifts empower him to know God's will and to devote himself to it intuitively. Supernatural prudence, for instance, will enlighten his reason to see in a certain situation which course he must take for the glory of God. The Holy Spirit with the gift of counsel makes him aware at once of the right course and enables him to do it with readiness.

To redeem the world God sent forth His Son, "born of a woman, born under the law", to take our human nature upon Him. The glory of God was revealed in a way that man could grasp with his natural senses and in some measure understand. St. John's saying "And the Word was made flesh" still breathes the adoring love which filled the apostle as he contemplated such condescension—"and we beheld His glory, the glory as of the only begotten of the Father, full of grace and truth". In the Sacraments, as we know, Christ perpetuates the wonder of His Incarnation, that all men so long as the world lasts may share in that grace and truth. But in conveying to us divine grace, and Christ's very self, they impress upon us certain fundamental principles of God's dealings with us.

(1) It is the act of God. God, as we have just said, takes the initiative. He must take it, if salvation is to come to man at all.

D

For man can do nothing of himself to remedy the disaster of his fall. But " God so loved the world that He gave His only begotten Son ". Read slowly the prologue of the Fourth Gospel, or the opening words of the Epistle to the Hebrews, and mark the emphasis on God and His action, while man does nothing but reject His love, blind to His presence. And yet God redeems him. Julian of Norwich, marvelling at this, exclaimed in her vivid way: " Our Lord God showed that a deed shall be done, and Himself shall do it, and I shall do nothing but sin, and my sin shall not hinder His goodness working."[1] The Sacraments form the abiding token of this divine prevenience though they are of course much more than this. They proclaim to man in his darkest hours, when he is most aware of his own helplessness, that God comes to seek and to save. They are, as it were, the voice of Christ ever saying " I will not leave you desolate: I come unto you ".

(2) Thus God conforms Himself to our weakness, and comes to us in palpable ways, through the material, through things we can touch and see. It is like a blind man's friend putting into his hands the thing he is groping for, setting before him the food he needs. " O that I knew where I might find Him," the penitent cries, and our Lord answers in the Sacrament, " Behold, it is I myself". " This is my Body which is given for you."

Further still, the material itself is taken up into the process of redemption and made the instrument of the glory of God. The visible creation does reveal the glory of God. In that sense the whole world is sacramental, though the eyes of fallen men are too dim to realize its significance. But in the Sacraments things that are made receive a new dignity, becoming the effective instruments through which the grace of God is conveyed at definite moments for definite purposes. " The heavens declare the glory of God and the firmament showeth his handiwork"; but the Sacraments not only declare that glory, but convey divine power to the penitent believer. Nor does the bestowal of grace depend on the individual's powers of spiritual perception. It is given to him however cold or blind he may feel at the moment, and it works secretly. Just because God is spirit and His gift a spiritual gift, the senses are not necessarily aware of His coming. Its primary effect is hidden in the spirit of man, though it does often also affect the

[1] *Revelations*, Ch. XXXVI. (Methuen & Co., London.)

senses too. It is received by faith—and a living faith enables it to work more powerfully on the soul.

One more thought here: this sacramental method from another angle stresses the value of the body. Writers on the spiritual life tend too much to speak of God's dealings with the soul, rather than of the whole personality, and of the soul in the feminine gender. (It is a mark of the independence and virility of Julian of Norwich that she usually speaks of the soul as masculine.) Such language is apt to be misleading. It suggests that the soul alone matters. But the Sacraments keep the full truth of man steadily before us. The body must be dealt with and met on its own level. The words used in the administration of the Blessed Sacrament drive home the lesson at that supreme moment: " The Body of our Lord Jesus Christ preserve thy body and soul unto everlasting life."

(3) The initiative is God's and the power is God's, but there is one condition laid upon us. We must bring what we have to be given to God and in the way He has appointed: bread and wine, the best we can provide and the product of our labour, symbolic of our desire and need to offer to God of our best, symbolic of the offering of our own selves, offered and blessed according to the appointed rites and ceremonies. This, together with faith, is our part in the Sacrament to be fulfilled as faithfully as we can. God will do the rest. The Eucharist illustrates the principle most fully, but the other Sacraments also bear witness to it. Bread that strengthens man's body, and wine " that maketh glad " his heart, the best he has, but in themselves only able to serve his physical needs, brought and offered to God, become the immortal Food that renews the soul and fills it with the joy of the divine Presence. Pure water, able only to cleanse the body or quench its thirst, becomes in Holy Baptism the means through which the soul is cleansed from sin and its longing for God satisfied.

Thus the Sacraments teach us to regard the whole of life as potentially sacramental. They teach us to bring to God all its details and events—our work, our interests and recreations, our possessions, to be taken and blessed by Him that they may be channels of grace and the means of manifesting His glory. Holy Church encourages us to do this by the use of what are called

" sacramentals ", e.g. holy water, ikons, ordinary things caught up into the prayer of the Church and henceforth become in some degree purveyors of heavenly grace.

Further still, the Sacraments point the way to the transformation of the whole creation, when " the earth shall be full of the knowledge of the Lord, as the waters cover the sea ". Very gradually our Lord taught His disciples to realize both His own power over the material world and its potentialities in His hands. He used a few loaves and fishes to satisfy the hunger of thousands: He used clay and spittle to restore sight to the blind. On the Mount of Transfiguration His body was transformed by a strange and wonderful glory. After the Resurrection that same body possessed new unheard-of capacities, fit for the revelation of the Risen Christ. So in His hands bread and wine were lifted into the heavenly sphere and charged with a new significance to be His own Body and Blood. It was not difficult in such a context for the disciples to believe His word. They learned to look forward to the renewal of all creation by the same power, glorified and made fit for the people of God.

(4) Finally, the Sacraments never cease to proclaim the essentially social character of the Christian life. There is no need to repeat here what we have already said on this subject. Once again it is the Eucharist that drives home the lesson most completely. Without the ministrations of another, even this most necessary food of the soul cannot be obtained. Even the priest (except in certain quite abnormal situations) cannot offer the Holy Sacrifice without at least one other to represent his fellow-members. And what scores of hands and brains have gone to the making of the bread and wine, and other things needful for the service! In offering the elements the priest offers with them the labours of that multitude—to be taken up and sanctified by God—and priest and congregation are united with them " to be a reasonable holy and lively sacrifice ", to be taken up by God and accepted in the one perfect and sufficient sacrifice of Christ, and to be used for God's glory.

II

So far we have spoken of the inestimable privileges of membership in the mystical Body of Christ, His Holy Church. To receive them repentance and faith are needed and Baptism, as St. Peter told the Jews. But there is still the question: "What must we do now?" For privileges demand obligations. Although God takes the initiative and does all, we may and must co-operate in the work, for to do so is part of His plan for us.

Those obligations may be summed up in the one word "worship". For worship (worth-ship) is the rendering to God "the honour due unto His Name". "Worship the Lord with holy worship", and that includes the offering of the whole life. St. Thomas Aquinas for this reason declares religion to be a part of the virtue of Justice, the creature paying what is due from him to the Creator. Here we will use the word in its narrower sense of prayer and praise, offered directly to God. Man has a special obligation to render such worship. All creation bears the impress of God and proclaims His glory. But it does so unconsciously, by the faithfulness of each creature to the law of its being. The bird sings because that is its nature: the lily spreads forth its three-fold splendours because it is made that way; in so doing they unwittingly proclaim the glory of Him who could create such wonders. Only man has the gift of reason to recognize that glory and whence it came, and the power to offer free and rational praise therefor. So he is the appointed mouthpiece of creation, to give conscious and significant expression, as it were, to the song of the bird, or the fairness of the lily, as also to the grimmer aspects, as of the tiger or the thunderstorm. The world waits for him to fulfil this duty. "The earnest expectation of the creature waiteth for the revealing of the Sons of God." (Rom. 8. 19.) The Apocalypse records a glorious vision of the Church's worship before the throne of God, with the Lamb in the midst "standing as it had been slain". The seer hears the voices of ten thousand times ten thousand lifted in adoration—and in that act of worship all creation joins. Every creature at last has found in them its tongue: "Every created thing which is in the heaven and on the earth and under the earth and on the sea, and all things that are in them heard I saying, 'Unto him that sitteth on the throne and unto the Lamb, be the blessing, and the honour, and the glory, and the dominion for ever and ever.'" (Rev. 5.)

The Holy Catholic Church provides man with the opportunity to offer this praise in its liturgical worship. (There is some dispute as to the exact limits of the Liturgy, but at least it includes the Divine Office, the Sacraments, and the sacramentals.) The Liturgy forms so essential a part of the Church's life that we must consider briefly some of its main features.

(1) The objective of the Liturgy is primarily the glory of God —that and nothing else. In countless other ways, e.g. through his works, through his friendships, through his recreations, man may and should indirectly be serving and praising God. But here he renders immediate honour, laying aside everything else for the time, that he may voice creation's worship of the Creator. Whether he himself feels any the better while doing so, or whether he feels more devout when otherwise employed, has little or nothing to do with the matter. He takes part in that worship primarily to pay his due of praise to God—to give, so far as the creature can give anything to his Creator, that amount of time and attention solely to Him and for no other purpose. And no man can sincerely attempt that without being the better for it. This aspect of the Liturgy particularly needs emphasizing in these days. Men tend far too much to estimate things according to their present utility; what will be their effect on the individual's conduct or on society? They can see a certain value in prayer as a means to guide and strengthen action here and now. But the prayer of adoration, directed purely to God with no other object in view, seems a waste of time. In the Middle Ages men raised magnificent churches to the glory of God and many of them still stand bearing their witness. They still convey some breath of the eternal, of aspiration that seeks God for His own sake, prodigal of labour and expense, if so it may glorify Him. They are pregnant with the spirit of the Liturgy. Our tendency has been to consider the number of seats to be provided and then to reckon on how economically they can be housed. However, recently signs have appeared of a better understanding, and churches have been raised which have caught something of the true spirit, and their architects have sought to express in stone what the Liturgy expresses in its rites and ceremonies.

(2) Just because the Liturgy is the expression of man's adoration of his Creator it must be as full and as splendid as he can make it. He brings to it all his gifts of mind and body, consecrating them as a kind of first-fruits to God's glory. Nowhere does

Puritanism show more clearly its Manichaean affinities than in its attitude towards public worship. It minimizes the part the body has to play, as though the body must be ignored, for the soul alone matters. But in the Catholic Church, East and West alike, specially at the Eucharist, the whole personality is called into play to give of its best. All the resources of art and music are employed to enrich the offering, and the body by its postures accompanies the worship at every turn. This has its dangers. The appeal to the senses may grow too strong and swamp the adoration. The rite then becomes overlaid with elaborate and meaningless ceremonies, the music an end in itself. That happens where the spirit of worship fails—just as the body rots uncleanly into life when the soul has gone. Something of that kind happened in the Middle Ages when the Cluniac revival had spent its force. The Cistercians in reaction went to the other extreme, and inaugurated an almost Puritan simplicity, the plainest of vestments and holy vessels, the barest of sanctuaries, the simplest of chants. But even they gave of their best in their worship, and their ruined abbeys still proclaim in their stark severity the glory of God.

(3) The Liturgy is a corporate *act* of the Church rather than a corporate recitation of words (though of course it is also that). It is the performance of a duty. We may mark here the choice of the word "Liturgy": for it is the Greek word, λειτουργία, the performance of a *work*, generally of some service to the state. For instance, it was a "liturgy" incumbent on the richer citizens of Athens to provide ships for the defence of their state. The Eucharist is the enactment of a drama—the drama of Christ's incarnate life and passion. But, once its dramatic character is realized, all the otherwise puzzling actions of the service fall into their proper place. Not only the priest at the altar, but the acolytes moving silently about the sanctuary, even the candles burning, all play their part. The Mass as it proceeds gathers up the life of Christ, His Incarnation, His Ministry, till the climax is reached in the consecration, where the celebrant reciting the words of the Canon with lowered voice performs certain prescribed acts, fore-ordained in the Upper Room to re-present the Sacrifice of Calvary, linking up the Sacrifice with the Resurrection and the Ascension and the coming of the Holy Ghost. And throughout the service the congregation join in the drama, praying, responding, now standing, now kneeling, now genuflecting.

(4) As corporate worship the Liturgy is the act of the whole
Church, and the prayer of the whole Church. It is never merely
the worship of the few individuals gathered at any one moment
in any one building. Round them stand always "the angels and
archangels and all the company of heaven"—and the few present
join in the prayer of the whole company which is the Body of
Christ, of Him who said: "Where two or three are gathered
together in my name there am I in the midst of you." More still
it is the prayer of Christ Himself, just because they also are members
of His Body. The Russian Orthodox have perhaps an even deeper
sense of their oneness with the rest of the Church in their Liturgy
than ourselves. The ikons and paintings of the saints, which adorn
their churches, impress it visibly upon the worshippers. The
Church, militant, expectant, and triumphant, is a living whole, and
through the Liturgy the whole joins at every moment in adoration
of the Blessed Trinity. That is one reason why the psalms still
keep their place in the Divine Office. They form the medium
through which the Church in all ages, and our Lord Himself
during His life on earth, poured forth its praise—and we to-day
are caught up in its harmony. No fitter medium could be found.
Inspired by God, the psalms move incessantly round the thought
of God's majesty and power, of His care for His people, of their
unfaithfulness and their need of His grace. Moreover, they provide
the opportunity for the individual to merge his own idiosyncrasies
and limitations in this great stream of prayer. He is caught up
into a world of devotion far beyond his own limited outlook or
modes of self-expression into the mystery of the saints. The
words may not always be the words he would himself choose to
address God, or which he would dare to use. He may not, for
instance, feel "like a bottle in the smoke", nor may he be able to
say sincerely at the moment, "My soul is athirst for God", yet he
is enabled as a member of Christ and of the new Israel to share
in the raptures of devotion as in the depths of penitence of the
saints of God, and his own spiritual stature is enlarged thereby.
That applies also in some measure to the other fixed forms of
liturgical worship. They may not be the individual's choice of
phrase, but with the accompanying ceremonies they help to liberate
him from self and make him realize his oneness with the whole
Church. Some years ago Stephen Graham, present in the cathedral
of Kiev at the offering of the Liturgy, had this sense of unity
vividly brought home to him. The effect was enhanced by the

frescoes of saints on the walls and pillars, and, above the altar, a
picture of the Madonna and Child. " There is ", he wrote, " always
a crowd, a promiscuity of rich and poor, of well-dressed and
tattered, a kaleidoscopic mingling of people and colours, people
standing and praying, people kneeling, people prostrated. . . .
There is no organ music but an unearthly and spontaneous outburst of praise from the souls of the choir and the clergy and the
laity worshipping together. . . . And from the back and the sides,
and from the pillars and columns, look the pale faces of antiquity,
the faces of the dead who are alive looking over the shoulders of
the alive who have not yet died, all praising God, enfolding in a
vast choric communion the few who in the church have met on
the common impulse to acknowledge the wonder and splendour
of the mystery of God. . . .

" It is not necessary to pray or to fall upon one's knees. It is
only necessary to exist in the great choric throng and to look over
a thousand heads to the awful and yet altogether lovely vision of
the Virgin to feel one's heart almost stand still and one's soul
become rapt in wonder, awestruck, thrilled. . . . You lose the
sense of the Ego, the separated individual, you are aware of being
part of a great unity praising God. You cease to be *man* and
become the *Church*, the bride of Christ."[1]

In spite of the apparent *abandon* of that scene the Liturgy, even
of the Eastern Church, strikes a note of restraint which it is
important to remember and which seems to some too cold and
remote. It speaks in measured, rhythmic tones; the actions it
prescribes are dignified and controlled. It possesses, as it were, an
old-fashioned courtesy, both wise and invigorating. Any well-
ordered society must preserve some measure of restraint in its
public conduct. It needs to have its emotions canalized in fitting
symbols rather than allowed free play according to the whims of
the individual. The raising of the hat to a lady, or the handshake,
may seem foolish or inadequate to many as an expression of their
feelings towards women or acquaintances, yet they serve as symbols, recognized by all, misunderstood by none, signifying ideals,
yet saving people from the embarrassment of unbridled emotions.
What is more, they not only signify ideals, but the fact of observing
them helps to inculcate interior attitudes of respect, courtesy, and

[1] *The Way of Martha and the Way of Mary*, pp. 78 and 74.

the like. So the actions in the Liturgy help not only to express but also to inspire reverence, faith, and adoration.

Such restraint deepens another characteristic of liturgical worship—its restfulness. It seems to be imbued with something of the eternal peace of God. The individual may come to it weary and distracted, too tired to make the effort necessary in mental prayer. He is like the underground traveller in London emerging from his train, far below the level of the street, much too tired to climb the stairs. But whatever time he arrives he finds a staircase always in motion. He steps on to it and is carried up to the top. So the Christian steps into the stream of the Church's worship and is carried up on the wings of its praise into the divine Presence. Its very sameness brings peace. The words are the same, the actions are the same all over the world. "As it was in the beginning, is now, and ever shall be." No mere clinging to a dead past, but joining with the living Church.

(5) The Liturgy revolves around definite historical facts. True, it directs itself always to God the Blessed Trinity who exists outside all time and all history; nevertheless it does so through the Incarnate Life of the Lord Jesus, God the Son, who revealed Himself to man at one definite point in time and in one defin te place. Worship centres in the commemoration of the great acts of His redeeming love. The Church's year provides thus a rich variety, as it leads the faithful through that life of Christ: the first half of the year a sequence of preparation for, and rejoicing in, its great moments; and then the steady plodding on in the strength of them through the rest of it, lit at intervals by the festivals of the saints. Such a system is in itself an education in the Christian Faith. The teaching powers of the Liturgy are enhanced by such accessories as the ordered sequence of colours to fit the different seasons, e.g. the sober Lenten office, specially of Holy Week, the stripping of the altars on Maundy Thursday, and then the outburst of praise and light at Easter.

The cult of the Saints impresses on the faithful still living in the world their oneness with those beyond, who are yet more alive than ever, and sets before them the example of their devotion. All this attention to events and facts has enormously facilitated the weaving of the gospel into the ordinary life of the people

—birth and marriage and death, seed-time and harvest; that is to say, where liturgical worship has had free course. In other words it teaches and unites two great lessons of the Gospel, mystery and simplicity—the ineffable mystery of God linked with a homeliness that the simplest peasant can understand. Nothing distinguishes the Christian Faith from other religions more than this emphasis on historic fact. Contrast with the richness of its Liturgy the monotonous repetition by the Moslems of the oneness and greatness of Allah as their one mode of worship. The old mystery religions had, it is true, elaborate ceremonials, but they were concerned with imaginary deeds of the gods, which had no reference to history or time. They but reproduced the cycle of Nature, winter and summer, seed-time and harvest, under the guise of dramas of the gods. But the bull slain by Mithras never trod this earth, nor did any moment in history witness the death of Osiris. The devotees were aware of it and it imparted a sense of unreality to their most solemn moments, forcing them to seek yet further for the satisfaction of their deepest needs. That is why they often became adherents of one religion after another, vainly hoping to find something real to support them in the end. All these myths disappear like bubbles before one solid statement in the Catholic Creed, " suffered under Pontius Pilate "—the mystery of redemption pinned down, as it were, to one definite moment in history.

Moreover, the Church in thus, year by year, celebrating the mysteries of Christ's Incarnate Life is not merely recalling past events in history. Its worship is far more mysterious than that. When the faithful, for instance, keep Holy Week they are not like children saying " Let's pretend, pretend we are accompanying our Lord through His Passion ". Nor are they like those South Africans who some years ago wished to celebrate the anniversary of the Great Trek. Those men procured replicas of the old Cape bullock-wagons, dressed themselves up in the costumes of their forefathers and trekked up into the Transvaal. It was a deliberate attempt to reproduce a bygone scene. Something far more real takes place in the Liturgy. For the Church is the Body of the Living Christ, and there is a sense in which His incarnate Life is still manifested to the world and lived out in His followers on earth. So in Holy Week they mystically take part in our Lord's own experiences. So in every Mass they do not sacrifice Him afresh, but they join mystically in the one perfect offering on

Calvary, or rather they are in Christ as He offers Himself there once for all. The Apocalypse in that fifth chapter, to which we have already referred, teaches the same lesson. It shows the whole Church of all time gathered at one and the same moment before that one sacrifice, and lifting its voice in praise and adoration.

Since liturgical worship plays so vital a part in the Church's life it is only right that a solemn obligation lies upon her members to take part in it. Furthermore, it is fitting that some should be set apart to make it their main concern, all the more as the majority of mankind are too much absorbed in social duties to give much time to it, even if they would. The Religious Orders and Congregations, especially the contemplative communities, have that special honour and obligation placed upon them. Their daily life is so ordered that the worship of God forms its central business. Their time-table reflects the psalmist's cry " Seven times a day do I praise Thee ". Many of them rise at midnight in order that even when the world sleeps, some here should join in the never-ceasing adoration of Heaven. St. Teresa wished her Carmelites to recite the night office earlier because it was a time when few others on earth were at prayer. In these highly specialized days the dedication of men and women to such lives of prayer ought to be easily understood. If men are set apart to give themselves wholly to the discovery of an antidote for some disease, or for the manufacture of some death-dealing explosive, it is at least fitting that some should be called to give themselves wholly to the worship of God the Creator and Redeemer of all.

But the Liturgy forms only one part of the Christian's response to God in prayer, and we must now consider the individual's private prayer.

CHAPTER IV

MENTAL PRAYER

THOUGH Liturgical Prayer is of vital importance in our worship of God, our private prayer has its own unique place—and nothing must be allowed to supplant it. Some enthusiasts of the liturgical revival have recently tended to lose sight of this, and to say that attendance at public worship included everything else. But that is to ignore the example of both our Lord and the saints. Our Lord was punctilious in His observance of the worship in temple and synagogue alike, but we know also that He spent long hours in private prayer. More than once the Gospels tell us that He passed whole nights thus. St. Luke was particularly careful to record some of those occasions, when He went out into the desert for prayer or up into the Mount of the Transfiguration. "It came to pass in these days that he went out into the mountain to pray; and he continued all night in prayer to God." (Luke 6. 12.) It was when He was "praying in a certain place" that the disciples asked Him to teach them how to pray, and He gave them the Lord's Prayer (11. 1). Prayer burst forth spontaneously from His lips on the return of the Seventy (10. 17). There is His agony of prayer in Gethsemane; there is also the "high-priestly prayer" recorded by St. John (Jn. 17).

We must remember, in talking of private prayer, that there is a sense in which even the hermit praying in the desert is never offering a merely solitary prayer. He prays always as a member of the Church, and his prayer is caught up in the stream of the Church's devotion. For some, more than others, the Liturgy forms the setting and starting-point of all their prayer. It was in the recital of the psalms that the hermits looked to be raised to ecstasy. The great Benedictines found chiefly in the Liturgy the material for their private prayer. So, many of the visions and revelations of St. Mechthild and St. Gertrude came to them as they joined in the community Mass, or meditated on it afterwards. In a convent,

where liturgical worship gives the pattern and chief occupation
for the day, the individual's private prayer is woven closely and
consciously with the corporate prayer. Elsewhere the connection
is not so obvious. Most people in the world need a lengthier
preparation to reach the recollection and devotion which the office
has already brought to the religious. That is one reason why the
Ignatian method of meditation with its careful preparation and
"composition of place" proved and still proves of such value to
the secular. It taught him how to withdraw, shut the door on
worldly interests, and join the saints around the throne. But it is
essential for everyman's spiritual progress that sometimes he should
be free to join in that stream in his own way, and according to
his own special *attrait*. For God deals with each one of His children
individually, inasmuch as no two souls are exactly alike, and each
has his own problems and outlook.

Our Lord not only set an example in this matter of private
prayer: He gave special injunctions to His followers how they
were to pray alone: "When thou prayest, enter into thine inner
chamber, and having shut the door, pray to thy Father which is in
secret, and thy Father which seeth in secret shall recompense thee.
And in praying use not vain repetitions" (Matt. 6. 6).

He also laid great stress on the need of petition in prayer, and
did so although "your Father knoweth what things ye have need
of before ye ask him" (Matt. 6. 8). It was not enough that blind
Bartimaeus called out to Him for mercy. Our Lord knew perfectly well what the man wanted and He knew his faith. Yet He
required more. He stopped, waited till Bartimaeus came to Him,
and then made him utter his petition specifically before He healed
him (Mark 10. 46). We are not only to ask for what we need,
but to be urgent and importunate in our asking, like the widow
in the parable. And He assures us that, if we have faith, our prayers
will be answered: "All things whatsoever ye pray and ask for,
believe that ye have received them and ye shall have them." (Mark
11. 24.) "Whatsoever ye shall ask in my name, that will I do,
that the Father may be glorified in the Son. If ye shall ask anything in my name, that will I do." (Jn. 14. 13; cf. Matt. 7. 7;
Jn. 15. 7; 16. 23; 1 Jn. 5. 14; Jas. 5. 16). St. John in this connection and
with regard to our attitude towards God uses the word παρρησία,
"boldness", "confidence". But literally the word means "saying

everything ", almost " freedom of speech ". Is not that exactly the
right attitude of the child with his father, whom he loves and
trusts? He says just what is in his heart, feeling sure that his father
understands, likes to hear him, and will give him whatever is best
for him. That solves all questions about what we may pray for.
Everything that seems to us of importance at the time may be
brought to our Father, provided that we desire that His will
should be done, that we should be co-operating with Him, not
seeking to bend His will to ours.

But prayer has a far wider range than petition. As it grows,
petition occupies a smaller space. The familiar definition of prayer
as " the lifting up of the heart to God " teaches us that. " Prayer ",
says a modern writer (closely following St. Thomas Aquinas), " is
the unfolding of our mind before the Most High and in His
presence."[1] Too often it is regarded mainly as a means of obtaining strength for doing our work in the world—a kind of heavenly
lubricant for the machine. Men contrast it with action. But
prayer, ordinary prayer at least, is itself action, the highest activity
in which a human being can be engaged. The intellect is man's
highest power, that which distinguishes him most from the animal
creation, and makes him most like God—and the use of it forms his
greatest prerogative. He uses it to the best advantage when he
turns from the consideration of creatures to the consideration of
the Creator. And it is there, in that highest power of the soul,
that he communes with God. Everyone who has persevered in
prayer knows how costing an effort it can be. But it is action
directed immediately towards God, whereas other activities are
directed towards others. And God is the " end " of all action.
Through all our other activitives we are seeking something else
—our own pleasure, our own good or that of others, if ultimately
God; but in prayer at its highest we seek nothing else, for there
we have the goal of all our action, God Himself. St. Mark tells
us that our Lord, before choosing the twelve apostles, spent the
night in prayer and then called unto Him " whom he himself
would " and appointed them—not, mark you, primarily to cast
out devils, heal the sick, or preach, but " to be with him ". Union
with Him first; then " that he might send them forth to preach,
and to have authority to cast out devils " (Mark 3. 15). So
on another occasion He commended Mary because, in placing

[1] Leen, *Progress through Mental Prayer*, p. 19. (Sheed & Ward, London, 1935.)

communion with Him before activities, she had chosen the one thing needful, " the good part which shall not be taken away from her " (Luke 10. 42).

The Catholic Church has always maintained this truth. That is why she values so highly the contemplative life, and has given a recognized place to those who have felt the call to that life and drawn apart from the world to practise it. In itself it stands as an emphatic protest against the constant tendency to absorption in this-world ends, a noble insistence on the value of prayer, and on the fact that union with God is man's true goal and the source of all his power here and now. The realization of this fact of God will result in our prayer becoming increasingly *adoration*—the attitude of the creature in the presence of the all-wise, all-loving, all-perfect Creator. The tendency to worship is deep-rooted in the human soul. It begins with the child as he grows into consciousness of a world around him, strange, beautiful, terrible, and above all incomprehensible. It fills him with wonder, bewilderment, and fear, with a sense of his own littleness and at the same time of desires which can be satisfied only by something or someone outside himself. It is the creature's sense of his own inadequacy and need of his Creator. There is no one more pitiful or more *borné* than the man who has lost the capacity of wonder or worship, through the distortion of his critical faculties, or through the delusion of his self-sufficiency. He must " be converted and become as a little child " to regain that capacity before he can enter the Kingdom of Heaven. Adoration is the expression of childlike wonder, the sense of dependence of a soul made aware of and directed towards its first cause—God Himself. It combines both awe in the presence of the All-Holy, All-Mighty, and delight in the presence of the All-Beautiful.

Another all-important element of prayer is *thanksgiving*. It is closely linked with adoration. Its necessity is too obvious to need stressing here. But we have to learn this note: we are apt to take our blessings too much for granted. It is good to go through each day and thank God for its mercies both material and spiritual. Neglect of thanksgiving more often than not lies at the door of a lack-lustre, despondent soul.

Realization of the holiness and goodness of God brings home

to the soul its own unworthiness. *Penitence* therefore forms a third element in our prayer. So it was with St. Augustine. Not the degradation of his sin, nor the fetters it laid upon his will, but rather the growing glimpses which he caught of the all-holy God, first brought home to him his sinfulness, showed him, in his own expressive phrase, that he was " far away in the land of unlikeness ". So it was with Job. In the midst of his calamities, his wife's want of sympathy, and the insinuations of his friends, Job protested his innocence. At the end God manifested Himself. In that moment Job saw himself in true perspective: " Now mine eyes have seen thee: wherefore I abhor myself and repent in dust and ashes." (42. 5 f.) This sense of sin persists and even grows, long after the soul has confessed its particular sins and obtained the peace of forgiveness. The lives of the saints stagger us sometimes by the keenness with which they felt it. We are tempted to think some of them hypersensitive. That is because, while we are familiar enough with sin, we lack their experience of God. However, our penitence must go further than a sense of sinfulness; it must be sharpened by the recognition of those particular sins which we have actually committed. That is why we must practise self-examination to see where that general sinfulness has led to definite acts of sin. Sorrow for them only becomes true penitence when it passes beyond remorse, or disgust with ourselves for falling below our standard, and becomes sorrow for having offended God and crucified the Lord Jesus. It is the truth brought home so vividly to Saul of Tarsus on the road to Damascus. Fra Angelico tried to depict it in his fresco of St. Dominic kneeling in tears at the foot of Christ on the Cross, while the Precious Blood streams down to cleanse him. Or we find it expressed in the simple words of the hymn:

> It was my pride and hardness
> That hanged Thee on the tree;
> Those cruel nails, O Saviour,
> Were driven in by me.

The fifth element of prayer, *intercession*, we shall consider in a later chapter (Chapter VIII).

Writers usually divide prayer into two kinds, vocal and mental. The distinction is not an illuminating one, though it serves as a rough classification. For vocal prayer, prayer expressed in words

E

and set forms, would scarcely deserve the name of prayer at all
if no mental effort was given in the reciting of them. And mental
prayer, where the mind and heart are mainly occupied, often finds
expression in words. The first stage in mental prayer is nowadays
generally called *Meditation*. It may be defined simply as thinking
about God and His will for the soul, in order to do that will.
Such thinking leads to conversing with God. The substance of
the prayer, therefore, consists in reflections, petitions, and resolutions.

The old writers also spoke of meditation, but they used the
word in a rather more restricted sense than we do. Walter Hilton
said, for instance, "Three means there be which men most commonly use, that give them to contemplation; as reading in Holy
Writ and of holy teaching, ghostly meditation and busy prayer
with devotion."[1] He may have read the *Scala Claustralium*, written
still earlier, which taught that the ladder reaching to God had
four rungs—Reading, Meditation, Prayer, and Contemplation.
We include the first three, Walter Hilton's three, all under the
name of Meditation, though we should recommend most of
the reading to be done as a preparation for the meditation, as
indeed they did. That does not mean that the reading is com-
paratively unimportant. Far from it. Some people find it most
helpful to have the book in front of them and read with
frequent pauses for thought and prayer. But that method,
valuable as it can be at times, has a tendency to result in very
little prayer.

It is well to remind ourselves at the outset that the first object
of mental prayer, as of all prayer, is communion with God and
conformity with His will. But we start with the fact that we are
already united with Him through our Baptism. It is sometimes
an immeasurable comfort to fall back on that fact of our union
with Him and of His eagerness to enter into closer communion
with us, of His abiding presence within us. As Meister Eckhart
once boldly expressed it: "You need not search for Him here and
Here: He is no further away than the door of your heart. There
the stands waiting and watching till He finds you ready to open
and let Him in. You need not call into the distance for Him: it
is harder for Him than for you to wait till you open." Our union

[1] *Scale of Perfection*, I. 14. (John Watkins, London, 1923.)

with Him exists independent of our feelings, however far away God may seem, however cold our prayer.

Mental prayer is an attempt to realize that fact, the spending of a certain time each day in conscious communion with Him who already dwells within us. So there will be no unnatural straining after the unattainable but a turning to our Father. God is our home, and home is the one place where we can be just ourselves, where we have no feeling of strangeness, where we need not strain or pretend to be something other than we are, and where we have no fear of being misunderstood. So our Lord taught us when He said, "When ye pray say Our Father."

Now, to know and love God demands some likeness to Him—and we, like St. Augustine, are aware of being "far away in the land of unlikeness". In only one man has that likeness been perfect, the man Christ Jesus, who is also God's perfect revelation of Himself to the world. He is our model which we must continually study. He therefore will form the main, though not the only, subject of our meditations. "I am", He said, "the Way, the Truth and the Life". "No man cometh unto the Father but by me." God, it is true, reveals Himself in countless ways in His creation. For the most part men, blinded by sin, fail to recognize Him. The world's tragedy lies in their failure. There is an almost unbearable pathos in the words, "He was in the world, and the world was made by him and the world knew him not" (Jn. I. 10). But Jesus Christ is the perfect revelation. Only in Him does creation become intelligible as a revelation of God. So a poet who loved Him could write:

> I see His Blood upon the rose,
> And in the stars the glory of His eyes.
> His body gleams amid eternal snows,
> His tears fall from the skies.
>
> J. PLUNKETT

If all this be true the study of our Lord's life on earth is of supreme importance. For here God sums up and explains His self-revelation to man: "And this is eternal life to know Thee, the only true God, and Him whom thou didst send, Jesus Christ." (Jn. 17. 3.) He will not miraculously make up for our lack of knowledge, if it has been through our own fault that we have neglected His teaching.

Meditation is an invaluable method of training the soul in this knowledge of God. If the knowledge of God is eternal life, to gain it is the supremely important business of life, knowledge worth employing every faculty we possess to obtain. God is no philosophical abstraction. He is a personal, loving God, and therefore we can in some measure know Him here and now. A child's education is both an unconscious and a conscious process, or more truly a passive and an active process, and of the two the former constitutes the larger part. Long before he is capable of reasoning, or even of talking, a multitude of facts is being impressed upon his notice. His growth consists largely in his reaction to these, in other words in his response to his environment. There are things soft to the touch and pleasant; others hard and painful; things which satisfy his hunger, others which make him ill. There are faces round him which he learns to distinguish, sounds to notice, things to see. And always that pressure of environment will continue, and he without effort will have knowledge thrust upon him. Very soon the other process begins. He sets himself to learn new truths for himself. A long succession of things to be learnt by deliberate effort stretches before him, walking, reading, writing, etc. Still all the time he is learning from his surroundings infinitely more than he realizes.

So it is with the children of God. He is our environment and we have to respond to Him with all we are. Chiefly our growth is a passive process under the moulding influence of grace. God is within us and around us teaching us, guiding us, feeding us, long before we are aware of Him. But the more conscious we become of Him the more eagerly must we task every faculty to know Him better. All our study should aid us in this. His handiwork lies around us. Everywhere through His creatures He waits to teach us the great lesson. Whether we are learning about plants or sciences or people, they can teach us something more of Him that made them, or point the way to Him. Old writers on the spiritual life loved to explain how to use the study of Nature to climb to the contemplation of God. Such a book as Bellarmine's *De Ascensione Mentis* applies this method and still has value for us. We have altered our method of approach to these things since his day, but the principle remains the same. Our interest lies more in knowing what Nature contains: he was mainly interested in what it signified. George Tyrrell once wrote: "The great aim of the spiritual life is by observation and reflection to enrich the significance of the word 'God', to crowd ever more and more meaning into its simplicity."[1] That, as it stands, is an overstatement, but it contains a great truth. The Church has always maintained that the want of learning is no bar to the highest sanctity. We recall the story of Brother Giles delightedly hailing a peasant woman and bidding her be of good cheer, because she could be as holy as the learned doctor St. Bonaventura. The saint himself had just told him so. And we remember the long list of saints who had no learning. But the Church has never taught that ignorance was an asset. Clearly one of the most direct ways of "enriching the significance of the word God" apart from prayer is the study of theology. Professor Maritain, in the very valuable little book written by himself and his wife, *Prayer and Intelligence*, speaks emphatically on this point: "Prayer, particularly in the case of intellectuals, can only preserve a perfectly right direction and escape the dangers which threaten it, on condition of being supported and fed by Theology. Knowledge of the Sacred Doctrine has a peculiar tendency of its own to shorten and render safer the spiritual journey."[2]

Saints continually proclaim the power of the name "Jesus". The Bible relates how the apostles cast out devils and healed the sick in that name. Most men find that hard to realize, because the word "Jesus" has so little significance for them. Nothing of course can equal the value of practical experience to "enrich its significance", e.g. the reception of the Sacraments, public worship, answers to prayer, victory over temptations. But that in its turn is deepened enormously by learning who Jesus is, what He did on earth, what was the meaning of His death on the Cross, and what He still does for man in Heaven. That is theology—though many put theology on one side as a mere intellectual exercise, barren of spiritual results! Yet meditation, say, on Bethlehem must be enriched by some knowledge of the meaning of the Incarnation, or that on Pentecost by some knowledge of the gifts of the Holy Spirit.

Islam provides an interesting illustration of this point. It insists

[1] *Faith of the Millions*, I, p. 303. (Longmans, London, 1902.)
[2] *Prayer and Intelligence*, p. 6. (Sheed & Ward, London, 1928.)

nobly on the unity of God. God is one and God is to be worshipped.
But Mohammed was almost ignorant of theology. He knew little
else about God. The result is not only a pitifully inadequate creed,
but also a pitifully inadequate prayer, and a pitifully inadequate
ethical response. We referred in the last chapter to the poverty of
his ritual. Prayer consisted for Mohammed mainly in the performance of certain ceremonial acts and words, almost entirely
lacking the inner lifting up of the heart to God and communion
with Him. For creed and prayer go hand in hand. *Lex credendi,
lex orandi.* There is a minimum of theology which every Christian
must have for right living and right praying. Whatever else
beyond that a man learns about God can be of great assistance to
him in his spiritual life. With Mohammed contrast St. Paul.
There we have the same insistence upon the unity of God. There
is "one Lord, one faith, one baptism, one God and Father of all,
who is over all, and through all, and in all" (Eph. 4. 5). Yet
what a difference! The word God is charged with meaning for
him. Into it is packed all the doctrine of the Jewish Church: to it
is added all the richness of the Christian revelation; and the whole
is crowned and interpreted by his own vivid personal experience.
It resulted in a tremendously enriched knowledge of God, bearing
abundant fruit in his moral life and social relationships. That does
not mean that St. Paul owed his driving power to his learning
and his knowledge about God. As he very well knew and stated
repeatedly, it was the power of God, Christ living in Him. But
such knowledge did, as it were, make fresh windows in his soul,
through which the sun could pour. It helped him to understand
more fully the mystery revealed to him by God, and to explain it
more clearly to others.

If what we have been saying is true, it makes clear how great a
value meditation possesses as a method of soul-training. It seeks
in four ways to assist our growth in the knowledge and love
of God:

(1) *By enlightening the understanding.* This is not the most
important, but it comes first in the method itself and forms its
distinctive note. Hence meditation is often called "Discursive
Prayer"—the form of mental prayer where the reason busies
itself most—"running about", as it were, to seek fresh light on
the subject. It may not be amiss to remind ourselves here that the

knowledge sought is personal knowledge of a personal God—not the knowledge of an abstract system, or impersonal force. Therefore, like other knowledge of persons, it is largely intuitive, even at this stage. Facts about God, reasons for faith and love which meditation suggests, are not that knowledge, but they aid us in its acquisition. So in forming a new friendship knowledge of the friend grows in ways not to be defined: it certainly does not consist in knowledge of the things he has said and done, yet somehow all those things have their significance in revealing the man to us, though he himself is always something more and richer than they. Even when we are studying the life of someone we have never met, that indefinable thing called personality betrays itself through what we read and hear of him. Now we cannot see God here, nor grasp Him by our senses. More than ever, therefore, are the things we can learn about Him of value. Yet He is never absent from us, but within us and around us and acting upon us at every moment.

(2) We possess one capacity of enormous assistance in our meditations—the *imagination*. More will be said about this capacity later on (see Chapter VI). Suffice it to say here that imagination enables us to bring home to ourselves the reality of some past experience, or grasp more intensely some experience of the moment, or taste beforehand in some degree an event yet to be experienced. It is essentially realistic, though it can transform itself into fancy. By means of it we can enter more fully into the subject of our meditation. If, for instance, we were considering the Passion of our Lord, it would bring home forcibly to us His sufferings, deepen our love for Him, and make us eager to serve Him better. So when writers on prayer stress the importance of using the imagination, they are not urging their readers to be fanciful, to work themselves up into an unreal state or picture things which never happened nor could happen, but to realize the truth. None has laid greater stress on the use of the imagination than St. Ignatius Loyola. What he calls in his *Spiritual Exercises* " Composition of place " is where it is specially to be employed. He teaches that, so far as the subject allows, all five senses in detail must be applied to realize the scene. Supposing, for instance, the subject was the Passion, we must try to imagine the scene as vividly as we can—*see* the thronging crowd, *see* the Pharisees and scribes exulting in their victory, the soldiers cold and callous, and

in the midst our Lord Himself—and so on. But St. Ignatius would have us go further still—try to *hear*, as it were, the shouts of the crowd, the words of our Lord, the taunts of His enemies; to *feel* the driving in of the nails, and the agony of our Lord—and even so far as possible to apply the senses of taste and smell.

All people possess this capacity in greater or less degree. But there seem to be different kinds. The imagination of some seems to be mainly pictorial, a capacity for realizing the scene as a picture before the eyes. Others find this very difficult, but can enter intensely into the feelings entertained by the actors in the scene. We might call their imagination psychological rather than pictorial. We must discover along which line our imagination works best and use it in that way. If one's imagination is not of the pictorial kind there is little use in trying to form a picture of scenes in one's meditation.

We said that in meditation the reasoning powers play a considerable part. But that does not at all mean using the time as an opportunity for sharpening the critical faculty, or for working out intellectual problems. Too readily meditation will degenerate into this, and become mere speculation, or, it may be, a time for composing sermons, or indulging in imaginary argument. Instead of that, the mind must be employed in considering the spiritual lessons of the subject, taking the thoughts that come and quietly pondering over them. There must be nothing controversial, aggressive, distracting: it should be a chewing of the cud (*ruminatio*) rather than a searching for new food. Invaluable as the study of theology may be, our meditation is neither the time nor place for it. Even to spend the time reading a devotional book may be merely to read someone else's meditation rather than meditate ourselves.

(3) *By kindling the heart.* Our perfection after all consists not in knowing much but in loving much. It is union with God through love—and God is love. Though knowledge and love must go hand in hand, the first commandment is not " Thou shalt know ", but " Thou shalt love the Lord thy God with all thy heart ". So we are brought to the very centre of the meditation. All that quiet pondering over the subject, e.g. over one of the mysteries of our Lord's life, with the help of the reason and imagination, brings home to us the wonder of God's love and power, and of

our own poverty and need of Him. Little by little the heart begins
to glow with devotion, which will show itself in expressions of
love, humility, faith, penitence, etc.—informal expressions, or
sentences from the psalms or well-known hymns. The mere utterance of such expressions helps to fan the flame of love, even though
the heart as it utters them feels cold.

The emotions have their part, and a very important part, to
play in the spiritual life. A man is incomplete without them and
God claims the whole man, body, soul, and spirit. The masters of
the prayer life quite rightly warn us against the danger of relying
upon feelings, or being dominated by them, but that does not
mean they have no value for us. It is right to pray for fervour,
though wrong to depend on it. Without it our devotion will
tend to lack the *élan* that inspires generous self-giving. There is a
curious insistence in medieval writers on the "gift of tears".
Even so robust a saint as St. Catherine of Siena held them in high
esteem, distinguishing five kinds. It strikes our modern ears as
mawkish and unbalanced. But did it not rather symbolize the fact
that the emotions have their importance in human nature, and
must figure in any complete response to the call of God? To-day
we do not set such store on tears, but we must not despise the
emotions.

On the other hand, at the door of our emotional nature lies
the foe of all true religion, sentimentalism, which is sentiment
gone bad. It involves the erection of feelings to be the be-all and
end-all of religion. Nothing can be more fatal. The remedy is
not to worry much about feelings. They come and go. They
have their place in true love, but love is infinitely bigger.

(4) *By inspiring the will.* The test of love is not in feeling but
in action. Understanding, sympathetic love will always seek an
outlet in service. Moreover, the doing of such acts of service,
however insignificant, reacts upon the love, increasing it still more,
like dry wood thrown on to a fire. If our meditation has been
fruitful at all, it will have filled us with a desire and determination
to serve God more faithfully. The question arises, How? for true
devotion is always practical. The time we have spent thus with
God must have its effect on the day. Generally it cannot show
itself in any revolutionary act or decision: it must find expression

in something smaller. Hence the value of the *Resolution* at the end. It will be something practicable—something if possible to be done that very day (though not necessarily arising out of the subject of the meditation), e.g. say a prayer at a certain time, write a neglected letter, be watchful over the tongue, or kind to a trying neighbour. It scarcely matters how trifling the thing is: it is a symbol of our love. Sometimes for weeks and perhaps months our resolution will vary little, as we try to eradicate some fault or grow in some virtue.

Little by little, if we persevere in prayer, we shall grow more quick to recognize the will of God and the inspirations of His Holy Spirit. In spite of many failures, much confusion, and even rebelliousness, God comes to mean infinitely more to us than ever before. " I said, I will water my garden . . . and lo, my stream became a river, and my river became a sea." (Ecclus. 24. 31.)

> Each faculty tasked
> To perceive Him has gained an abyss, where a dew-drop was asked.
> R. BROWNING, *Saul.*

Methods of Meditation

The question arises: How are we to conduct our meditations? Innumerable books have been written on this, so it will not be necessary to enlarge upon the various methods in use. There is the three-point meditation—a subject with three thoughts about it—as admirably put forth by Bishop Challoner's *Meditations for Every Day in the Year*. The Ignatian method is perhaps the most familiar in some form or other, with its preparation, preludes (composition of place, etc.), points, colloquy (which includes a resolution).

St. Ignatius in his *Spiritual Exercises* regards the soul in its relation to God. He fastens attention upon it. The exercitant must examine his soul in all its bearings, its end, its setting, its capacities. And he must employ every effort and every means to achieve perfection that he may fulfil the purpose of his creation. The *Exercises* were the epitome of St. Ignatius' own experiences. His conversion had revealed to him the state of his own soul, how far he had forgotten his " end ", and the process by which he had sought to regain the right track had been a painful one. He had prayed and agonized, and in the process he had organized all his faculties, seen to their purification and their concentration on God. Just because his experience was the experience of countless others, his method proved, and still proves, of inestimable value. It met their needs as it had met his own.

But it was not the only method. The Sulpician method, taught by the French Cardinal, de Bérulle, is probably less well known. It is in some ways simpler and leads more readily on to Affective Prayer. We will therefore consider it briefly. Cardinal de Bérulle had a different outlook. No sudden experience of conversion had come to him. Instead, an overmastering sense had seized him of the majesty and glory of God, incarnate in Jesus Christ. "The Word was made flesh and we beheld his glory." That was the stupendous fact which riveted his attention. In the face of it his own soul seemed to shrivel into nothingness. "What is man that thou art mindful of him?" He was conscious only of his sin and his frailty. God was all and self nothing. This was in itself a reaction from the humanism of his day with its self-sufficiency and facile contentment with the merely human. Hence, whereas St. Ignatius began with an examination of self and its surroundings, its attitude to God and to its fellow-creatures, de Bérulle began with an act of self-renunciation. St. Ignatius began with self-examination and worked up to adoration: de Bérulle began with adoration and worked down to self-annihilation. The difference between the two must not be pressed too far. Both alike sought the glory of God. *Ad majorem Dei gloriam* was St. Ignatius' motto, not de Bérulle's, but the latter would have subscribed whole-heartedly to it. The approach was different: the end the same.

The method of mental prayer taught by de Bérulle is generally known as the Sulpician method owing to the fact that it was his pupil, M. Olier, *curé* of the parish of St. Sulpice in Paris, who first systematized it and taught it widely. What is it? We will omit the preliminaries and go straight to the main part of the prayer. It consists of three parts, (1) Adoration, (2) Communion, (3) Co-operation, and it is modelled on the first clauses of the Lord's Prayer. The keynote of the prayer, be it remembered, is devotion to God Incarnate, and the subject for meditation always one of the Mysteries of our Lord's life. De Bérulle himself had a particular devotion to the Incarnation itself. Our first task lies in setting before us the mystery, chosen beforehand, and in considering it in the light of some special virtue which we desire to think of in connection with it.

(1) *Adoration*—or "Jesus before the eyes".

As an illustration let us choose the Crucifixion. We think of our Blessed Lord on the Cross, picture Him hanging there for our salvation. In particular we will consider on this occasion His self-sacrificing love. Then we remind ourselves that this is God Incarnate suffering for us: it is the love of God Himself revealed here on the Cross. Other considerations will occur to us as we bring our minds and imaginations to dwell upon it all, revelations of the Divine love, it may be, in previous ages, thoughts of the world's sin and our own sin that caused the sacrifice.

As we do this, more and more the wonder and richness of that love will come home to us—the glory of the God who thus humbled Himself and thus gave Himself—the utter worthlessness of ourselves in treating Him so. So the first part of our prayer pours itself out in adoration and thanksgiving before that stupendous revelation. It is an expansion and adaptation of the first clause of the Lord's Prayer, "Hallowed be Thy Name".

(2) *Communion*—or "Jesus in the heart".

We go on to meditate on the desirableness of that love in ourselves. We are conscious of our own selfishness; we realize the necessity of being like our Lord, and how far away we are. Here our thoughts turn to ourselves, but only in the light of God's revelation of love. There can be no room for self-centredness, morbidity, or day-dreaming in such a context. So our prayer changes into penitence and petition, beseeching our Lord that He would come and reign in our hearts. Such communing with Him is rightly named communion. But the name has a deeper significance. It is so called because it means that Christ does come and fill our hearts. His grace meets our prayer, and His love takes possession of us.

De Bérulle and his followers play constantly on two notes, *adhérence* and *anéantissement*, and it is important to understand what they meant by these terms. The main purpose of the spiritual life, they taught, was that Jesus Christ should possess and rule the disciple's soul, without any opposing will or desire on the disciple's part. As Christ's human nature had no separate personality, for there was in the God-man only one Person, God the Son, so, in so far as it was possible, there must be in man's soul only the one ruling person, Jesus Christ, the Word. Not only this, but the different "states" of our Lord's earthly life were also to be reproduced in the soul—of His humiliation and self-naughting at Bethlehem and Nazareth, of His patient service of others in His ministry, of His love and self-sacrifice on Calvary, as of the glory of His Resurrection and Ascension. The disciple clung to Jesus throughout the whole life, and in a sense reproduced the experience of H.s Incarnate life, or rather Jesus reproduced it in His disciple. That process, that clinging to Jesus Christ, was what these teachers meant by *adhérence*. *Anéantissement* summed up the whole process of self-naughting, of mortification and detachment, by which the wayward will and ill-regulated desires were brought under control, that *adhérence* might be possible.

Now just as the first clause of the Lord's Prayer summed up the first stage of this method, so the second clause sums up this second stage, "Thy Kingdom come"—the reign of Christ as undisputed King in the soul.

(3) *Co-operation*—or "Jesus in the hand".
Here we consider how we can co-operate with our Lord to carry into effect His will. It brings us to the third clause of the Lord's Prayer, "Thy will be done in earth as it is in heaven". In the mystery of Calvary we have adored God Incarnate on the Cross: we have considered the meaning of His love and prayed that it might rule our hearts. Now we stop to think how we can realize it in action. Thus the method is as practical as the Ignatian, for it too brings us to resolutions. And care must be taken, as we said above, that our resolutions at the end of our prayer (whatever method we use) should be practical and definite.

So the meditation ends. But there is one thing further to be done and it consists of three parts—(1) an act of thanksgiving to God for the time spent in His presence thus and for the light He has given; (2) an act of penitence for our shortcomings, want of fervour, or distractions; (3) a brief recollection of one or two thoughts which have most helped us in our prayer. These we take with us to recall during the day. They help to keep us mindful of God as we go about our work.

What is generally called the Ignatian method is not the only method of mental prayer taught by that saint. At the end of his *Spiritual Exercises* he too suggests the Lord's Prayer, though not in quite the same way as the Sulpicians. He bids us take the prayer word by word, stopping at the end of each word to think what it means and then to pray about it. It is a way of praying which anyone can use sometimes as an alternative to his usual method, or later in the day. Incidentally it helps one to realize something of the depths of that prayer, given by our Lord Himself. St. Ignatius also tells us that we can take any other set prayer, e.g. the Collect for the day, and go through it in the same way. He describes the method thus: " The second method of prayer is that the person, kneeling or sitting, whichever he finds more suitable and making for greater devotion, keeping his eyes shut or fixed on one place, without moving them hither and thither, says *Father*: and remains pondering over that word so long as he finds meanings, comparisons, relish and consolation therein. And let him do likewise with every word of the *Our Father*, or of any other prayer, which he wants to pray in that way." Perhaps most people would find it more helpful to take it clause by clause rather than word by word.

Whatever stage of mental prayer we have reached, it is wise to choose the subject beforehand. The last thing at night, if one is not too tired, is a good time for that. It has two advantages. For one thing the mind has a way of working during sleep. Nearly everyone has had the experience, after trying hard to solve a problem or remember a forgotten word, of going to bed and waking up with the answer ready. So during sleep the mind to some extent works on the subject chosen for mental prayer. Secondly, the preparation beforehand saves wasting prayer-time, wondering what to meditate about.

It is good when coming to prayer not to be in a hurry. One needs to get recollected first, to let the world and its clamour, as it were, die away, and to stop to think whom one is approaching. Our Lord's words about entering into one's room and shutting the door before praying suggest a measure of deliberation, of shutting out the world, and the heart getting still first. And it is good too, sometimes, during the prayer, towards the end, to still the clamour of our thoughts or prayers which we are offering, and stay silent, waiting for a short time for the Holy Spirit to show us His will.

We must have fixed times of prayer, but we must not confine prayer to those times. St. Paul says, "Pray without ceasing", and we have to learn not only to use "ejaculatory prayer", offering up short prayers or words (vocally or mentally) at any time, but to train ourselves to become aware of God at all times. It involves what is often called the Practice of the Presence of God (see page 179).

Affective Prayer

Meditation will not always hold the field. A time comes when both imagination and ideas seem no longer so necessary. It happens to some people much quicker than to others. Some find that thinking much over the subject chosen only sharpens their critical faculties or leads them off on to divers intellectual problems, which, however important in themselves, do not facilitate prayer. They would be wise to take at once to a more affective type of prayer. This comparative failure of the imagination is different from the dullness and dryness which befell us on occasions during meditation. It has become our more or less permanent state. Prayer has now taken a stronger hold on us and become part of our life. Moreover the power to converse with God has grown: so has our fervour, on the whole at any rate. In other words, the "colloquy" part of meditation now absorbs most of our time and attention. It means that God is leading us to another, simpler kind of prayer. It involves a more immediate relationship to God, more like that of a child talking freely to a loved father. For the child does not need to form pictures of his father and his doings, or ponder over different aspects of his character. His knowledge of him is more direct, and he talks to him freely of his hopes and plans, and expresses his affection quite naturally. The new kind of prayer is something like that, and is usually called "Affective Prayer". Yet no hard and fast line can be drawn between this and our former prayer. In meditation we made acts of prayer, acts of adoration, of love, etc., which will form the main part of this other prayer. In what does it consist?

(1) Whereas formerly the greater part of our prayer time was spent in thinking over the points of the meditation, and much less time in actual praying, now the conditions are reversed. The latter

demands more and more space, the former gets less and less. For a subject it will be sufficient to take one of the great elementary truths about God, e.g. one of His attributes, His love, His power, His eternity, or one of the Mysteries of our Lord's Incarnate Life. Yes, most of all one of the Mysteries. We shall not need to rack the brain for fitting thoughts about the subject. All that is necessary will be to place it before us and allow the mind to dwell restfully upon it. One or two considerations will arise and they will probably suffice for our time of prayer.

Those considerations will give rise to thoughts and feelings of devotion, which can be expressed in acts of adoration, thanksgiving, penitence, faith, love, and hope. Father Baker at the end of *Holy Wisdom* gives a list of such acts. He also in that book (Sect. III. 1–3) gives careful directions about this kind of prayer. Some of the acts he gives may seem a little stilted in phrasing or a little extravagant in content, but they will help us to form acts more exactly expressive of our own mood. To go back to laborious thinking, or even to follow out some line of thought that suggests itself at that time, is to miss the whole point of our prayer. The object of such thinking in meditation is to kindle the heart to love God. If that happy condition has come almost spontaneously, so much the better. Let us go on our way rejoicing, offering our prayer in these simple acts, or even silently. As St. Vincent de Paul once put it in his homely way: "When we want a light, we use a steel, we strike it, and as soon as the fire has caught the prepared material we light our candle, and he would look foolish who, having lighted his candle, continued to strike the steel."[1] Well, we don't light candles that way nowadays, but the saint's lesson holds good all the same.

Perhaps at first the acts will not come easily: we shall have to force ourselves to make them. To do so helps us to learn the language of prayer. In time they rise more naturally to our lips. Sometimes, indeed, our prayer will seem to fail altogether. Then we must return quietly to our subject and find some new consideration which may form the centre for our acts. Only there must be no busy working of the brain. Those times are past. Our prayer has now become a prayer of the heart and will, rather

[1] Quoted by Saudreau, *Degrees of the Spiritual Life*, p. I, 261. (Burns, Oates & Washbourne, London, 1926.)

than of the mind. We hold ourselves, as it were, before God, no matter how dull and undevout we may feel, and offer ourselves to Him, tell Him of our love and pray for His grace. The repetition of the acts will help to prevent distraction and rekindle devotion. We bring what we have: it may be only a cold heart and tired brain, but it is the best we have at the moment, and God knows it. Nothing else matters much. We can repeat with the psalmist: " O God, my heart is ready, my heart is ready: I will sing and give praise with the best member that I have " (Ps. 108. 1), however poor that best may be.

Sometimes the simple thought of the presence of God will suffice for a subject. Nor shall we need a great variety of acts. A few will best serve our purpose. Occasionally one single act will be all we shall need for some minutes, perhaps for the whole of the time. If that happens, it is best to surrender to it and not to force ourselves to go on to another. St. Ignatius expected that in using the Lord's Prayer one might spend a whole hour over one word. What actual words are said matter very little. Often the acts will be made mentally without repeating them with the lips. If the mind wanders, verbal repetition will aid recollection; it may be the repetition of a single phrase, or of the Holy Name. The use of a rosary has the same effect. The very feel of the beads passing through the fingers, combined with the repetition of the same few familiar words, serves to occupy the superficial activities of the brain, and leaves us free to cling to the real subject of our prayer. It is good to make a resolution at the end of this prayer as at meditation, and for the same reason.

Thus our prayer goes on, ever towards a greater simplicity, as we climb the ladder towards contemplation. To that we shall come later in this book.

CHAPTER V

COMPLICATIONS

WE have tried to consider the purpose of our creation and the glorious destiny which God has for mankind, nothing less than fellowship with Him in Christ Jesus, and eternal life. Then we examined the ways in which He has enabled us to begin that life here and now, together with the opportunities He affords us of renewing and deepening our fellowship with Him. Once again it is good to remind ourselves of the joy of that life with God. It is the ultimate full satisfaction of all the deepest desires of the soul. Real happiness can only proceed from such satisfaction. That is why merely worldly things can never give full lasting happiness. Always something is lacking to the soul that was created for union with the infinite eternal God—God who is spirit—until it finds God. Only in and through Christ can it so find God.

Yet, even when we have grasped the purpose of our creation and as members of the Church become partakers of the life in grace through word and sacrament, all is not accomplished. It is not even a smooth progress to the final consummation. Great difficulties stand in the way. There are few who cannot say with Browning's Paracelsus:

> I had a noble purpose and the strength
> To compass it; but I have stopped half-way,
> And wrongly give the first fruits of my toil
> To objects little worthy of the gift.

St. Paul's reproach to the Galatians comes home to most of us to-day, "Now that ye have come to know God, or rather to be known of God, how turn ye back again to the weak and beggarly rudiments? . . . Ye were running well; who did hinder you that ye should not obey the truth?" (Gal. 4. 9; 5. 7.) We know well enough who hinders us and what. But before passing on further we must look closer at these obstacles, and consider

ways and means of dealing with them. Those obstacles are the
world, the flesh, and the devil—to quote the words of the Catechism,
" the devil and all his works, the pomps and vanities of this wicked
world, and all the sinful lusts of the flesh ". These, as it compels
us to confess, we promised to renounce at our baptism (by proxy
at least), but they still retain a greater or less control over us. For
a short space we shall examine each of these three separately. In
thought it is possible to do this, even though in practice the three
are almost inextricably intermingled, a fact which makes the
struggle against them so much the more difficult.

(1) *The Devil*

Satan is the first and greatest enemy. Though at times he
seems to leave us for a season he is never far away, and lies in
wait for us to the end. We may well pray in the *Anima Christi*:
" From the malignant enemy defend us." Belief in the devil forms
no part of the Christian creeds. Yet he figures so prominently
both in the Bible and in the tradition of the Church that it would
be foolish to ignore their witness. Moreover we meet with such
experiences both in our own souls and in the world that we should
have to invent him, even if hitherto he had remained unknown.
For nothing else is adequate to account for those experiences, not
even the theory of the Unconscious. People in the past have often
attributed to his agency events which are better explained more
naturally, but there still remains much, both in our own selves and
in human society, which points to supernatural powers at work.
Our Lord showed no doubt about his existence, took it for granted,
and was quick to mark the first signs of his activity. His own
coming was in part a mission to destroy the devil and his works.
He faced him and defeated him at the beginning of His ministry.
The first mission of His disciples led Him to declare, " I beheld
Satan fall as lightning from heaven ".

In after years Christ's saints also had their open conflicts with
the devil. Indeed the further they advanced in holiness the more
quick were they to perceive his presence. Many of them have
affirmed that they have seen him and heard him, even smelt him.
That was not because they grew more superstitious as they grew
holier. Rather it was that their spiritual senses were quickened,
so that they discerned more clearly spiritual powers both good
and evil.

In the Middle Ages the devil loomed large. He seemed to sprawl over both the cloister and the world. Dr. Coulton went so far as to label him " the monk's God ",[1] and in doing so showed his inability to understand the medieval mind. It is true that the devil and his minions appeared to pervade every department of life, and the monk had to be ever on his guard against them. Old Irish regulations insisted that monks should make the sign of the cross on their spoon for fear a devil should insert himself in their food. St. Benedict orders a visitor to be taken first into the oratory for prayer for fear of illusions. Lurid pictures of the Last Judgement and hell and of the devil's triumph abounded.

But there was another side to all that. To a certain extent much of that belonged to old pagan folk-lore. It revealed in what a pixie-ridden world our forefathers had lived. But the Christian could rejoice in the redemption of the world by Jesus Christ and in the completeness of His victory over the powers of evil. Hence it was that the devil, dangerous though he might be, came to figure as part dupe and part fool. He provided the comic relief in the Mystery Plays of the day. And a gleam of laughter played round the dark cloud of their fear. Julian of Norwich had a glimpse of this in her vision of Christ's Passion and His victory over the devil. " I saw our Lord scorn his malice and set at nought his unmight; and He willed that we do so. For this sight I laughed mightily, and that made them to laugh that were about me." [2]

Nevertheless the devil remained then and still remains a sinister, terrible figure, bent on the ruin of souls. The office of Compline opens with St. Peter's grim reminder, " Be vigilant, be watchful, for your adversary the devil goeth about as a roaring lion, seeking whom he may devour ", though it does not forget the note of triumph, " whom resist, stedfast in the faith. But thou, O Lord, have mercy upon us." St. Paul teaches that there is something still bigger at stake than the welfare of individual souls. We have to deal with a mighty foe, and it forms mankind's real struggle; " Our wrestling is not against flesh and blood, but against the principalities, against the powers, against the world rulers of this darkness, against the spiritual hosts of wickedness in the

---

[1] *Five Centuries of Religion*, vol. I.
[2] *Revelations*, Ch. XIII.

heavenly places." (Eph. 6. 12.) Like the Apocalyptist's portrait of the Antichrist, the apostle seems to suggest in the man of lawlessness a kind of satanic parody of the Incarnation. In the course of history, more than once, rulers have arisen who appeared to their contemporaries to fit the picture. It is evil on a gigantic international scale, organized under a single master-mind, and for a season triumphant. We may not know exactly what the writers meant by these pictures. One thing is certain: they bring home with startling force the truth that evil is something far more than the absence of good. It has an immense positive power, capable of taking possession of human personalities, and working untold ill and suffering.

However, in whatever guise the devil appears each member of Christ must learn to be quick to recognize his presence, and as quick to reject his advances. His most insidious form of attack is to persuade folk that there is no such creature as himself. The old masters of the spiritual life show a remarkable insight in distinguishing between the temptations which come from the main enemies of the soul. The devil is specially concerned with the spiritual sins—pride, jealousy, hatred, malice, unbelief. But he lies behind all others, ready to mark the first yieldings of the soul and to seek to strengthen the temptation by innumerable devices of his own. They would say, for instance, that the temptation to intemperance springs from the man's own corrupted desires. The devil thereupon would use all his cunning to play upon that temptation. Not being able to get inside a soul in grace, he can only guess at what is going on there from such signs as the man gives. So sometimes, in spite of his deep knowledge of the nature he corrupted, he makes ridiculous mistakes. More often his diabolical skill enables him to use the most deadly means. For his object is always to secure the soul's damnation, and he is ready to seize on every opportunity that presents itself.

But it is not necessary to pursue further old opinions about the devil. For we ourselves "are not ignorant of his devices". It is enough to repeat their warning that we must renounce the devil and all his works utterly, always and everywhere. In a sense dealing with him is simpler than dealing with the world and the flesh. For there the renunciation cannot be and ought not to be so complete.

(2) *The World*—the rest of the visible creation outside ourselves. Two initial complications present themselves here.

(*a*) God made the world as the sphere in which man was to live and glorify Him—and He made it good. "God saw everything that he had made, and behold it was very good." And still it remains very good in spite of all man's sin. Still it remains the sphere in which we are to live for His glory. Nor does He demand that we should renounce it utterly, but only what is evil in it— the "pomps and vanities of this wicked world". "Wicked", for wicked the world is, when it means human society going its way apart from God. The New Testament thrusts the paradox before us, as in the writings of St. John: "God so loved the world" (Jn. 3. 16), and, on the other hand, "Love not the world neither the things that are in the world" (1 Jn. 2. 15). But we could not renounce it utterly, even if we would, not if we were to remain in it. For God has so arranged our life that we are dependent upon it. That "no man liveth unto himself" is one of those platitudes which from time to time bursts into a flaming and terrifying truth. No living creature is more helpless and dependent on others than a baby. And, all life through, man needs both the produce of the earth and the labours of his fellows, and intercourse with them if he is to live and grow at all or reproduce his species. Even the hermits who renounced the world and fled to the Egyptian desert still depended upon it for their sustenance.

Yet the world with all its attractiveness and goodness constitutes an ever-present menace to the soul. It has indeed its harsh side, where Nature (as we often term the physical and animal world apart from man) goes her way indifferent to man's needs or feelings, sometimes sweeping away in a moment's storm the labours of a lifetime. Or there is human society itself pursuing its course, offering a brazen face to the unsuccessful individual, true to the principle "each man for himself and devil take the hindmost". But not here lies the worst danger to the soul. That comes from its very attractiveness. It dangles its prizes before men's eyes, power, wealth, lordship, pleasure—all substitutes for God. And there are few who are not led astray by them in greater or less degree. Our Lord Himself faced the full force of its enticements in His temptation, and He alone could estimate the evil and remain heart-whole.

(b) But the world is not only outside ourselves. It has strong-holds within. It was at work within us long before we were aware of it. From our earliest childhood its influences have been helping to mould our character. Here again the good is inter-twined with the evil, and can scarcely be separated. Family cus-toms, social ideals, our own particular environment have all played their part. We have accepted them unconsciously, assimi-lated them so that they have become part of ourselves. So much of them is good and necessary for our Christian calling—friend-ship, consideration for others, loyalty to our country, the desire to play our part for the welfare of society. On the other hand, what evil gets mixed up with them! Each age, indeed each stratum of society, acquires its own false ideas and selfishness which create a curious social blindness to the truth. To-day most Christian people would agree that slavery is incompatible with their Faith. Yet only a little more than a century ago the agitation against slavery aroused bitter opposition from many otherwise loyal Christians. A strange situation existed in America. Abolitionists in the North thundered ceaselessly at the iniquity of the slave-owning South, but were blind to the fact that the white employees in their own business concerns were being subjected to more degrading treatment by their employers than most of the slaves in the South. At the present time there is a similar blind spot with regard to the colour bar—the relation between the black and white races. If such ideas are to be found in Christian homes, it is easy to understand how the world can lay hold of souls brought up in godless surroundings. Some years ago an ex-burglar pub-lished his autobiography.[1] It was a strange, sordid story. The child of a prostitute, he was brought up in the midst of vice. The ideal put before him and accepted by him was that of the successful criminal—the "wide" who by robbing and duping the "mugs" could find means to satisfy his desires and passions without work, live the "wide" life. "Every man for himself" was his motto, and morality in the ordinary sense of the word had no meaning for him. Yet even here the world had not complete sway. There were gleams of nobler ideals striking through the sordidness, and a sense of frustration, of failure to find the satisfaction for which he craved. It was one more case of a soul made for God and restless because it had not found Him.

[1] *Low Company*, by Mark Benney.

(3) *The Flesh*

This is our warped human nature, particularly on its sensual side. The Catechism says we are pledged to renounce "all the sinful lusts of the flesh". Not the flesh entirely. That would be impossible. The desires of the flesh were given to man to enable him to fulfil the purpose of his creation, to live for the glory of God. They belong to that creation which God made "very good". But now sin has deflected them from that purpose. They tend continually to entice the soul away from its true goal, and to seek satisfaction for its own sake. If we are to deal rightly with this misdirected tendency, it helps greatly to understand something of the workings of those desires, and of the composition of our human nature.

From early ages men have puzzled over the relations of soul and body. The Law of Nature, or sad experience, apart from the Christian dispensation, taught them that some strange conflict existed between the two. How was the problem to be solved? Some took the view that the body was the prison of the soul. A fundamental dualism existed. The soul belonged to the realm of light, the body to the realm of darkness. Life's business lay in setting free the soul from its prison. It involved a process of complete mortification of the flesh and all its desires, on the ground that they were evil and a barrier to the soul. Only few, however, who held this creed had the courage to follow its relentless logic. The rest abandoned themselves to the flesh. Here and there, singly or in groups, holy men, fakirs and their like, tortured their poor bodies in the attempt to kill all desire, that the soul might be set free and swallowed up in the All. Others, such as the Epicureans, maintained that in a life so short and fleeting men must make the most of their time to taste to the utmost every pleasure the senses could give. It meant indeed for the discerning a measure of discipline, lest the edge of their finest sensations should be blunted. The creed always has its adherents, though most of them follow it blindly. Walter Pater dressed it up again in its most attractive and least sensual form. But even the languorous beauty of his words cannot conceal the despair that inspired them. The sentence of death has already passed over them. "To burn always with this hard gem-like flame, to maintain this ecstasy, is success in life. . . . While all melts at our feet we may well grasp at any exquisite passion, or any contribution to knowledge

that seems by a lifted horizon to set the spirit free for a moment.
. . . With this sense of the splendour of our experience and of its
awful brevity, gathering all we are into one desperate effort to
see and touch, we shall hardly have time to make theories about
the things we see and touch."[1] Both these attitudes towards the
body have had their reflections in the Church. In the early days
of its history many hermits tended in practice at least to a dualistic
view. They tortured the flesh as though it were evil in itself.
Yet the purity of their intention to follow Christ and their own
fervent belief in the resurrection of the body kept them in the
right path. That is well illustrated by St. Bernard of Clairvaux
some centuries later. He was steeped in the teaching of those
hermits and ruined his already delicate health by his austerities.
Yet he insisted on the importance of caring for the body as the
" good and faithful comrade " of the spirit, and on its value both
for this world and the next.

At the time of the Renaissance the reaction swung too far in
the other direction, and a revival of its teaching is widespread
to-day. We are told that, as God made all things good and gave
us senses to enjoy them, enjoy them we should to the utmost of
our capacity, short of deliberate sin. The doctrine contains much
truth: the difficulty, indeed the impossibility, lies in the stopping
short. No, there is a further difficulty. Walter Pater could have
pointed it out. Man cannot give all his senses free play, for the
more the lower senses are indulged the more incapable does he
become of enjoying the highest and most delicate pleasures of
mind and spirit. Even here he has to make choice, and it calls
for some kind of self-discipline, or asceticism.

The word " asceticism " has gained an ill-favoured significance.
Popularly it connotes excessive mortification. But that is foreign
to its original meaning. The Greeks used the word *ascesis* to
express training—and it had no necessary connection with over-
severity. St. Paul loved to draw the parallel between the training
of the Christian and that of the soldier or athlete. The Christian
is like a man running in a race or a boxer (1 Cor. 9. 25), or like a
soldier on a campaign (2 Tim. 2. 3), or like an athlete stripping for
the contest (γύμναζε δὲ σεαυτόν, 1 Tim. 4. 7). The Epistle to the
Hebrews contains a similar picture (12. 1). " Athleticism " might

[1] *Renaissance*, p. 236. (Macmillan, London, 1910.)

give a more accurate idea of what is meant by Christian asceticism. For the modern athlete knows very well the necessity of training, if he is to gain proficiency in his sport. Moreover he knows that that training must be precisely adapted to the end in view. The footballer will need a different training from the pugilist, and the oarsman from the runner. Further still, if the training is too severe the athlete goes stale: if it is too light, he cannot stay the course. The need of adequate training came imperatively to the fore at the beginning of the recent war. The military authorities discovered that the existing system was totally inadequate for the demands of modern warfare. They therefore revolutionized the whole system. But they proceeded scientifically. A gradual intensification of training increased the physical capacities of the recruits to an almost incredible degree. They became able to endure long marches on short rations, and exposure to cold and wet and other hardships, which without such discipline would have broken them completely. It revealed to them capacities which they had no idea they possessed.

However, discipline merely for discipline's sake has little value, and the body quails before it. What is needed is some sufficiently inspiring motive to carry a man through. T. E. Lawrence, who exercised so extraordinary an influence over the Arabs, and achieved so much in the war of 1914-18, saw that clearly and has given fine expression to it. By stern self-discipline he raised his own physical powers to an amazing degree of efficiency. But there was something more behind his success than that. "Such liberties", he wrote, (victories over needs of flesh, food, and sleep) "came from years of control (contempt of use might well be the lesson of our manhood), and they fitted me peculiarly for our work: but, of course, in me they came half by training, half by trying, out of mixed choice and poverty, not effortlessly, as with the Arabs. Yet in compensation stood my energy of motive. Their less taut wills flagged before mine flagged, and by comparison made me seem tough and active. . . . During the revolt we often saw men push themselves or be driven to a cruel extreme of endurance: yet never was there an intimation of physical break. Collapse rose always from a moral weakness eating into the body, which of itself, without traitors from within, had no power over the will."[1]

[1] *Seven Pillars of Wisdom*, p. 467. (Jonathan Cape, London, 1935.)

Unfortunately Lawrence himself never found a sufficiently inspiring ideal to carry him right through. He flung himself with selfless devotion to the achievement of victory and the cause of the Arabs. It had steeled his will, fired his imagination, and enabled him to perform prodigies. But when the victory was won and the Arabs, as he thought, betrayed, there was nothing left. His literary ambition could not fill the gap and he fell into a curious state of disillusionment and uncertainty. Not long before his death he wrote, "One of the sorest things in life is to come to realize that one is just not good enough. Better perhaps than some, than many almost, but I do not care for relatives, for matching myself against my kind. There is an ideal standard somewhere, and only that matters, and I cannot find it."[1] The words show that he was not far from the kingdom of God, and he has probably found that standard now.

Now Christianity in demanding a strict "asceticism" or training supplies an adequate motive. "They do it", said St. Paul, "to receive a corruptible crown, but we an incorruptible," and he went on to say, "I therefore so run as not uncertainly; so fight I, as not beating the air: but I buffet my body, and bring it into bondage" (1 Cor. 9. 25 ff.).

"To receive a crown?" Is the motive then so selfish? The Quietists loudly repudiated this. They maintained that the Christian, so far from seeking reward, must be indifferent even to his own salvation, utterly surrendered to the will of God. God's will must be his sole aim. But the gospel is more discriminating, and our Lord is content to deal with human nature as He knew it to be constituted. He speaks indeed without qualification of the need for the entire giving of self, if any one is to be His disciple, and of the paramount claims of God. All that is summed up in His call to the cross. It is illustrated in the garden of Gethsemane where He deliberately accepts the will of God though it meant the cross for Himself. Yet side by side with that there runs the promise of reward, repeated again and again. The Beatitudes in the Sermon on the Mount are crowned with such a promise. The disciples who leave all to follow Christ are told that they will receive a hundredfold even in this life, and in the world to come life everlasting. The apostles will sit on twelve

[1] *T. E. Lawrence and His Friends*, p. 22.

thrones judging the twelve tribes of Israel. The labourer is worthy of his hire, and he shall be paid generously even if he does not enter the vineyard till the eleventh hour.

Our Lord speaks thus because He knows that man is so constituted that by his very nature he seeks the fulfilment of his own personality. Finite, cramped by sin, and incomplete, he must seek completeness. No ideal will satisfy him unless it holds out to him some sure hope of ultimately attaining to this. Modern psychology has fastened on this need of man, but too often it expects him to find that satisfaction in the readjustment of his own ego with the claims of society and with his own subconscious self. "Every one's ultimate aim and strongest desire lies in developing the fulness of human existence that is called personality "; and again: " The ideal of personality is an indestructible need of the human soul."[1] So writes Professor C. G. Jung, and he is more aware than most that something must come from beyond to meet the need. What our Lord knew, and what the psychologist generally does not know, is that that fulness can only be obtained through the giving of self to God. For man was made for God and can only reach his perfection in Him. The saints sometimes expressed the truth in vivid terms. " Nothing is necessary for you except God," Blessed Angela of Foligno told her disciples. She is but echoing our Lord's words to Martha: " One thing is needful." Here lies the central paradox of the gospel, that man must by his very nature seek his own self-completion, yet can only obtain it by the sacrifice of himself, which is a clumsy paraphrase of our Lord's saying: " Whosoever would save his life shall lose it; and whosoever shall lose his life for my sake and the gospel's shall save it." (Mark 8. 35.) So He corrects both the Quietist and the psychologist.

[1] Jung, *The Integration of the Personality*, pp. 281, 298. (Kegan Paul, London, 1940.)

CHAPTER VI

THE CHRISTIAN ASCESIS

I

THE prophet Isaiah foretold the coming of God to transform the desert: "Then . . . in the wilderness waters shall break out and streams in the desert. . . . And an high way shall be there, and a way, and it shall be called the way of holiness; the unclean shall not pass over it; but it shall be for those: the wayfaring men, yea, fools, shall not err therein." (Isa. 35. 6, 8.) It is a beautiful picture. The first Christians realized that the prophecy was fulfilled in Christ Jesus. He had proclaimed Himself the Way, and so they spoke simply of following Him as being "in the Way". In the previous chapters we have been considering the meaning of the Way, the obstacles that confronted us, and the need of self-discipline. It is time now to study the kind of training we must undergo if we are to overcome those obstacles, and follow the Way to the end. The training must be stern, for the road goes uphill right to the summit of the Mount of Vision. It involves a fight as well as a climb. St. Paul harps on that idea of Christian warfare. The thought kindles him: more than once he calls it "the fine fight" (τὸν καλὸν ἀγῶνα). What must we do? How can we best take our part in it?

First of all the Way itself imposes upon us a certain measure of discipline—the most valuable of all because it is none of our own choosing, but laid upon us by the Church. The rendering of a glad obedience to her ordering demands an initial surrender of self-will. Every society or club must have rules which its members must obey. But the Church stands to us in a unique relation, different from that of any other society. For the Church is the Body of Christ, and we are members (limbs) of that Body, in a sense in which we can belong to no other society. She imposes the obligation to fast, to join in public worship, to receive the sacraments and observe her other precepts. In this she is like a wise mother, placing before her children such "good things as pass man's understanding", but teaching them how to prepare to receive them.

Nevertheless each individual has to face the task of dealing with his own refractory self. He can learn from others: he has the inestimable privilege and comfort of their fellowship and support, but he cannot escape his own special responsibility of self-discipline. The process of adapting and absorbing one's environment is a mark of life. Soil passively accepts whatever is thrust into it. But the plant that is thrust into it at once sets to work to take into itself, and adapt for its own use, the elements that it finds in soil and air, to grow to its perfection.

In the past men sometimes regarded too negatively the Christian training. Some of the old hermits, for instance, or, much later on, the author of the *Spiritual Combat* (Scupoli), seem to have fixed their eyes almost exclusively on the struggle against besetting sins, and on how to deal with temptation. They seem to picture the struggle as nothing else but a battle royal against the devil and his myrmidons. The *Spiritual Combat* gives elaborate directions about facing temptations, recalling them, reasoning with them, and then finally vanquishing them—almost like a dog worrying a rat. Such directions have their value. But modern psychology has revealed certain dangers in such a method. It tends to keep the mind turned towards the evil, which may lead to unhealthy reactions. So often the cause of the temptation lies hidden. One may crush the temptation for the moment, but it only drives the evil further underground, and like the creeping rootstock of some poisonous weed, it appears in another part, more virulent than ever. It is true that it can be dealt with there again in the same manner, but it all involves an enormous waste of energy and is apt to have a depressing effect on the soul.

Now there is one factor which plays a decisive part in our training—the imagination. It may be employed in two quite different ways, and it is important to distinguish these. The one provides an escape from reality into a world of fantasy; the other illuminates reality. A Walt Disney technicolor film displays imagination run riot, amusing because of its fantastic fancifulness. A young recruit in the Army may picture himself heading a charge against an impregnable position, single-handed bayoneting the enemy, then receiving the thanks of the commander and being decorated with the V.C. That is pure fancy, divorced from reality. But the same recruit gets a letter from home, in which his mother gives an account of some family events. His imagination calls up the scene before him: for the moment he is back with his people, sees them, hears them speaking. That is the more valuable use of the imagination: it enables him to appropriate, as it were, reality. Or again he may be set to cross a narrow plank bridge, high above a torrent. If it were a foot above the ground, it would cause him no hesitation. As it is, he begins to picture himself losing his foothold and falling headlong, and he either shrinks from it or else tries and fails. But his imagination might work the other way. It might enable him to realize that the bridge was quite wide enough and that he could get across easily—and cross it he would.

Well, in the fight against temptation the first secret of victory is to realize for ourselves the reality of the grace we have received, what it means to have Christ within us, to know the power of God. St. Paul tried to drive home this truth to the Ephesians. Living in their cosmopolitan pagan city they were apt to give up the struggle too easily as hopeless. So he wrote to kindle their imagination, piling into one sentence almost every word he could think of to express power, praying that God might show them "what is the exceeding greatness of his power to usward who believe, according to that working of the strength of his might which he wrought in Christ" (1. 19 f.). It needs imagination to realize that—and that kind of imagination can be trained to some extent. A well-known psychologist, Dr. W. Brown, says: "One essential element in self-control is the ability to imagine success. If we wish to control any instinctive tendencies, or any desires or impulses, just as if we wish to control any fears or worries, an essential condition is that we should expect to succeed. . . . We can define will as a desire qualified and defined by the belief that, so far as in us lies, we shall bring about the end that we desire because we will it."[1] What is needed is a lively faith, and the right use of the imagination is an immeasurable help to this. It is that kind of faith which the Epistle to the Hebrews calls "the assurance of [R.V. margin, the giving substance to] things hoped

[1] *Mind, Medicine and Metaphysics*, p. 69. (O.U.P., London, 1936.)

for, the proving of things not seen " (11. 1). Most of us are so aware of our own weakness that we seem unable to grasp the fact that we have all the power of God at our disposal. To meditate often on our Lord and on the lives of the saints helps to bring it home to us. And this can be supplemented by some form of self-suggestion. An elementary form of this is to get thoroughly relaxed and recollected, think of the Risen Christ dwelling within us in His might, and then repeat some short *positive* statement slowly as to our ability to do this thing we have to do, or be this which we desire to be, looking always to what we desire, and not at what we wish to avoid. It points the way towards St. Paul's triumphant " I can do all things through Christ who strengtheneth me " (Phil. 4. 13). Then we can go forward with confidence. Our Lord told the man with the withered hand to stretch it out. The man had a lively faith, and Christ's healing power could work. He made the attempt without doubting and found his hand healed. How many of us in his case would have said: " I can't: my hand is withered: if Thou wilt first heal it, I will stretch it out "!

If we follow this method, it will lead us to a different way of meeting temptations than that laid down by the *Spiritual Combat.* We shall as far as possible ignore them instead of dealing with them in detail. Occasions indeed arise when Apollyon seems to straddle the path and he has to be faced as our Lord faced him with " Get thee behind me, Satan ". There are times when the evil seems so mixed up with the good that for the moment it is difficult to see the right course. The devil often seeks to pervert those who are definitely " in the Way ", not by temptation to obvious deadly sin, which they would detect at once, but rather by first suggesting some lesser good—something perhaps harmless and good in itself, but not what God wills for them. So it was with Eve in the garden of Eden. To know good and evil might seem a valuable piece of knowledge, and it was to be obtained by eating fruit, and she often ate fruit. But it happened this time to be the forbidden fruit, and Eve knew it. But " to be as God knowing good and evil "! Surely God would understand. Yes, Apollyon was right across the road. It is instructive too to study our Lord's temptations in the wilderness and see how appropriate each was and how plausible—each time a temptation not to gross evil but to something which might seem to help forward His mission. But it was not what the Father willed for Him, and in the end it would have meant devil-worship.

When such temptations assail us, the best way is not to argue with them but to turn from them and hold resolutely to the light we have. The beginner on a bicycle soon learns how necessary it is for him to keep his eye straight on the road in front of him. If he looks at the oncoming vehicles they seem to exercise an irresistible attraction, and he wobbles towards them. So the Christian following the Way must keep his eyes forward, " looking unto Jesus the author and perfecter of our faith ". It means his pressing on towards God, without allowing himself to be diverted. There is something to be said for the quaint refrain of an early Salvation Army hymn, " Satan, don't bother me. Satan, don't bother me. Satan, don't bother me. I'm saved and happy be."[1] Most of the temptations that crowd upon us day by day are clear and bear the mark of the beast, temptations to impatience, to pride, to contempt, to lust, or to greed. Some of them are probably due to hidden complexes seeking some outlet—some part of our life-force imprisoned. To ignore them does not mean to repress them. Repression has disastrous consequences. Certain temptations, especially lustful ones, so surprise and shock some souls by their foulness that they refuse to recognize them as their own, and seek to force them into oblivion. But as we have already remarked, they then tend to reappear in other more dangerous forms. Such a damming of the life-force reduces the soul's energies and prepares the way for nervous breakdowns. The individual must, on the contrary, accept them, recognize them as symptoms of yet ill-regulated desires or of some hidden complexes, realize that they run counter to his scheme of life, and then deliberately choose not to be diverted from it by them. Instead he will give himself as generously as he can to follow Christ, confident in His power to set things right, waiting with earnest expectation " to be delivered from the bondage of corruption into the liberty of the glory of the children of God " (Rom. 8. 21), in some measure here and now. As his faith grows stronger such an attitude brings an increasing sense of relief. Trying to fight temptation in his own strength involves an almost intolerable strain. To take refuge in the heart of Christ and leave the fight to Him is to rid himself of the burden. " Come unto me all ye that labour and are heavy laden, and I will give you rest." To come to Him thus is like

[1] Quoted St. John Ervine, *God's Soldier*, p. I, 514. (Heinemann, London, 1934.

G

reaching a sunny sheltered spot after struggling against a blizzard.
"Thou shalt keep him in perfect peace, whose mind [imagination,
R.V. margin] is stayed on thee: because he trusteth in thee."
(Isa. 26. 3; cf. Ps. 18. 29–40.)

Further, Christ himself has pointed the way to the sublimation
of such unruly temptations. Sublimation is perhaps the wrong
word. For here it is not a question of finding satisfaction other
than the natural ones for instinctive desires: it is rather a question
of centring those desires on God, who is their true satisfaction, the
end for which they were created. The self-assertive instinct makes
a man seek a position of some importance and respect amongst his
fellows. Our Lord did not content Himself by saying he must
crush that desire. But He showed that in the Father's Kingdom
there is a different scale of values, and that the true distinction is to
seek the lowest place. Let a man have faith to realize that and he
will eagerly make for it, and his self-assertion will find its proper
satisfaction. "Ye know that the rulers of the Gentiles lord it over
them, and their great ones exercise authority over them. Not so
shall it be among you: but whosoever would become great among
you shall be your minister; and whosoever would be first among
you shall be your servant: even as the Son of Man came, not to be
ministered unto but to minister, and to give his life a ransom for
many." (Matt. 20. 25–28.)

Sacramental confession at regular intervals is of priceless value
here. The earlier it begins the better. So many of the soul's
problems and temptations owe their origin to unpleasant experiences, too shameful or humiliating to be told to others, but kept
revolving in the mind, till at last thrust beneath the surface. The
mere unburdening of such experiences to another brings relief,
helps to clear the air, and prevents complications. The secrecy of
the confessional guarantees one from exposure and contempt or
ridicule, and therefore invites confidence. A wise confessor can
help us to deal rightly with the trouble for the future. The ancient
Irish had an apt name for their confessor: they called him "soul-
friend". Best of all, the grace of absolution cleanses the soul from
the stain of sin and gives it strength to go forward in peace. "Go
in peace," says the confessor, "for the Lord hath put away thy
sin." Hence if we are being assailed by violent temptations it is
good to reveal them to our confessor, even if we are not conscious
of having deliberately yielded to them. They gather force when

locked in one's own heart, and dissipate when uttered. Lady Macbeth's doctor had no satisfactory answer to her husband's agonized question:

> Canst thou not minister to a mind diseased;
> Pluck from the memory a rooted sorrow;
> Raze out the written troubles of the brain;
> And with some sweet oblivious antidote
> Cleanse the stuff'd bosom of the perilous stuff
> Which weighs upon the heart?

The doctor could only say that in such a case the patient must minister to himself. The Catholic can give a better answer. Only God indeed can bring such healing, but the Sacrament of Penance is His chosen way of bestowing, if not oblivion, at least peace and relief.

Even more important than the training of the imagination is the training of desire. It concerns all those instinctive urges which form so much of a man's make-up, the raw material of his being. They are the very stuff of his future sanctity, and he must learn to direct them aright to achieve the purpose of his creation. His heavenly destiny demands all he is and has, all his thoughts and desires purified, liberated, and directed to the glory of God. God wants in him that fulness of which we spoke in the last chapter (p. 92. Cf. Ch. v, p. 121f). None of the great spiritual masters has insisted on this regulation of desire so forcibly as St. John of the Cross. It is in order that the self may be given to God in its full strength. Moreover, he makes it clear that the "natural desires", i.e. those instinctive urges, do not hinder the union with God, provided that they are not yielded to, for "when we do not consent to them, and when they do not pass beyond the first movements, they do but slightly or not at all stand in the way of union".[1] It is the "voluntary desires", the unregulated, more or less deliberate, hankering after and clinging to the satisfactions of the world and the flesh for their own sake, that ruin the soul's progress. So Ruysbroeck posits as one of the essential preparations for union a "free turning of the will with a gathering together of all the powers . . . cleansed from every inordinate love".[2] Mark that "gathering together of all the powers". It is the opposite of their destruction. One of the aphorisms of the teachers of Yoga describes physical perfection as "beauty and grace and power and the compactedness of the

[1] *Ascent*, I. 11.

[2] *Adornment of the Spiritual Marriage*, Bk. II.

thunderbolt ".[1] The words might stand for a description of the soul perfected in Christ. A modern writer has said: " Asceticism in the Catholic sense is essentially the asserting of the body, not its negation. The aim of asceticism is to strengthen virtue. . . . Mortification is to mortify or deaden, not the senses, but those unruly appetites that weaken the sense of purity, that weaken the moral fibre of a man. To make a man pure, to make a man strong, such is the aim of mortification."[2]

To deal thus with the regulation of desire means that the whole man is disciplining his *concupiscentia* or *libido*, as it goes out in various directions. That seems a better way of considering the matter than to think of the purification of various faculties, like a worker cleaning his tools. Nevertheless, it is useful to treat separately the different avenues through which the *libido* functions. This book is not a manual of Ascetic Theology, so we must content ourselves with a few suggestions.

Our first business will be with the animal side of our nature, that which we have in common with the beasts. Two things must be considered here.

1. *Simplicity*

In the first place we have to discipline those desires which are " inordinate ", i.e. which create disorder in our life by diverting it from its main purpose, causing us to love creatures for their own sake and to seek our satisfaction in them, irrespective of God. Self-examination, for instance, will regard the use of our five senses. And our question will be not so much whether we have given way to gluttony or to lust, whether we have too many luxuries or are too fastidious, as whether we are held in bondage by the desire for physical satisfactions. Of course we must also come to definite things: " Is my desire for food (perhaps some particular food) or warmth or rest inordinate, and how am I trying to deal with it? " The examination will go on to other things, all included under the head of " creatures ", mental, æsthetic satisfactions or friendships, anything in fact which can get between the soul and God. It may be a passion for music or golf, or for reading novels—all good things in their place but it often requires

[1] Behanan, *Yoga*, p. 120.

[2] Vonier, *Human Soul*, 3rd ed., p. 93. (Burns, Oates & Washbourne, 1939.)

stern self-denial when they have grown "inordinate". George Russell, whose poems are known to many under the initials A.E., possessed great artistic talent, and painting was his favourite pursuit. But it was not the main business of his life, and he felt it was hindering that. He therefore deliberately laid aside his brushes, and refused to touch them till he had mastered "the temptation". "He feared it as a self-indulgence which if yielded to might stint his life."[1] As St. Benedict pointed out, it is possible for a man to have given up great possessions, and yet still hanker after some trifling thing like a pencil, which can divert him as much as something great. A silk thread, as more than one saint has suggested, can hinder a bird from flying as effectually as a cart rope. And we must be free. There is a medieval story of a friar who had to travel long distances to preach. A wealthy layman gave him a valuable ass to carry him on his journeys. With great delight the friar mounted it and set off for his next sermon. Arrived at the church, he tethered it outside and went in to Mass. But all through the service his thoughts kept recurring to the ass. Had he tied it securely? Perhaps some thief had come and stolen it or at least gone off with the saddle and reins? When he got out of church the ass was there safe and untouched. The friar unfastened it, gave it a blow on the flank and drove it away. He himself walked off in the opposite direction saying: "God forbid my soul should be tethered to an ass!"

Moreover, too much dependence on creatures argues a pitiful bareness of resources within oneself, a failure to find the sufficiency of God. "Godliness with contentment is great gain: for we brought nothing into the world, for neither can we carry anything out; but having food and clothing we shall therewith be content" (1 Tim. 6. 6 ff.)—"contentment" or rather self-sufficiency in the sense of being so far as possible independent of other creatures. Bossuet has expressed it a little differently: "What is the love of riches but a borrowing of external things, and so a sign of poverty within? And what is the love of sensual pleasures, but something which the soul borrows from its body and its surroundings, and so again ever poverty within? . . . instead of becoming rich once and for all by abandoning oneself to God, and by taking hold of everything in Him, or rather by taking complete hold of Him Himself."[2]

[1] A. E., edited by Monk Gibbon, p. 26.
[2] Quoted de Caussade, L'Abandon, II, p. 321.

Or to quote a modern British philosopher: "It is just in letting go the cherished possession when the call comes, that we learn the true strength of the personality, which can let so much go and yet survive, because it is not tethered. What we should really learn from these experiences is that there is that in our personality which is not fettered to any temporal good and can emerge enriched, not impoverished by the surrender of them all."[1] Mark Rutherford relates that at one period he had to take wine for reasons of health. Later he found it getting the mastery of him, so eventually he gave it up altogether. "The most powerful inducement to abstinence in my case", he adds, "was the interference of wine with liberty, and above all things its interference with what I really loved best, and the transference of desire from what was most desirable to what was sensual and base. . . . What enabled me to conquer was not so much heroism as a susceptibility to nobler joys."[2]

(2) Virility

Those words lead to the second point. The body must be trained to its utmost capacity to serve the soul in the quest for God. (See Chapter V, page 89f.) The Christian ideal reaches much further than that of physical perfection. It looks beyond this-world satisfactions. The Christian is travelling to a far country and he must carry no superfluous fat or baggage. There are nobler joys for him, and he must not spoil his palate for them by over-indulgence in coarser ones. "Thou, therefore," writes St. Paul to Timothy, "suffer hardship with me as a good soldier of Jesus Christ. No soldier on service entangleth himself in the affairs of this life." (2 Tim. 2. 3 f.) First attempts at such training often lead to weariness and distaste, perhaps to actual pain. The tendency then is to abandon them as injurious to our health. An athlete playing his first strenuous game of the season finds himself tired, stiff, and sore. But he does not thereupon decide to give up that form of exercise, for he knows that with a little more practice his body will stand the strain easily. So when a man first begins to fast it may cause a headache and tiredness. But, if he perseveres, his body adapts itself to the new conditions, provided his training is gradual and with discretion. How far have we tried to fit ourselves for following in the Way, which is Christ? If an apple-tree

[1] A. E. Taylor, Faith of a Moralist, I, p. 307. (Macmillan, London, 1937.)
[2] Autobiography, p. 38.

is planted in too soft a bed, it tends to develop a tap-root deep
in the soil. The tree flourishes and bears abundance of leaves, but
little or no fruit. The fig-tree cursed by our Lord may have done
the same. So with the soul. If we treat it too softly, it fastens its
roots too deeply into this-world pleasures. The outward forms
of piety may remain but there is little fruit, and it becomes insensitive to spiritual things and incapable of seeking them. In the
service of Christ there is no place for softness or effeminacy. "They
that wear soft raiment are in king's houses." Our Lord's teaching
is permeated with a note of sternness, of a ruthless schooling of
self to be fit for the kingdom of God. Dom Aelred Graham is in
keeping with that when he writes: "Eight hours' sleep and three
square meals a day are adequate safeguards of comfortable living,
but it may be questioned whether the Kingdom of Heaven suffers
violence by such a régime. We have no reason for supposing
that the perfect love of God which casteth out fear can be bought
so cheaply."[1] But the training of the body forms only a small
part of the Christian ascesis. It is interesting to note what a small
place it occupies in the teaching of St. John of the Cross. He is
concerned far more with the discipline of heart and mind and
spirit. And indeed if this is rightly carried out it becomes much
more easy to deal with the body.

We shall have something to say later (page 179) about the
"Practice of the Presence of God". It is enough here to emphasize
the need of keeping before us the purpose of our life, the glory of
God. It gives point to all our thinking and doing. This positive
direction of the mind is of much greater value than the mere
rejection of wrong thoughts, necessary as the latter is. "Our
citizenship [πολίτευμα, the setting of our life] is in heaven," says
St. Paul, and we have to be mindful of that. "How will this look
in eternity?" was the question one saint used to put to himself
when deciding on some course of action. But such concentration
on the things of God does not imply a careless or absent-minded
attitude towards our work in the world. The author of the *Spiritual
Conquest* writes: "Perform such works as concern your calling
without solicitude of mind or enjoyment of affection" (3rd *Ambush*),
but he does not mean by that taking no interest in them. Precisely
because they are the works which God has given us to do they
must be done for Him with all our heart and strength. To be

[1] *Love of God*, p. 123. (Longmans, London, 1939.)

God-centred has nothing in common with a Johnny-head-in-air
attitude towards our work here. As Fr. Waggett once said, " To
have one's heart in heaven is a very different thing from having
one's head in the clouds ". So St. Paul exhorts Timothy to pay
heed to his duties: " Be in them," he adds [R.V. " give yourself
wholly to them "]. None the less it is necessary to remain detached
from them, always heart-whole for God, ready to drop them and
turn to whatever else He desires of us.

The lesson, therefore, to be learned in all this is purity of heart.
Pure gold is gold at full strength, free from alloy: pure wine is
wine at full strength, undiluted. And a pure heart is a heart at
full strength, unadulterated by wrong affections, but all for God.
Our Lord here, as in everything else, provides us with the perfect
model—the true love of creatures combined with the utter devotion to the Father and the Father's will. We are indeed so conscious
of His tender love towards mankind, His acceptance of, and simple
delight in, God's creation, that we are sometimes inclined to underrate the extent of His detachment. Emil Brunner has given striking
expression to it. He says Christ's " whole life is one of extreme
detachment. He does not shun the reproach of extreme lack of
family feeling, in reference to the family in general, as well as in
connection with His own relatives. He does not make the slightest
effort ' to preserve the sacred possessions of His people '. . . .
He is a stranger in this world, He has no profession and He tears
His disciples away from their callings and from their natural
conditions; He possesses no home, no income, and no property.
He does nothing which could bring Him even the slightest praise
from those who care supremely for civilization, although . . . He
is no ascetic. He is unmarried and He praises the celibacy of elect
souls, but He consorts without the slightest embarrassment or self-
consciousness with women. . . . He went to be the guest of women,
and allowed them to wait on Him. He speaks the harshest words
against being bound to those ' sacred possessions ', and yet He
makes no attack on anything. . . . He shares human experience
to the full, and yet He is completely detached. He stands in complete reality in the midst of the real world, without breaking a
single thread which binds it to the creation, and yet He is free
from all; He is rooted in nothing, and yet He has not been torn
up by the roots."[1]

[1] *The Mediator*, p. 367. (Lutterworth Press, London, 1934.)

Christ's perfect detachment followed from His perfect attachment to His Father's will. Nothing else can rightly replace this as life's dominant theme. Now in learning that truth the discipline of the mind plays an important part. And how contrary the mind can be! Wandering thoughts, for instance, plague all men at one time or another, most of all perhaps in prayer time. That great scholar, Benjamin Jowett, once said that nothing brought home to him so clearly the meanness and wrongness of his mind as his failure in prayer. Whereas a novel would absorb him completely, the thought of God, the Truth, often left him cold, and after two or three minutes his mind would wander off to trivial things. It is the experience of many others. Nevertheless the mind can to some extent be brought under discipline, and the effort must be made (cf. Thouless, *Control of the Mind*). Our practice of recollection and of ejaculatory prayer, which is the main secret of success, must be supplemented by other means.

Do what we will, it is impossible for most of us normally to keep our thoughts fixed for very long on any one subject. The interest flags for a moment, and the thoughts always on the margin of consciousness, some of them suggested by the subject itself, come thronging in and occupy the centre. After a shorter or longer interval we find our thoughts far from their original subject. The only thing to do then is to lead them gently back and start afresh. If some particular unwanted thought insists on obtruding itself and occupying the centre, it can be banished by the constant repetition of some short phrase or prayer, uttered more or less distinctly and rapidly, and the mind swung back to our subject. After a short time it may be that the thought returns, and the same process must be repeated. But it is important, not only in prayer time but at all times if possible, never to prostitute the mind to idle thoughts. Obviously we should try to prevent that in the case of definitely evil temptations, e.g. to lust or uncharitableness or pride. But the same rule should be observed even with regard to innocent matters. It may be merely a crossword puzzle that tries to dominate us when we want to be thinking of something else. We must choose our own subject and not be dictated to by the puzzle. The rule applies with even more force to day-dreaming. Moreover day-dreaming is nearly always concerned with self, a subtle form of self-love, which can lead to serious consequences.

Recently some people have maintained that if one is troubled with harmful thoughts the best plan is to give expression to them openly, that this relieves the pressure and the soul can then go on its way undisturbed. That is bad psychology as well as bad religion. Experience shows that to tell bawdy tales or to indulge in scandal serves to increase the temptation to lust or uncharitableness. What was only a tendency has become a finished act, and made a deeper mark on the soul. It is true enough, as we have already seen, that to attempt merely to stifle the evil, to pretend it is not there, can lead to worse complications. The good psychologist would insist on the importance of recognizing its presence, facing it, and then deciding what to do about it. To speak of it privately to one's confessor is one thing and of great value: but to give free tongue to it publicly is quite another thing and fraught with danger both to oneself and to one's hearers. Incidentally this reminds us of the imperative duty of disciplining the tongue. "I will take heed to my ways," cried the psalmist, "that I offend not with my tongue." (Ps. 39. 1.) St. James declared that no man can tame the tongue. It is good sometimes to read that third chapter of his epistle, and realize its terrible truth. One of the ancient Fathers pointed out that God had set over the tongue a double guard of lips and teeth. But neither apostle nor father said anything stronger than our Lord's own statement that "for every idle word that men shall speak they shall give account thereof in the day of judgement" (Matt. 12. 36), or "Let your speech be Yea, yea; Nay, nay: and whatsoever is more than these is of the evil one" (Matt. 5. 37). Yet our Lord did not hereby mean to banish from human life all that innocent fun which goes to quicken the spirit of fellowship and lighten the daily round, nor to reduce men to a perpetual taciturnity. He did not even say that every idle word should be condemned, but only that the speaker must give an account thereof. Many an apparently idle jest, uttered as an expression of friendship and encouragement, has proved itself far from idle. It would be very hard to believe, for instance, that the joke which St. Thomas More made on the scaffold about his beard[1] came under the divine condemnation. Nevertheless it remains true that nowhere are watchfulness and self-discipline

---

[1] More, "laying his head upon the block, bade the executioner stay until he had removed aside his beard, saying that *that* had never committed any treason".—R. W. Chambers, *Thomas More*, p. 19. (Jonathan Cape, London, 1936.)

needed more than in the use of the tongue—both in what we say and in what we leave unsaid.

II

So far we have discussed the Christian ascesis in general. But each individual must adapt its principles to suit his own needs, in the particular sphere in which he is to glorify God. The Middle Ages knew a great deal about the spiritual life. They provided a rich full spirituality which produced many saints. Their writings and examples remain an inexhaustible reservoir on which future ages can draw. But the ascesis they taught ran too much on one line, that of the evangelical counsels. This resulted in a tendency to believe that truly to follow Christ meant, either entering the Religious Life, or else living in the world according to the monastic pattern of life. It was this that led St. Bernard of Clairvaux to urge his brothers to enter with him the monastery of Cîteaux, including the one who was married to a devoted wife. The wife was persuaded to seek the same kind of life in a nunnery. Those who did not feel called to such renunciation were content for the most part with a frankly worldly life, modified by the conventional observance of a few precepts of the Church. It led to a dangerous cleavage in the Church between Religious and Seculars. The Tertiary movement inaugurated by the Franciscans did little to check that, for the Tertiaries themselves, though living in the world, adopted, so far as possible, the ascesis of the Religious. It was perhaps the greatest contribution of St. Francis de Sales to the Church to go beyond merely acknowledging the possibility of perfection in ordinary life, and to provide a spirituality for secular folk. It was not modelled upon monastic observances, but it was admirably adapted to encourage those living in the world and to lead them on to perfection.

To-day the pendulum has swung too far in the other direction. We talk about every walk in life as a " vocation ", and treat all as on the same level. Moreover there is much misunderstanding about the place of what is technically called " the Religious Life " in the Church as a whole. A short digression on the subject may therefore serve a useful purpose. A generation boasting loudly of its emancipation from the sex repressions of the Victorian age, yet none the less obsessed by sex, talks of marriage as necessary to the individual's full development, and regards the Religious Life as an attempt to escape from life's problems, social or personal. Now it cannot be too clearly stated that God has His purpose for every single soul, and the particular work which He wants him to do in society, whether he be a dustman or a monk. No child of Christ should be allowed to think that God does not care much what he makes his life-work. On the other hand, though in all rightful occupations the soul can find its perfection, they are not all on the same level. The Church has always maintained, and rightly maintained, a distinction. In doing so she only repeats our Lord's own teaching. For He did hold out to the rich young man the life of complete renunciation as a higher life for him, and He did call His apostles to make such renunciation, and pronounce special blessings on those who should follow in their steps. So also the Church has always held in special honour consecrated virginity, even though at the same time she has ever upheld the sanctity of marriage. In an army the clerk in the office at headquarters, with a comfortable billet far from danger, is just as much a part of the war machine as the man lying in a muddy trench under shell-fire. But every soldier is aware that there is a difference between the two posts, and knows which is held in most honour both by his comrades and by the nation at large. So the soldiers of Christ are taught to value most those vocations where the self-offering for the glory of God is most complete. The Religious Life has always held its place of honour, not because its members are holier than other members of the Church, for very often they are far from being so; but because it forms a state in which the opportunities for the life of renunciation and of worship are most fully provided. And it is renunciation of a particular kind, for there lies no value in renunciation for its own sake. It is renunciation according to the "evangelical counsels" of poverty, chastity, and obedience. These three are called "evangelical", because they are taken from Christ's own words; and "counsels", because He did not say that it was necessary for all to follow them. They constitute a special vocation. The Religious binds himself by vow to observe these three counsels for life in a special community according to its Rule. Stability is of the essence of that life. There is no such thing as a temporary Religious. He gives himself once for all. The bridegroom at the altar vows fidelity to his bride "till death us do part". But the vow of the Religious is more permanent still, for it outlasts the incident of death. But the observance of these counsels is not confined to the Religious life. Men and women will be found everywhere living in the world, following one or more of them for love of Christ, and leading a heroic life of poverty and sacrifice, at any rate for a period of years. Fr. Damien, for instance, as a missionary on the leper island, underwent hardships and privations far greater than any he had to submit to in the community to which he belonged. But one great value of the Religious Life lies in the fact that it is adapted to suit men and women of normal strength, and gives them the support of others in their self-giving. St. Benedict in his Rule deliberately avoided the excessive austerities of many of his predecessors, in order that ordinary men might find their joy in the life of the counsels, wholly given to them, yet not pushed beyond their strength. Hence the Religious Life remains one of the greatest aids towards the attainment of Christian perfection. For we must remember that the Religious has precisely the same end in view as every other member of the Church. King and monk and baker, duchess and nun and charwoman, within the Church have but one and the same aim—to keep the great commandments, to love the Lord God with all their heart and soul, and their neighbours as themselves. St. Basil the Great, in one of his monastic Rules, states that clearly. He begins with repeating those two commandments as the aim of every Christian and then goes on to ask what is the best way of fulfilling them. His answer is to point to the evangelical counsels and draw up his Rule for monks. St. Basil did not mean that it was the only way to follow Christ perfectly, but the most direct way. Sanctity does demand real self-sacrifice, a reaching out beyond what is necessary for salvation. And the more we do so reach out, the more help we can be to others. As Professor Maritain has expressed it: "If a man does not seek first of all for the secret of heroic life, the work he does for the common good will remain of little value."[1] Where the morale of an army stands high there is no lack of volunteers for posts of special danger and hardship, even though only a few are required. It seems improbable that God will ever call more than a small percentage of His people to the Religious Life or similar special vocations, but it is good that the younger members at any rate should be eager to offer themselves.

However, before attempting to draw up a scheme of training for himself a man must first know what is the particular calling in

[1] *Degrees of Knowledge*, p. 434. (G. Bles, Centenary Press, 1937.)

which he is to glorify God, whether as religious or secular, soldier
or sailor, grocer or miner, or any of the other manifold occupations which exist for the good of society. In the world his life will
probably have at least two main aspects, a business aspect and a
home aspect. Yet he must not allow it to become divided in aim.
They are both channels through which he is to fulfil the love of
God and of his neighbour, and in so doing to achieve his own
perfection. Let him remember, too, that his work in the world
may be none the less God's will for him although it came to him,
as it were, inevitably. It seemed the only opening possible for him.
Perhaps it is safer so. God has His own plan and works it out in
His own way. It brings an immense assurance to find Him thus
arranging our life, preparing our place for us, instead of all depend-
ing on our receiving some strange interior call. So the son may
take his place in his father's business and none the less may it be
the work God has prepared for him. But he must recognize it as
God's plan for him and carry it out as unto the Lord. Most of us
want to choose our own way and seek our own ends. So we ruin
both the work and our own happiness. Not many would recognize
the fact so clearly as Dr. John Baillie did: "Deep down within me,"
he says, "I always knew that He had His own plan for me, His own
place for me, and in a sense even His own need for me; and I knew
also that this plan, which was laid with a view of His sole glory,
was laid also with a view to my own greatest happiness and welfare—because only in His glory could my happiness and welfare
ever be found. But I was not content thus to allow the issues of
my life to rest in His hands alone. I had certain little plans of my
own. I wanted to arrange things a little differently. . . . By so
doing I put the whole nature of things out of joint. That which is
in its proper nature subject I was making sovereign. That which
is relative I was making absolute. I, a creature, was aspiring to
independent creation."[1] No, that will not do. We must not only
realize what God's plan for us is, but we must work it out in His
way, not in ours. For we cannot love Him with all our heart and
soul unless we are trying to do His will.

Once a man has grasped both the main purpose of his life and
the sphere in which it is to be realized, he can set about his training.
It involves certain principles, which will guide him in forming his
Rule of Life.

[1] *Invitation to Pilgrimage*, p. 54.

(1) All other aims and interests must be regarded as subsidiary and harnessed to the main purpose. He will cultivate specially those virtues which his calling most requires (though neglecting none)—justice, patience, firmness in a schoolmaster; honesty, courtesy, incorruptibility in a business man; courage and obedience in a soldier, etc. His friends and recreations will be such as will best aid him to fulfil his duties faithfully. And his whole style of living will be in keeping with this. The test of any action will be whether it enables him to fulfil God's will in his calling.

(2) Whatever means of self-discipline he adopts, his first obligation is to observe those laid down by the Church, such as the use of the Sacraments, the keeping of certain festivals and fasts, the duty of learning his faith, and the duty of almsgiving, in addition to the discipline required by the laws of Christian morality. Both fasting and almsgiving are closely associated with prayer. Almsgiving, which need not necessarily be offered in money, looks out towards others, as well as symbolizing the giver's duty and desire to offer himself and all that he has to the service of God. Fasting, like almsgiving, is bound up with the gospel message. It lies embedded too deep in the teaching of the saints for us to ignore it. Yet there is an increasing tendency to do so. Our Lord Himself fasted, and gave instructions to His disciples how they were to fast. The Gospels only mention one fast of His, during the forty days of the temptation, but presumably He observed the statutory fasts of the Jewish Church, though He refused to force His disciples to keep the extra ones established by the Pharisees. Incidentally, only a body inured to fasting could stand the strain of a forty days' fast. Ever since His ministry His Church has insisted on the importance of fasting, and the lives of the saints have borne witness to its value. Few people to-day probably could go without food so long as some of them did without injury to their health, and some, either because of the nature of their work or physical infirmity, ought not to fast at all (apart from the fast before making their communion). All others can derive benefit from it, if only as an act of obedience to the wisdom of the Church, and as a token of their desire to be linked more closely with our Lord in following in His steps. Fasting means going without food, or having much less food than usual; it does not mean substituting one dish for another, e.g. a tasty fish for cold meat. Originally a fast day meant having only one meal in the day and that not before noon—and

in the Eastern Orthodox Church it still means that. The Western Church has in her wisdom made some relaxation, while maintaining the principle. It may be easy to obtain dispensations from fasting, but if we remember what an aid it is to the spiritual life, we shall be eager to practise it, if our health allows.

Hunger is one of the most imperious natural desires of the body. It tends to dominate us too much. Fasting symbolizes our resolve not to be enslaved by the flesh, but to live by the Spirit. It is an emphatic witness to our faith in our Lord's own answer to the devil that " man shall not live by bread alone ". Moreover the body itself benefits by the abstinence, if it is done with moderation. Many doctors nowadays say that we tend to eat too much and that most of us are all the better for having less food, at any rate one day in seven. Most people, it is true, do not nowadays indulge in the prodigious repasts in which our forefathers seem to have revelled, but neither do they normally expend so much physical energy, and they feed more frequently. But the object of fasting is not to check excess, but to increase self-control and assert the supremacy of the spirit, to turn attention to God. The Eucharistic fast is primarily an act of reverence to our Lord in the Blessed Sacrament, but it also emphasizes the fact that there is something of more importance even to the body than material food. Moreover, when the body has grown accustomed to it, fasting tends to sharpen the spiritual faculties, both making the mind more alert and the soul more attuned to spiritual things. It helps us to gain a certain sense of freedom, and to realize the power of the spirit to rule our bodies as well as our souls. That in its turn helps us to deal with our fallen human nature when it becomes rebellious in other ways. To gain that is well worth the discomfort of an occasional fast. But it must be undertaken, as our Lord insisted, not grudgingly nor ostentatiously, but with a glad heart, as an act of love to God (Matt. 6. 18). St. Benedict names the love of fasting as one of the " instruments of good works ".[1]

(3) Self-denial will involve a glad acceptance of all the demands made upon a man by his work and by his circumstances, e.g. hours of duty, dealing with trying people, personal discomfort, enduring the vagaries of climate, even sickness. They represent the most valuable form of self-discipline, just because they are not self-chosen, and give him the training which he most needs. It is possible

[1] *Regula*, Ch. IV.

to choose other ways of self-denial, which do not touch the root of self-love.

(4) The next step is for a man to ask himself whether there is anything in his life which is hindering its main purpose. It may be a friendship grown dangerous; it may be some luxury or some form of recreation become too engrossing, or a dissipation of energy amongst a variety of unnecessary interests. Lawrence of Arabia tells of a British officer in Arabia whose whole work was spoilt because of such variety. "His shadow," he adds, "would have covered our work and British policy like a cloak, had he been able to deny himself the world, and to prepare his mind and body with the sternness of an athlete for a great fight."[1] The Holy Spirit quickly makes the man who keeps in touch with God aware of such over-indulgence. He must take steps to remedy the trouble, if necessary by complete renunciation. Nothing must be allowed to get in the way to bar his progress. Our Lord even went so far as to say that a man must be ready to cut off his hand or pluck out his eye, and enter heaven maimed rather than not enter it at all.

First amongst such renunciations comes the avoiding of occasions of sin. It is a mockery to pray " lead us not into temptation " if one wilfully puts one's self in its way. Tertullian tells a grim story of a Christian woman in his day. She insisted on frequenting the gladiatorial shows, though the Church had forbidden her members to attend them on account of the moral perils involved. One day she was there possessed by a devil. On her return home the exorcist was sent for. In accordance with the rubrics for exorcism he questioned the devil, and asked him how he dared to enter the soul of a Christian. " I had every right," came the answer, " I found her on my ground."

Sometimes, however, the occasion of sin comes right in the line of the man's calling. His work may involve the handling of sums of money and the temptation to embezzlement be strong, or it may take him amongst those who urge him to intemperance, or lust. Here the temptation is none of his own seeking, and he must humbly throw himself on the mercy of God, trusting in His power to keep him unspotted. Even so it might be right for him, if the danger of falling into mortal sin were very great, to seek another post. Some occupations there are which no Christian ought to

[1] *Seven Pillars of Wisdom*, p. 57. (Jonathan Cape, London, 1935.)

undertake, but it is hard to draw the boundary line. The man, whose aim is to seek God's glory and his neighbour's good, will come to recognize some as being incompatible with his ideal, and he may have to make great sacrifices. In the old days men like Tertullian drew the line more sharply. To the idol manufacturers who said that they would have nothing to live on if they gave up their trade he gave the ruthless answer, " Must you live? " And occasions arise to-day when a man must be prepared to risk all to be true to his Lord and Master, Jesus Christ. At least it means that he should make as sure as he can that the work he undertakes is compatible with his Christian profession in its main direction. But how important it is that the Church in every district should be ready both to encourage her children to make such sacrifices when necessary, and also to see that they are supported till fresh employment can be obtained! It was a work nobly fulfilled by the Church in the first centuries.

(5) In the midst of all his activities, trials, and triumphs he will keep before his eyes the ideal of ultimate perfection, of taking his place amongst those who " have washed their robes in the Blood of the Lamb ", and stand before the throne of God, and see Him face to face. As we have already said, the Christian " Way " goes uphill all its length—to the city of God. His temptation is to be content to stay at the beginning, to be content with avoiding mortal sin, and not to expect to go forward towards that perfect love of God. The first and great commandment, however, points straight to the summit. It suggests no half-measures. " Thou shalt love the Lord thy God with all thy heart and with all thy mind and with all thy soul and with all thy strength." To fulfil that is the work of a lifetime, and then only achieved by the grace of God. But God wills that perfection for each single soul. " Be ye therefore perfect " was our Lord's injunction to all, " even as your Father which is in heaven is perfect." It is to be transformed into the likeness of Christ, to be united so closely with God in love that one can say with St. Paul, " I have been crucified with Christ; yet I live; and yet no longer I, but Christ liveth in me " (Gal. 2. 20).

Those who have received the gift of contemplative prayer must submit to a sterner traini. r—indeed they will embrace it eagerly. Others seek, and rightly seek, God in the exercise of their powers amongst things and persons. Some rivers reach the sea in one strong stream; others find their way to it more slowly through many openings. Both reach their goal. The contemplative concerns himself more directly with God; makes, as it were, straight for the ocean. His ascesis will have much the same principles as others, but he will have to travel more lightly. Things which aid them only encumber him and he must put them aside. His attention to God calls for and gives him a much greater detachment. Something will be said later in this book about his ascesis, and the special dangers that lie in his way. We will not anticipate that now. Sometimes we read of great lovers of God who not only embarked on a course of extreme self-denial, but who performed actions which seem to us senseless and even revolting. The story of St. Catherine of Genoa drinking the water in which filthy bandages had been washed is one instance amongst many. Father William Doyle in our own enlightened days flinging himself naked into a bed of nettles, or scourging himself with razor blades, sounds almost as bad. The truth is that these people saw their goal and took what they believed to be the quickest way to it, whatever the cost. St. Catherine, delicately brought up in a Genoese palace, knew that she must get rid of her fastidiousness. It was hindering her progress. We may learn a parable of the skater. Learning to figure-skate demands some measure of courage as well as skill. Two men will set about the task differently. One will go very cautiously to work, gingerly trying to find his outside edge or scraping a turn, with his unemployed foot ready to drop at the first sign of a fall. The other goes full tilt from the start. He will take many a toss and often look ridiculous to the bystanders. Both men will learn to skate, but the second man will learn the quicker. What is more, there will be a thrust, a poise, and a freedom about his skating, a capacity to hold out his edges at a good speed to the end, which the first will never achieve. The saints were and are something like that as they learn to give themselves to God.

CHAPTER VII

PSYCHOLOGY AND THE SAINTS

THE athlete, or his trainer, must take into consideration his physical capacities and needs, and arrange his programme accordingly. So the Christian athlete contending for the crown of life needs to understand something about his own soul and its make-up. Modern psychology looks at it somewhat differently from our forefathers. They regarded the individual as a conscious being endowed with a number of faculties—the powers of the soul. These could be dealt with more or less separately and trained by good habits into the way they should go, as the branches of a fruit tree might be pruned and trained to grow along a wall. It is possible, in thought at least, to separate the capacities of the soul and in some degree to treat them so. But it leads to a too mechanical view of it. To-day we think rather of the person as a being who thinks and wills and feels, and whose thinking, willing, and feeling are inextricably involved in every activity or mental process. Moreover, he is far from being wholly a rational creature, able to order himself according to plan. He is still more a creature of instinct, moved by strange and primitive desires and emotions, which tend to insist on their own satisfaction, leaving him to " rationalize " them as best he may. Some years ago psychologists were arguing about the number of the instincts possessed by each human being. They maintained, moreover, that an emotion was attached to each instinct. If the instinct did not obtain its satisfaction, the emotion was lost or forced itself out elsewhere and upset the balance of the self. If, for instance, the instincts of parenthood and reproduction did not obtain their natural satisfactions, the whole personality would be seriously impoverished; the emotions would crop up in other ways liable to bring disaster in their train. Other psychologists, and in particular Professor Jung, teach that there is, rather, a common life-force (*libido*) possessed by the individual, which is not portioned out amongst the instincts, but can be sublimated or diverted from some instinctive satisfaction to function all the more forcibly along other lines. Jung's *libido* has much in common with St. Augustine's *concupiscentia*. Thus, the woman deprived of the opportunity of motherhood does not thereby lose a measure of her life-force: to a large extent she may sublimate it in such ways as work amongst children. Dr. Axel Munthe relates in his delightful book, *San Michele*, how he found many such women in a nervous listless state, and how their lives were transformed by his discovering for them interests which enabled them to deal satisfactorily with their frustrated instincts. The Catholic knows that the dedication of those instincts to God by the vow of chastity brings an enrichment, not an impoverishment, of the personality.

Religious people have sometimes criticized the psychologists because few of them have found any place for a religious instinct amongst the other instincts. But surely the psychologists are right. For if there were a special religious instinct it would mean that religion was only one amongst many human needs. But God is the beginning and end of every soul. All the instincts derive from Him and tend towards Him as their goal. Religion, therefore, is like the main stream of a great river which makes for the sea through many channels. If one channel is dammed, the stream will find a fresh outlet or pour itself in greater volume through the others. So the rightly directed soul will seek the glory of God through all its different instincts, and, inspired by grace, will use its natural gifts to render Him praise. The psychologist will admit that the natural instincts can be more or less satisfactorily sublimated, and the lives of the saints have proved it throughout the ages. St. Francis of Assisi, devoting himself at the call of God to the single life and the way of the Cross, did not thereby impoverish his powers. Rather he gained an immensely increased capacity to pour himself out for God in the love and service of others. If religion were but one instinct amongst others, it too could be sublimated. But there is no satisfactory sublimation of the desire for God, for it is the goal of the man's whole being. Some individuals seem never to have been conscious of this desire, and it is curious to mark how they have tried unconsciously to find some substitute for it—in vain.

In one other important respect our view of human personality differs from that of our forefathers. It is in what has been called the "psychology of the unconscious". Until recently, men believed that a person was at least conscious of his mental processes and sensations. The fulfilment of the demand "know thyself" was, if not easy, at any rate within his compass. As a rational being he could decide on the course he would take and order the powers of his soul accordingly. But it is a more complicated business than that. Psychologists have forced us to recognize phenomena in human personality which point to the existence of a part of it outside the sphere of the conscious ego. They have given this various names—the "subconscious self", or "the unconscious"—and even divided it into a personal and a collective unconscious. All such names are open to criticism. but one cannot well ignore the results of their investigations. The psychologists are not agreed amongst themselves as to the extent or content of this unconscious. Freud held that it consisted simply of mental states which had been forced out of consciousness owing to their unpleasant character. But they still remained in the background, affecting the attitude of the individual towards life and threatening to manifest themselves with disastrous effects. A child, for instance, might have received some paralysing fright once in the dark. After a time he would forget the agonizing experience, but nevertheless it would remain in the unconscious, exercising its influence on his life and likely to reassert itself later with serious results, e.g. nervous breakdown. Jung, on the other hand, maintains that there is here something much more than this, though he admits its existence and calls it the "personal unconscious". He considers that deeper still the unconscious derives from a kind of "collective unconscious" from which the individual conscious sprang. Again, men have long been aware of differences of temperament and character in human beings, though they have not always classified them in the same way. There is the sanguine person, the melancholy person, the intellectual, and the sentimentalist, etc. Such a one each man is with the qualities and defects of his temperament, and such he remains, however much he may modify any extravagance into which it may lead him. Professor Jung maintains that there are four main types, though any individual temperament may represent a mingling of two or more of these. But he does not rest there: he goes on to say that the opposite of that temperament exists in the individual's unconscious, apt to manifest itself in strange and sometimes harmful ways. The intellectualist, for instance, possesses, unknown to himself, strong sentimental characteristics, which may break in upon him unexpectedly. Thus a learned middle-aged bachelor may suddenly fall violently in love with a young and sentimental girl just out of her teens, or a materialist and *bon viveur* with a poetess. So a Nelson may be infatuated with an Emma Hamilton.

However, it is beyond our purpose here to discuss the new psychology in detail. It is enough to point out some of its main features. At least they force us to reconsider former methods of soul-training. Have the old masters of the spiritual life been following wrong lines, and must their teaching be scrapped? Is there to be a new spirituality based upon a new ascetical theology? The answer is emphatically in the negative. There is much that we can learn from the new; modification that we can make in the old. But the old stands firm. Those great masters were better psychologists than they knew. A brief study of St. Ignatius's *Spiritual Exercises* or of the writings of St. John of the Cross would be sufficient to convince us of this. After all, human psychology has remained much the same through the ages, and men learnt a great deal about how it acts and how to treat it, enough at least to deal with ordinary men and women and guide them on the way to heaven, even if they would have been less successful with more distorted types. They needed no one to remind them that "the heart is deceitful above all things and it is desperately sick" (Jer. 17. 9). Or, as the author of the *Spiritual Combat* (Scupoli) expressed it: "Nature doth so secretly seek herself in our enterprises, that those very things which thou thinkest please or displease thee only for the love of God, are principally willed or refused for thy self-interest" (Ch. V). On the other hand, the pressure of modern society has created all kinds of psychological tangles seldom found in earlier days or in more primitive societies. In fact, it was the urgency of such problems that revolutionized the study of psychology. Men examined these abnormal cases and worked back from them to the normal, arguing that characteristics that appeared so plainly in a distorted form must also have their place in the normal.

It is interesting to see how modern psychologists but repeat the emphasis laid by the old writers on certain fundamental principles. The latter based their doctrine on the teaching of Holy Scripture and the Church, whereas the former are generalizing from their practical experience. If we mention some of these here we do so, not in order to show that the old masters are right because they agree with the modern psychologist, but rather to show how little they need to change, whatever new theories are put forward. Yet it is good to see their teaching through modern eyes and learn to understand it better.

(1) The saints have always insisted on self-knowledge as an essential for spiritual progress. They have repeated the Delphic oracle " know thyself" and placed it at the threshold of the spiritual life. From St. Paul's " Let a man examine himself" it is caught up and echoed through the ages. St. Catherine of Siena put it picturesquely when she said that there are two cells in which the devout soul must always live—the cell of the knowledge of self, and the cell of the knowledge of God. St. John of the Cross, two centuries later, sets out in his two first books an almost devastating method of self-knowledge, probing deep into the hidden workings of the soul.

At the same time the saints insisted on the importance of confession—not only of definite sins, but, in the case of the devout, even of the temptations and spiritual experiences that came to them, as a guard against self-deception. St. Benedict in his Rule ordered his monks to practise this openness with their abbot, as later writers counselled others to practise it with their directors. " Counselled " is a mild expression for the emphasis they laid upon the value of a director.

Now it would scarcely be an exaggeration to say that self-knowledge is the one and only method of modern psychology. Psycho-analysis is but an elaborate device for obtaining this. Once a true knowledge of self is obtained, difficulties, it maintains, can be overcome and the personality free to work harmoniously. Of course the psychologists teach that there is a great deal more to be known than men used to think. There is all that mysterious realm of the unconscious. All kinds of complexes lie there, and these create disturbance in the conscious life and lead to nervous diseases and breakdowns, which cannot be dealt with by superficial methods of self-examination. To obtain this deeper self-knowledge the aid of a skilled psychologist is needed, and a far more detailed confession must be made to him than ever confessor demanded of a penitent. But it is interesting to find the old emphasis on confession repeated still more forcibly here, though the psycho-analyst has taken the place of the director.

The saints, however, meant something far wider and deeper by self-knowledge than do the psychologists. To the latter it means an understanding by the individual of the inner workings of his personality, instinctive and mental, and of his relations to society. But the saints are thinking primarily of his relations to God. They maintain that, if he is to order his life aright, he must know at least whence he is, what he is, where he is, and whither he is going. *Whence:* that he is a being created out of nothing by God, and owing his existence from moment to moment to his Creator's care. "Remember, O man, that thou art but dust. Dust thou art and unto dust shalt thou return." *What:* that he is made in the image of God, and capable of communion with God, fallen yet redeemed by Christ. *Where:* that he has his place in the hierarchy of the creation—"lower than the angels" yet possessing a special honour as the child of God, and a special duty to his fellow-beings. *Whither:* his destiny is eternal in the heavens, to be satisfied at last with the vision of God. These are the things that a man needs to know about himself, if his self-examination is to be fruitful.

(2) The psychologist of to-day lays, and rightly lays, enormous stress on the value of what we might call wholeness. The object of self-knowledge is to achieve this. His point is that, in nearly every individual, large stores of energy are unavailable owing to the inhibitions and complexes which life has brought in its train. Until these are dealt with, his personality lacks its full expression. It is incomplete. Track the evil to its source, show what has caused the trouble, and the patient can be helped to reintegrate into his life those broken bits. This will mean the source of new power. Professor Jung declares that the medieval alchemists were aiming through a multitude of confused symbols at precisely this liberation of human personality. No other psychologist, it may be stated, has insisted more strongly than he on the attainment of such wholeness. For this reason he lays less stress than Freud on psychoanalysis. What matters is not so much what happened in the past, as what faces a man at the moment.

Even a glance at the New Testament is sufficient to reveal how large looms the idea of wholeness in the Christian Faith. The very word salvation suggests it. The Beatitudes uttered by our Lord promise it. St. Paul loves to speak of Christ as the fulness (τὸ πλήρωμα)—the fulness of God, as also the fulness of the Church and of the individual soul. It is all in keeping with his teaching that the gospel is the fulfilment of God's ancient covenant with man, for "in Christ", he tells the Colossians, "dwelleth all the fulness of the Godhead bodily and in him ye are made full [have been filled], who is the head of all principality and power" (Col. 2. 9 f.). He prays again that the Ephesians may be "filled with all the fulness of God". His prayer for the Thessalonians breathes the same thought: "The God of peace himself sanctify you wholly; and may your spirit and soul and body be preserved entire, without blame at the coming of our Lord Jesus Christ." (I Thess. 5. 23; cf. Jas. I. 4.) The same principle manifests itself in the Church's triumphant insistence on the resurrection of the body, in the face of strong and constant pressure to belittle or deny it, for without the body the personality would be incomplete, lacking its proper means of expression. It is an essential element in the gospel message. The need of mortification and detachment has been so much stressed by many saints, that they have seemed to many to preach only destruction in order that some remnant of personality might be saved, as though all who reach the kingdom of heaven, if they enter it at all, must enter it maimed. But it is only with that background of wholeness, of fulness, that they write at all. Few of them, perhaps, thought much about achieving wholeness here and now. That did not seem to matter greatly, provided it was gained finally and for ever. In thinking in terms of eternity a few years more or less did not seem to them of great importance. A closer acquaintance with their writings reveals the positive aspect more clearly. St. John of the Cross was well aware that he might be misunderstood. "It may perhaps seem," he wrote, "that we are destroying the road of spiritual practice rather than constructing it . . . but, since we are here giving instruction to those who would progress farther in contemplation . . . it is necessary to proceed by this method of . . . causing the natural jurisdiction and operations of the faculties to be denied them, so that they may become capable of infusion and illumination from supernatural sources."[1] And again: "Man is commanded to employ all the faculties and desires and operations and affections of his soul in God. . . . Now when these faculties, passions and desires are directed by the will toward God, and turned away from all that is not God, then the strength of the soul is kept for God, and thus the soul is able to love God with all its strength."[2]

[1] *Ascent*, III. 2.   [2] Ibid., III. 16.

The idea is carried a step further. The end of the soul's quest is union with God in love. It brings with it " transformation "— the transformation of the soul into the likeness of Christ. Some saints have boldly spoken of " deification " to express the completeness of the process. It brings with it an amazing liberation of power, often physical as well as spiritual. With most of them it has burst forth after a long period of darkness, inhibition, and physical weakness. Physical disabilities frequently remain, yet they are incapable of preventing an astonishing output of energy. The whole being is filled with a new-found joy and sense of freedom. St. Paul was a brilliant example of this, and he constantly pointed to the possibility of it for all Christians. It was one way in which the fulness of God manifested itself in the soul. He made no secret of some disabling " thorn in the flesh ", yet it did not prevent him from performing incredible labours, supported by a strength not his own. " When I am weak," he cried, " then am I strong "; or again, " I can do all things through Christ who strengtheneth me ". He trusted himself to the promises of Christ and found they came true. The lives of almost all the great saints echo the experience of St. Paul. There is St. Bernard of Clairvaux, with his ruined health, undertaking long perilous journeys at the instance of the Pope, in touch with almost every great movement of the day and maintaining a prodigious correspondence, yet immersed in supernatural peace and joy, which communicated themselves, sometimes with miraculous effects, to those who came in contact with him. St. Catherine of Siena offers an interesting parallel—one more shining light in the long roll of saints who have thus revealed to the world something of the wonder of union with God in Christ. St. Francis Xavier and St. Teresa of Spain are two others familiar to modern readers: St. Sergius of Russia is better known in the East—names picked out at random from the roll.

Miracles are nearly always associated with the lives of the saints, sometimes fantastically so. But it would be a vast. mistake to dismiss them all as due merely to the credulity of their age, or to the desire of their biographers to fit their saints into a conventional frame. The real importance of that miraculous element lies in the fact that something about those men and women so enlarged the stature of their personality that they seemed more than human. Men felt that, whether they performed a miracle or not, there was

something miraculous about them, and the power to perform such
deeds easily within their compass. Miracles they certainly did work
and, wherever saints arise, there marvellous things will happen, as
our Lord foretold (Jn. 14. 12).

But we have journeyed far from the psychologist's conception
of the liberated personality. And it is of supreme importance to
mark the difference. It exhibits itself mainly in two ways:

(a) The psychiatrist aims merely at the restoration of his patient's
health. He seeks to enable him to gain the full use of all his powers,
so that he may play his part usefully and happily in his life here.
His function resembles that of the doctor. The doctor's business is
to restore his patient to physical well-being, whereas the psychiatrist
is chiefly concerned with his psychic health. If he thinks religious
ideals will facilitate this, he will encourage them. (The deterministic
outlook of many psychologists, however, would leave little scope
for this.) The Christian director has a very different objective.
We have already seen what the purpose of life is—" Seek ye first
the kingdom of God ". " Thou shalt love the Lord thy God with
all thy heart, with all thy soul and with all thy strength." In
other words, man is to give himself wholly to God. That is the
all-important consideration. His whole personality is involved in
the venture. If the teaching of the new psychology will help
towards this, then he will recommend its use, but only as a means
to that end.

Perhaps here we might call attention to a cult hoary with age
and hailing from the East, which has recently gained prominence
in this country. It derives from Brahminism with its ideal of the
merging of the individual soul in the whole—a pantheistic ideal,
put forward in language which at first sight resembles closely the
Christian mystics' ideal of union with God. It sets forth a technique
of its own, a modification of the Yoga taught by the Easterns, with
a side-glance at Christian spirituality. Thus a form of contemplation is to be reached by the devotee's own exertions, and so "union"
takes place. But the real objective is not the glory of God, or the
giving of self to God: it is the soul's own liberation and satisfaction.
The technique is devised to remove the barriers which hinder this.
Moreover, the divine source so tapped has little resemblance to the
intensely personal, self-revealing God of the Christian faith. It is

something much vaguer, a kind of indefinite stream of life which seems to differ little from what Jung more cautiously terms the "Collective Unconscious".

We are brought back again to the old paradox, that man by his very nature must seek his own fulness, yet he can only obtain it by aiming at the glory of God. It is possible that God's purposes are best served in some souls by delaying that liberation of personality which is the goal of the psychologist and oriental. In this crooked world God sometimes uses crooked tools, personalities warped or stunted by physical or psychic maladies. One may well ask whether, for instance, Blessed Angela of Foligno or Blessed Henry Suso would have set forth the praise of God as they did had they been balanced souls, living a normal life. Or, if the poet Shelley could have had his complexes resolved on leaving school, would he have written poetry still more beautiful or with a deeper, more poignant note? The two saints seem to have obtained their liberation; Shelley never did, but the saints were looking beyond it all the time.

(b) The psychiatrist, like the oriental, expects the individual to achieve his aim in his own strength by the successful use of a technique. Even the dark and terrifying powers of Jung's Collective Unconscious must not be allowed to take possession of his ego, but they must be reckoned with and assimilated by him. Jung himself is insistent on this point.

The Christian saint is looking for the coming of another, not himself, to restore his ruined personality, that he may give himself away more completely. He is seeking union with God in and through Christ, and he is mindful of Christ's own words: "Ye shall know the truth, and the truth shall make you free. . . . If the Son shall make you free, ye shall be free indeed." (Jn. 8. 32, 36.) This is in its deepest meaning the liberty of the sons of God of which St. Paul speaks, the liberty of those who are "led by the spirit of God". Perhaps the psalmist had a dim sense of it when he said, "I will run the way of thy commandments, when thou hast set my heart at liberty" (Ps. 119. 32). It means freedom both from the bonds of sin and from all the inhibitions and the self-centredness which cramp the soul's response.

Here there is no bland confidence in the power of a technique. The saint brings nothing but a vivid realization of his own sinfulness and helplessness, and he throws himself thus at the feet of God. By God's grace he is cleansed, lifted up, and strengthened to undergo the purifications which will fit him for God's own possession. The liberation of his natural forces comes when God wills. But he himself is aware that that does not matter greatly. All that matters is that he should be forgiven, and have strength to fulfil the will of God so far as he can see it. For thus shall God's name be glorified.

And, just as the aim and the methods of the Christian saint differ from those of the psychologist, so immensely does the result differ. For here something far more is achieved than the harmonization of the conflicting aims and desires of a personality. The personality is taken up into union with God to be the vehicle of His grace. " Yet no longer I, but Christ liveth in me " (Gal. 2. 20). That was how St. Paul expressed what had happened to him. " Christ in you, the hope of glory" (Col. 1. 27): it was to be the same for his converts. There was scarcely any limit to what they might achieve, so filled with Christ. A story from the ancient hermits gives vivid expression to this realization of vast possibilities thus opened. A young monk came to the aged abbot Joseph and said, " Father, according to my strength I keep a modest rule of prayer and fasting and meditation and quiet, and according to my strength I purge my imagination. What more must I do? " The old man rose from his seat, held up his hands against the rising sun, and his fingers became like ten torches of fire, and he said, " If thou wilt, thou shalt be made wholly flame ".[1] The thought brings an inestimable comfort. For Christ is Lord of the whole self. All this talk of the unconscious has a terrifying aspect. It was bad enough to have to deal with the refractory self of which we were conscious. We need for that, we know full well, all the grace God offers to us. But what if there are unknown depths within us, containing unregulated desires which may burst upon us at any moment and wreck our best-laid schemes of spiritual progress! Thank God, if Christ lives in us thus, our King and Lord, He is Lord also of that unconscious realm, whatever it may be. And " the word of God is living and active, and sharper than any two-edged sword, and piercing even to the dividing of soul and spirit, of both joints and marrow, and quick to discern the thoughts and intents of the heart. And there is no creature that is not manifest in his sight: but all things are naked and laid open before the eyes of him with whom we have to do." (Heb. 4. 12 f.)

[1] H. Waddell, *The Desert Fathers*, p. 157. (Constable, London, 1936.)

So we can enjoy, in a deeper sense than we knew, His peace, "which passeth all understanding". Normally the Holy Spirit will work there in His own way and time, smoothing out the complexes and removing the barriers far more wisely than any psychiatrist. Yet the psychiatrist may sometimes have a useful part to play in the process. His difficulty usually is to find some satisfactory centre round which his patient's newly recovered emotional forces can be gathered. At first they tend to be transferred to himself, which is both embarrassing for him and dangerous for the patient. If he himself has a strong faith in God, he knows where to look for the solution of his problem. Otherwise his patient may be left, as it were, "in the air", and after a temporary improvement relapse. An American journalist, a globe-trotter and close observer of her fellow-creatures, writing recently of her life's adventures, made an interesting statement *en passant* on this subject: "Three of my most intimate friends have been psycho-analysed. With two of them their last state was worse than the first, because the analyst left them in a state of disintegration. They saw themselves stripped of fantasy, but they had nothing to build on. The third benefited, because at each stage of the analysis her mind was thrown back on to the reality of God. She had a basis for reconstruction."[1] I quote this the more readily as it corroborates my own experience of those who have submitted to the treatment. Few of them even with a belief in God seem to have gained anything worth the strain of the analysing process. It is only right to say that I have read of others where the result has been much more successful. Moreover, psycho-therapists have recently considerably modified the method of analysis and now attempt a more constructive policy.

Again, the real barriers are barriers of sin, and sin can only come from conscious processes. Holy Church supplies us with abundant grace to deal with it. The rest God will disentangle some day. The more generously we yield ourselves to His will, the quicker will that work be accomplished. In this we are reminded and comforted that what God values most in us is our deliberate, willed responses. The Church with her usual wisdom here maintains the truth. God gave us reason that we might offer Him reasonable service instead of merely the instinctive reactions of an animal. Psychology by its very nature tends to over-estimate the importance of our instinctive and irrational impulses. They must

[1] Janet Mitchell, *Spoils of Opportunity*, p. 288.

be reckoned with, but in the last resort it is the conscious response that matters.

(3) We have one more comparison to make. It follows from the last. The Christian *ascesis* is aimed at the discipline of the " unruly wills and affections of sinful men " in order that Christ may rule in their hearts. We have already seen how positive in this respect is the teaching of even so rigorous an ascetic as St. John of the Cross. In a man's life many interests compete for the mastery: pleasure, family, honours, riches. His affections are squandered in various directions. If he is to fulfil the true purpose of his creation he must undergo a vigorous self-discipline in order that the will of God may be the ruling desire. There is a scathing description in the second epistle to Timothy of certain women who thought themselves religious, yet without any definite purpose in life, at the mercy of every whim, and an easy prey to humbugs who crept into their houses, " holding a form of godliness, but having denied the power thereof ". " Silly women," they are termed, " laden with sins, led away by divers lusts, ever learning and never able to come to the knowledge of the truth "(2 Tim. 3. 5ff).

The psychologist of to-day is equally insistent that man must have what he calls a " master sentiment " if his life is to have any definite coherence. A sentiment in this sense " involves an individual tendency to experience certain emotions and desires in relation to some particular object ".[1] Home may be such a sentiment. The thought of it arouses in a man feelings of affection: if it is attacked his anger is roused and he will fight for it: if misfortune befalls it he is filled with grief. His profession or his hobby may form another sentiment, his political convictions another. His character is built up of the number and order of such sentiments. But if he has no master sentiment he will show no clear purpose in his life, being at the mercy of the sentiment prominent at the moment. The psychologist maintains that all those who possess character have such a master sentiment, though they are not all aware what it is. Such a sentiment gives them a tremendous driving power, for it harnesses all the other interests in its service. A man's power indeed depends on the strength and the value of that sentiment. Not only do his emotional impulses gather round it, but the other main interests or " sentiments " of his life are subordinated to its

[1] McDougall, *Outline of Psychology*, p. 419. (Methuen, London, 1923.)

demands. So if political ambition forms his master sentiment, he will make all else give way to it or subserve its ends. He will seek a wife likely to forward his aims, and he will not allow his family life to absorb too much of his time; his recreations and friendships will be undertaken with one eye on the political advantages they may bring. Even his patriotism will be tempered by his chances of office, so that in a national crisis he may turn quisling, persuading himself that thus he is serving the best interests of his country. Perhaps all through his career he will imagine that patriotism is his master sentiment. History records the names of countless people who have acted in some such way. David Cecil, in his brilliant sketch of the English aristocracy of the early nineteenth century, gives this picture of Lord Melbourne's mother: " All her qualities, good and bad, were subordinated to one pressing motive—ambition. Since to her this world was the only one, its prizes seemed to her the only objects worth having. . . . To this end she dedicated her beauty, her brains and her energy. . . . A single purpose united every element in her personality. Here we come to the secret of her eminence. It was not that she was more gifted than many of her rivals but that her gifts were more concentrated. Amid a humanity frustrated by conflicting aspirations and divided desires Lady Melbourne stood out all of a piece; her character, her talents moved steadily together, towards the same goal."[1] Set beside that woman, for comparison and contrast, one of the saints, e.g. St. Louis of France, or St. Ignatius of Loyola, or St. Teresa of Spain. They too stand out amongst their contemporaries all of a piece, their capacities concentrated on one great ambition. But their aim is the will of God, and it is set against the background of eternity. It means " bringing every thought into captivity to the obedience of Christ " (2 Cor. 10. 5). We have already spoken of the paramount importance of a main purpose in life and in what that purpose consists for the Christian. But we must also look to two things. We must make sure that we are not subtly aiming at some more selfish goal under the cloak of devotion to God; and secondly, we must endeavour to make our other interests duly subordinate and sub-servient to the true purpose. Until our consciously willed objective becomes our real master sentiment they will tend to depose it from its throne, or at least to paralyse our action. For one thing is certain: the strongest desire of the soul, known or unknown, always wins in the long run. If our Christianity were but a matter

[1] *The Young Melbourne*, p. 26. (Constable, London, 1939.)

I

of the reason, a satisfactory philosophy, it would have little chance with most of us against the passions of our fallen human nature. But because its essence is love and union with Love Himself, it can become the most satisfying, the only wholly satisfying desire. It is, to use our Lord's own illustration, like the grain of mustard seed which, at first so small and overshadowed by other more clamant desires, grows to be the tree that harbours on its branches all the rest.

It seemed wise to call attention thus to modern psychology. Something has been happening in this sphere in relation to ascetic and mystical theology, as with modern science in relation to dogmatic theology. Many scientists, after years of patient investigations, have abandoned their old cast-iron materialism and speak tentatively of the possibility of a master mind behind creation, thus reaching up, as it were, towards belief in God. So the psychologists after laborious research have come to inculcate principles in some respects similar to those which the masters of the spiritual life have always taught And Mother Church goes serenely on her way, too wise to turn round and say, "I told you so". But she is also far too wise to turn a deaf ear to the voice of the learned, even if her children have sometimes earned the title of obscurantist. Nor can we afford here to ignore entirely the work of these psychologists. They have much to teach. On the other hand, we shall beware of thinking that they speak with one voice. From one point of view there is no such thing as Modern Psychology, if by that is meant a systematic form of teaching. There is a number of specially trained men studying psychology, and, if there is some measure of agreement on some points, they differ widely on many others. Freudians, Adlerites, Behaviourists, disciples of Jung—which are right? Perhaps most valuable is their method of approach. It is and must be an experimental method. Each individual has to be dealt with separately, and induced to reveal himself in his words and actions, to the expression of his inmost thoughts and desires. Even his dreams have their significance. At the end of the process he often discovers himself to be very different from what he had thought—and he is left to readjust himself more exactly to his environment. Spiritual conversion often has a similar effect on the soul.

In the matter of readjustment to environment the psychologists have brought home to us with alarming clarity the dependence of the individual on the society in which he lives. They have shown that his failure to gain that wholeness of which we have spoken is mainly due to the interaction of other personalities upon his own in the past, to codes of conduct which he has either accepted too readily or reacted from too violently. Dr. Jung has declared that most of the failures which have come to him for treatment have been due in the case of the young to fear of facing social life, the struggle to make good, and in the case of the middle-aged to fear of leaving it—the prospect of death. It all goes to emphasize the fundamental importance of the family life, and the proper upbringing of children by providing them with the right environment. But this is precisely what the Church has always taught from the earliest ages. It has always insisted that the individual Christian is a member of a body, the Body of Christ, and as a member is articulated into the whole, " fitly framed and compacted together "; that " if one member suffers all the members suffer with it ". So the New Testament insists on the duty of parents to children, and children to parents. " Husbands, love your wives, and be not bitter against them. Children, obey your parents in all things, for this is well-pleasing in the Lord. Fathers, provoke not your children, that they be not discouraged." (Col. 3. 19 ff.) It is the advice of a wise psychologist. If it had been always followed, the psycho-analysts would have had empty consulting-rooms. So again the Church permitted infant baptism, for it was fully aware of the power of spiritual influences on minds still barely conscious, and of the need for that process of growing in the Body to begin as soon as possible. Yet it only allowed the practice where there was some guarantee that the family environment should be favourable for the reborn child.

In this present age when family life is valued so lightly, modern psychology can perform valuable service in reinforcing from its own different angle the Church's age-long message. At the same time it forces members of the Church to ask themselves whether their homes are ordered in a way best calculated to enable the children to reach their full development and fulfil their divine vocation.

Again, the psychologists can help us to a truer knowledge of ourselves. Our self-examination will become more real. Not only shall we inspect the motives of our conduct more carefully and save ourselves from false ideas about ourselves, but we shall not be astonished to discover how unworthy many of those motives are, nor shocked at the revelation. Many of the saints passed through agonizing experiences of mind and soul in their upward reach to God. It was not merely that old and unsuspected temptations leapt upon them with terrifying violence, when they were already far on the way to holiness, but that their unexpectedness and foulness immeasurably increased their suffering. A truer knowledge of their own psychopathic make-up would have enabled them to meet the storm with far more equanimity, and in some degree to have forestalled them. No one but God knows what sufferings are needed for the purification of His saints, and for their own sake He will see to it that they are adequate. But in the struggle with the powers of darkness, whenever they come, His children may rightly take the whole armour of God, and with it a true self-knowledge.

CHAPTER VIII

INTERCESSION

I

THERE is one form of prayer which must always have its place in the Christian's life—the prayer of intercession. It runs through the whole history of God's dealings with His people. We are familiar with the quaint story of Abraham's pleading for Sodom and Gomorrah (Gen. 18). Moses stands forth as mediator between God and his people, whether he is holding up his hands in prayer for their victory in battle or, sometimes broken-heartedly, sometimes almost violently, interceding for their forgiveness. Always in those days God, as He made known to Ezekiel, seemed to be seeking one " that should make up the fence, and stand in the gap before me for the land " (Ezek. 22. 30), to offer the adequate intercession. But none was to be found. " He saw that there was no man, and wondered that there was no intercessor " (Isa. 59. 16). So at last in the fulness of time He sent His only-begotten Son to make on the Cross the " one full, perfect, and sufficient sacrifice, oblation, and satisfaction ".

Intentions at the liturgical services of the Church have a special value. They place our own feeble prayers in the mighty stream of prayer that flows from the whole Church with the saints and the angels to the throne of God. We should therefore never neglect this opportunity of intercession offered by our participation in the Divine Office. But to limit our prayers for others to those occasions scarcely seems an adequate interpretation of the New Testament in the matter, or of the practice of the saints throughout the ages. Our Lord Himself taught emphatically the importance of intercession—not only the importance of praying for people in general, but for specific individuals. " Pray for them that despitefully use you," He said, and He prayed on the Cross for those who caused His agony. He told St. Peter that He had prayed for him that his faith fail not. How tenderly intimate too is His prayer for His disciples in John 17! And surely our own great comfort lies in the knowledge that He " ever liveth to make intercession for us ", with the particular love of one who knows each of His flock by name. St. Paul again and again reminds his converts that he prays continually for them—" praying always for you "; " we do not cease to pray and make request for you ", and he asks for their prayers for himself—which implies something much more informal and personal than the rather formal intention at an office.

" Is any among you sick? Let him ", says St. James, " call for the elders of the church, and let them pray over him " (5 14). And St. John bids us pray for any brother in sin if it be not a sin unto death (1 Jn. 5. 16).

It is unnecessary here to quote all the passages in the New Testament where this kind of prayer is urged. All we need is to be encouraged by the example of our Lord and His Apostles to pray for others, and to pray for them individually. Intercession is not only the duty of the Christian, but his peculiar privilege, for in it lies the layman's best opportunity of exercising his priesthood, as a member of Christ. Mediation, pleading to God for others, forms the essence of priesthood. The Epistle to the Hebrews dwells much on this. The priest is " appointed for men " on the Godward side (τὰ πρὸς τὸν θεόν, " in the things pertaining to God "), " to offer gifts and sacrifices for sins " (5. 1). It is a solemn call from God. No man takes such an honour upon himself, but God appoints him in order that he may so act for his people. God's purpose was that the people of Israel should perform this office towards the world. It lies embedded deep in His dealings with them. But they failed. To-day the Church as the Body of Christ fulfils this ministry. St. Peter calls it a " royal priesthood ". And each individual Christian has his share in it, and his responsibility both for other members of the Church and for the world without. Herein lies the true priesthood of the laity, which in no way conflicts with the official priesthood. There is something extraordinarily moving in the picture of the ascended Christ given in the Epistle to the Hebrews in the verse we have already quoted: " He ever liveth to make intercession for us." For every Christian as being in Christ and Christ in him is caught up into that great work—and Christ, as Julian of Norwich expressed it, is the " ground of our beseeching ". The priesthood of the laity is not, of course, confined to intercession. Priesthood has two aspects. In the one it looks out

towards men, bringing to them the gifts of God in sacrament and
service. The other, the more important, looks towards God,
pleading for them, above all, pleading Christ's sacrifice on the
Cross. Thus the priest is an *alter Christus*, perpetuating our Lord's
work here on earth, both in His ministry of healing and teaching,
and in His offering of Himself to the Father, to fulfil the Father's
will. It pertains to the duly ordained ministry to offer the Holy
Sacrifice and administer the sacraments. But each communicant
in his measure is called to take his share in that work, on the one
hand by faithful witness and loving service, and on the other, on
the " Godward side ", by continual intercession.

Hence, although our intercessions are not confined to liturgical
services, the Eucharist remains the focus of all. All look towards
it, are gathered up in it. For there we in Christ and He in us offer
the perfect intercession, and all our prayers, wherever and however offered, have value only in so far as they are united with that.
Our intentions at the Eucharist therefore have a special importance.
We Anglicans need to be profoundly thankful for the recovery of a
truer understanding of the Eucharist as primarily this offering of
our Lord's sacrifice on Calvary. Some years ago it had dropped
almost completely out of sight. The author remembers as a boy
at school being presented at his confirmation with a popular manual
which dealt only with communion and entirely ignored the sacrifice.
But the implications of the recovery are far-reaching, and demand
amongst other things a very real participation in this work of
intercession. Indeed, it must be so if we are truly members of
Christ and united with Him there in His offering at Calvary.
The prominence given to the Prayer for the Church Militant in our
Liturgy drives home the lesson, a lesson which is reinforced and
brought to its climax in the prayer at the end: " Here we offer
and present unto Thee ourselves, our souls and bodies, to be a
reasonable, holy and lively sacrifice unto Thee."

Perhaps our greatest stumbling-block with regard to intercession lies not in the theory of it, but in our lack of faith in the
efficacy of prayer. It is so easy to fall into a desultory practice of
intercession where we never expect any definite results. St. James
evidently had to deal with the same difficulty in his day. After
insisting on the importance of praying for others he adds, " The
supplication of a righteous man availeth much in its working ",

and emphasizes his admonition by the story of Elijah and the
marvellous results of his prayer. And Elijah, he hastens to add,
" was a man of like passions with us ". One need not be a canonized
saint to offer effective intercession, because, after all, it is in virtue
of Christ's perfect prayer and one's union with Him that the prayer
is heard.

It is good to go back often to the New Testament and the lives
of the saints to recapture the strong restful faith in the power of
prayer that breathes there. Some of our Lord's sayings are staggering in the efficacy they attribute to earnest prayer: " Whosoever
shall say unto this mountain, Be thou taken up and cast into the
sea; and shall not doubt in his heart but shall believe that what he
saith cometh to pass; he shall have it. Therefore I say unto you,
All things whatsoever ye pray and ask for, believe that ye have
received them, and ye shall have them." (Mark 11. 23 f.) " Whatsoever ye shall ask in my name, that will I do, that the Father may
be glorified in the Son." (Jn. 14. 13.) " If ye shall ask anything of
the Father, he will give it you in My name." (Jn. 16. 23.) St. John
is only reminding his readers of these words when he writes:
" This is the boldness which we have towards him, that, if we ask
anything according to his will, he heareth us, and if we know that
he heareth us, whatsoever we ask, we know that we have the
petitions which we have asked of him." (1 Jn. 5. 14 f.)

God is the source of all creation and its life. All depends on
Him, and owes to Him all its change and movement. The word
that goeth forth from Him is not void but accomplishes the thing
whereunto it is sent. As the None hymn puts it:

> O God, creation's secret force,
> Thyself unmoved, all motion's source.
> (*Rerum Deus tenax vigor,*
> *Immotus in te permanens.*)

Now prayer links up the soul in a special way with God: it
taps the source of that cosmic power, if we may reverently use the
phrase. And the " prayer of a righteous man availeth much "
because the righteous man is most closely united with God, most
responsive to each whisper of His will, and therefore a " vessel
meet for the Master's use ", a means through whom He is best able
to work. The saints have well understood this and prayed

accordingly. It justifies the contemplative life, and saves it from the reproach of uselessness or of neglect of the world's need. "Contemplatives", wrote Father Baker, "do not, without a special and certain inspiration from God, interest themselves in external businesses . . . yet those inexpressible devotions which they exercise, and in which they tacitly involve the needs of the whole Church, are far more prevalent with God than the busy endeavours and prayers of ten thousand others. A few such secret and unknown servants of God are the chariots and horsemen, the strength and bulwarks of the Kingdoms and churches where they live."[1]

How exactly God answers our prayer we do not know. It sets a baffling problem to the intellect. Men have argued that, as God knows the needs of our brothers and loves them far better than we can, He is already giving all the help necessary, so it is useless for us to pray for them. Now it is true that God does not need man's help, yet in His wisdom and mercy He has chosen to make use of it. St. Paul tells us that we are "fellow-workers" with God. It is the Christian's glorious privilege. And quite certainly God depends upon us for the carrying out of His will in practical ways. Unless the Good Samaritan fulfils his part the wounded traveller will be left to bleed to death. Everywhere God seeks human agents through whom to work. The believer becomes the lever by which His power can function, or the wire through which His current can pass. The same holds good with regard to prayer. God has His purpose of love towards souls but He wills to fulfil it through His faithful, and their intercession forms part of His plan. Professor Maritain proposes the question why so many saints in heaven and the thousands of angels do not prevent the devil triumphing over sinners here. He gives the answer in the words of a French priest, Père Rabussier: "Let us remember that God does all things in order and that heaven and the Church on earth are different things. In the same way a single star holds enough fire to melt all the ice upon earth and yet we endure the winter; just as we require a point of contact to move the bar of a lever, so God wills that all the action of Heaven on earth should have a point of contact here on earth; and this point of contact is the saints who are still pursuing their pilgrimage in this life."[2]

[1] *Holy Wisdom*, IV, 1. (Burns, Oates & Washbourne, London.)
[2] *Degrees of Knowledge*, p. 449. (G. Bles, Centenary Press, London, 1937.)

To speculate on how that contact is effected, or how the lever works, does not carry us far. One writer may seek a solution in the solidarity of human nature: another may stress our unity in God, maintaining that, as God's spirit is in each, the prayer of one means the quickening of that spirit in others. There is doubtless truth in both theories, but what brings conviction is experience in prayer. The man who prays finds his prayers answered in almost startling fashion, though often he does not at first recognize the answers. The unbeliever may murmur coincidence, but when those " coincidences " happen frequently that theory breaks down. If a savage finds that a light goes on time and again when he moves a certain switch, he rightly concludes that there is some power at work which answers to the switch, though it does not teach him what the power is or exactly how it works. God's answers to prayer are not indeed on the same level as that, for we are dealing with a personal Being, who is God Himself, and prayer is a relation between Him and human beings. But the more we pray the more we find that things happen, and it is only reasonable to conclude that they happen because of our prayer. There will be enough recognizable answers to assure us of this, enough apparent failures to remind us that our prayer has nothing to do with magic. Christian prayer involves our seeking a personal God that we may learn His will, and then give our wills wholly to Him that His will may be done. Magic demands no faith beyond what is sufficient to carry out the necessary rites. But faith is the first essential of Christian prayer. Our Lord constantly insisted on the need of it: " Whosoever shall not doubt in his heart but shall believe "; " believe that ye have received them and ye shall have them." Yet we must remember that it is faith in God, which means trusting oneself and one's plans to Him, seeking to co-operate, not to force Him to fulfil our desire. Sometimes indeed it seems that God does yield to the impetuosity of His child and grant him his wish, and the wish fulfilled crumbles to dust in his hands. Did not the psalmist realize this when he said: " So he gave them their desire and sent leanness withal into their soul "? (Ps. 106. 15.) "Leanness of soul" is a heavy price to pay for self-willed petition.

According to St. John, our Lord attached a qualifying condition to granted prayer. It must be offered " in My Name ". " Whatsoever ye shall ask in my name, that will I do " (14. 13). The phrase obviously means something more than tacking the name of Jesus on to the end of a prayer. It seems to be

connected with that abiding in Him and He in us, which is the
leitmotiv of those chapters of the Fourth Gospel. It implies some
likeness to Christ, some realization of the character of God revealed
by Him, some understanding of His eternal purpose of love. That
would teach us to make the right kind of requests, those that were
in accordance with His perfect design. Anything outside that only
aims at some lesser good, the price of which is precisely " leanness
of soul ". Hence the intercessor needs, as it were, a double portion
of faith—not only faith to believe in God's almighty power that
can overcome all obstacles, but also faith to trust himself, and,
what is often harder still, those he loves and prays for, to God's
ordering.

Here we come to another complication in the granting of our
requests. God has given freewill to man, and of that He will
never rob him, even to save him from sin or damnation. We pray
for one living in sin. God hears our prayer: He surrounds that
individual with His care, sends His messengers to awake him,
warn him, draw him lovingly back to safety, but He will not
" compel him to come in ". That ought not to discourage us from
praying for such people. Is it really astonishing that prayers for
them should so often lead to their conversion, if they help that
power of God to work upon them?

Again, intercession for others often involves not only their
souls but material things, e.g. disease, money, circumstances. Do
these lie outside the sphere of prayer, as some people think? Our
Lord's answer to that is shatteringly clear: " Whosoever shall say
unto this mountain, Be thou taken up and cast into the sea; and
shall not doubt in his heart, but shall believe that what he saith
cometh to pass; he shall have it." (Mark 11. 23.) That may belong
to those paradoxical sayings of His like a camel going through the
eye of a needle, but at least it means that we are not to be daunted
in our prayer by material difficulties. And He Himself reinforced
the lesson in the feeding of the multitude and in the stilling of the
storm. But here too we must ask " in His Name ". It was because
He Himself was always so perfectly at one with the Father, so
perfectly in tune with His will, that prayer and answer were in
exact accord. The lives of the saints also reveal first the deepening
of their union with God and the understanding of His will, and then
prayers marvellously answered—so much so that we doubt the

veracity of their biographers, not because this or that event lacks evidence but because we do not believe it possible.

In the gospel our Lord teaches many lessons both as to the value of intercession and as to the way in which answer is given. The centurion comes to pray for his servant, and our Lord's answer is immediate and full, " I will come and heal him " (Matt. 8. 5). To the Syro-Phoenician woman He gave at first what appeared an abrupt refusal before granting her request for her daughter. The mother of St. James and St. John, making her bold intercession for her two sons that they might sit the one on the right and the other on the left hand of Christ hereafter, received no direct answer. Instead our Lord addressed Himself to the two sons with a challenging question, and even then promised them only a share in His sufferings (Matt. 20. 20). That promise met its fulfilment very soon for St. James, when Herod's sword fell and he was baptized with his Master's baptism of death. Nor did his brother drink less of the cup, for, if he was spared then, it was only to be driven into exile and to live to see the love of many wax cold, and the heavy hand of persecution descend on the Church he loved. There is one interesting case where He answered an acted intercession. It was when the friends of the man " sick of the palsy " brought him and let him down through the roof in front of our Lord. " Jesus, seeing their faith, saith unto the sick of the palsy, Son thy sins are forgiven " (Mark 2. 5), and then went on to heal him. " Seeing *their* faith ", not *his*—though apparently they spoke no word.

We need to ponder long on these lessons. They teach us God's graciousness and eagerness to answer our intercessions, however we present them, and also His power to fulfil them. Yet it is to be on His own terms and in accordance with His own plan. Furthermore, it means the submitting of ourselves to Him to be fitted for the part we are to play; and that may involve a time of testing and disappointment, even of suffering. We must put ourselves utterly into His hands, and here too it holds true that it is a fearful thing to fall into the hands of the living God—though it is at the same time the richest experience man can have. Those we pray for will also be subjected to His fire of love, testing, purifying, making them fit to receive the happiness we desire for them. This emerges with almost terrifying clarity in our Lord's last prayer for His disciples, as given in the seventeenth chapter of St. John's Gospel. He was leaving them to face the world alone. They would have to meet the aftermath of the Jews' fancied victory over Himself—a time of fierce persecution—and most of them would be put to death for His sake. Yet His prayer contains no petition for their deliverance from suffering, but only from the temptation to shrink from the challenge and yield to the evil. "I ask not that thou shouldst take them from the world, but that thou shouldst preserve them from the evil one." That is perfect love interceding for the loved ones. The saints sometimes reveal a similar strength which can only come from a very pure love, coupled with a deep insight into the will of God. St. Catherine of Siena had great gifts of healing. It is related of her that once she came to Pisa and healed many sick folk. Amongst the sick was a young friar, who begged to be healed. St. Catherine looked at him and then only said, "This trial is necessary for your salvation; it will accompany you to the grave, but it will not hinder you from serving God as a friar."[1] With that she left him. Most of us tend to pray first for the deliverance of our friends from suffering of any kind. Eckhart gives forcible expression to the lesson when he says: "He who would save a friend from suffering for one short day that which might bring him lasting profit, honour and prosperity, would be no true friend and would not really love him."[2]

Yet God in His mercy does have pity on human weakness and often answers prayers concerning mundane things, even when offered by ordinary Christians. Nor does He seem to look too closely at the manner of their offering, provided He sees true humility and faith in the heart of the intercessor.

Faith then is the first condition for effective prayer. But there is another which our Lord couples with it—the spirit of forgiveness. On this He laid tremendous emphasis, coming back to it again and again. Immediately after His statement which we have just quoted about removing a mountain provided one has faith, He added: "And whensoever ye stand praying forgive, if ye have aught against any one." Our own forgiveness, He says, depends on it, and He illustrates that by the parable of the two debtors.

[1] *St. Catherine*, 2nd ed., p. 183, by the author of *Mlle. Mori*. (Methuen London, 1907.)

[2] Quoted Lasson, *Meister Eckhart*, p. 256. (Hertz, Berlin, 1869.)

" Forgive us our trespasses," He taught us to pray, " as we forgive them that trespass against us." Finally He clinched the lesson by His own prayer for the forgiveness of His enemies. It is true that some sign of repentance is needed on the part of the sinner before forgiveness is possible. Our Lord Himself recognized this: " If thy brother sin, rebuke him; *and if he repent*, forgive him. And if he sin against thee seven times in the day, and *seven times turn again to thee, saying, I repent*, thou shalt forgive him." (Luke 17. 3 f.) That is a hard saying. Forgiving even once a serious wrong is difficult enough. But why should it be so necessary to forgive before our own prayers are answered? Is it not because an unforgiving spirit is essentially a lack of charity? it belongs rather to a spirit of hate—and a lack of charity means being out of touch with God, who is Love itself. St. John has expressed it with his usual insight: " He that saith he is in the light, and hateth his brother, is in the darkness even until now. He that loveth his brother abideth in the light, and there is none occasion of stumbling in him. But he that hateth his brother is in the darkness, and walketh in the darkness." (1 Jn. 2. 9 ff.) Hence an unforgiving spirit blocks the way to God. It breeds hatred, and the one possessed by it " walketh in the darkness and knoweth not whither he goeth, because the darkness hath blinded his eyes ". The result is that he cannot pray " in the name of Jesus ", and his actions tend to " lawlessness " or disorder because he is not co-operating with God's plan, God's order. Yet the need of repentance on the part of the wrongdoer still remains, and forgiveness is far from being mere acquiescence in wrong. What one needs most, perhaps, is first the realization of one's own frailty. The fault is seldom all on one side, and one's own attitude or weakness may have provoked the crisis. Secondly, one must keep alive love—the spirit of forgiveness, the eagerness to meet the first sign of repentance— like the father of the prodigal waiting and watching for his return, and running to meet and embrace him before he could stammer out his apology. We must beware here of a subtle temptation to adopt a wrong attitude to one who has wronged us. We do not take any definite steps against him: we are civil to him when we meet him. But we nurse the grievance: we do not particularly wish to heal the breach: we are secretly glad if some misfortune befalls him. At least we expect a formal apology. There is none of that eagerness to forgive which is of the essence of true charity, and an all-important condition of effective prayer.

We do not know exactly how God makes use of our prayer for others; neither do we know how far-reaching that prayer may be. So much of our intercession deals with people and events outside our ken, and no one knows what comfort and strength it brings to them. For it is not necessary to apply our prayer always to definite persons. God accepts it and uses it as He sees fit. One may be praying, for instance, for souls " in peril on the sea ", or for soldiers in battle, or for the sick in hospitals. The prayer goes forth to God, and He uses the praying soul to aid this person or that person according to His own loving purpose. Perhaps one of the joys reserved for us hereafter will be to learn what became of our intercessions, and to meet the souls they supported in time of need. And for ourselves, there will be the joy of meeting those who have prayed for us, and so of realizing from a new angle our share in the Communion of Saints. If so, we may learn then how much the Church owes, and we ourselves as members of it, to the artless prayers uttered by simple child-like souls, the value of whose intercession we should have little suspected. As a French writer has put it: " You priest, to what do you owe the grace of your priesthood? You know well enough that it is not due to yourself, but see! at the church-door in your native town there was a blind beggar selling matches. He used to pray with a simple heart for all those he could not see. One day his prayer caught you as you passed and marked you out for God. You apostle! to whom do you owe your sickle and your sheaves, your boat and bursting nets? You are well aware that your harvest is not the result of your own powers. But see! a little girl one day at school put her hands together before the statue of our Lady and asked God to have pity on miserable sinners. It was the joined hands of a child that touched the heart of God."[1]

II

The question arises as to the best method of interceding. One popular method is the rosary. The rosary is recited decade by decade in the usual way, but with a special intention for the cause or people for whom prayer is desired. It has much to commend it. It is a very simple form of devotion, which can be practised by the least advanced in prayer and by the least learned. The constant repetition of the same short familiar suffrages, coupled with the

[1] Père Charles, *La Prière à toutes les Heures*, p. 84. (C. Beyaert, Bruges, 1923.)

touch of the beads and the direction of the mind to one of the mysteries, makes for recollection. Moreover, this prayer looks primarily to our Lord and that is the first condition of right intercession. It counteracts the natural tendency to occupy the mind mainly with the objects of our intercession rather than with God's plan for them.

Nevertheless the use of the rosary in this way, like the intentions at the Divine Office, valuable as it is, should not comprise the whole of our intercessions. (The rosary is, however, a very adaptable devotion and can be combined with many kinds of prayer.) It does not follow the model given to us in the Gospels. When our Lord tells St. Peter that He has prayed for him that his faith fail not, He does not give the impression that He had said a psalm or versicle with that intention. Still less does such a method resemble the tender, almost brooding, love that breathes in His great prayer of St. John 17. The letters of St. Catherine of Siena reveal incidentally the same tender love for others possessing her in her prayers for them, and it gave her an extraordinary insight into their needs. "It happens sometimes," so she writes to Daniella of Orvieto, "that when one is praying for the same person, one occasion will find him in such light and holy desire before God that the soul will seem to fatten on his welfare; and on another occasion thou shalt find him when his soul seems so far from God, and full of shadows and temptations, that it is toil to whoso prays for him to hold him in God's presence."[1]

A study of that seventeenth chapter of St. John will teach invaluable lessons about methods of intercession. However much St. John may have interpreted and expanded our Lord's prayer, it is at least an interpretation, and not a substitution of his own ideas. And it harmonizes entirely with what our Lord Himself taught elsewhere about prayer.

(1) First of all comes His own continual absorption in the Father's will and the Father's glory. He prays that He Himself may be glorified in the supreme trial of the Cross in order that the Father's glory may be revealed and recognized. His whole object had been to reveal that glory to men. It had been the work the Father had given Him to do, and looking back over His incarnate

[1] *Letters of St. Catherine*, ed. by V. Scudder, p. 68. (J. M. Dent, London, 1906.)

life He saw that He had fulfilled it perfectly in every detail. Eternal Life lay in the recognition of that glory, in the knowledge of God and of His Son. "This is eternal life that they may know thee the one true God, ànd him whom thou didst send, Jesus Christ. I glorified thee on earth having accomplished the work which thou gavest me to do. . . . I manifested thy name to the men whom thou gavest me out of the world." He saw that His relations with them were a solemn responsibility entrusted to Him by the Father, and He had regarded them as such. So they had learned through Him that all things came from the Father.

(2) Therefore He prays first for them. They are going to be left to face the world alone without His visible presence, to carry on their mission to men, and to face the hostility and persecution that awaited them, as He Himself knew full well. But our Lord does not pray for their deliverance from those dangers, but that they may be kept "in thy name which thou gavest me", that they may be delivered from the evil. Further, He makes His prayer that they may have His own joy fulfilled in themselves, that they may be sanctified or consecrated in the truth, and that they may be one "as we are".

(3) That they might receive these benefits, He offers His own life: "For their sakes I consecrate myself that they may be consecrated in the truth." Such self-dedication must be the price of all true intercession.

(4) From the disciples our Lord's love goes out to all those others who should believe on Him through their ministry. For them too He prays that they "may be one". That unity with one another and with the Blessed Trinity sums up all that man can need for blessedness. Further still it will witness to the world the truth of Christ's own life and work on earth. He prays that that blessedness may find its consummation in heaven in the Beatific Vision.

One of the richest fruits of perseverance in prayer lies precisely in the deepening of our union with Christ in God. There grows within us an increasing sense of our Lord ever living to make intercession for us and for all men, and of our being caught up in Him and in His prayer. We become more and more conscious of the throbbing of His Sacred Heart, and our own hearts begin to beat in

K

unison with it. His all-consuming zeal for the Father's glory finds an echo in ourselves, and, as we turn towards those we love and for whom we are praying, something of the same desire for them to share it takes possession of us. That is the one thing that most matters for them—whatever else we ask for them must be subordinate to that and be asked for only in so far as it promotes it. In other words, we begin to " have the mind of Christ " towards them, to see them in their true setting in the Father's eternal purpose. St. Catherine of Siena used sometimes to speak of her prayers for others as a placing of them in the Blood of Jesus. Frequently she would begin her letters, "Dearest——in Christ, sweet Jesus: I . . . write to you in His precious Blood ", sometimes adding " This is what my soul desires—to see you in that Blood ", and she would bid them bathe or " drown " themselves in the Blood of Jesus. The forcible phrase betrayed her own strong sense of being herself in her prayer swept into the stream of Christ's redeeming life, and of those others being brought into the same stream to be cleansed, strengthened, and carried up to God. Union with the Sacred Heart expresses the same truth in a slightly different way. Indeed it suggests an analogy with the function of the natural physical organ. For the heart and lungs receive the dark exhausted blood from the veins, purify and renew it and send it forth in crimson stream through the arteries to invigorate the whole body. So in intercession we bring ourselves and the wearied, the sin-stained, and the suffering to the Sacred Heart to be cleansed and renewed, made strong to fulfil our mission for the glory of God. His perfect understanding and victorious life gather our hesitating prayer, our blindness and coldness, cleanse us and carry us with those others in the stream of His love. A grand confidence takes the place of our doubts, of that vagueness as to the value of our intercessions, which prevent us expecting any positive result. The question that remains is no longer whether, but how, our prayer will be answered.

No better framework for intercession can be found than that provided by our Lord Himself in the prayer which He gave to His disciples. God's glory and God's will stand in the forefront and give the right orientation to whatever petitions are offered. The prayer may be used in various ways. The following illustrates very briefly one method. The thoughts suggested may or may not find expression in words, for words are not necessary. We will suppose that the intercessor is pleading for certain sick folk, grievously ill.

The method consists mainly in pausing at each clause to realize its force for the particular need.

Our Father—

Thou hast created and redeemed us and drawn us together in Thee. Thou lovest these thy children and knowest what is best for them far better than I. I bring them to Thee.

Which Art in Heaven—

Thou art God Almighty, dwelling in light unapproachable, "the Holy One that inhabiteth eternity"; therefore I come in reverence and awe, yet confident in Thy power to do all things. "In Heaven" and therefore not far distant, but in the hearts of us all, "nearer than hands and feet, closer than breathing". Our home is with Thee in heaven, not on earth: teach us to "set our affections on things above", for there alone lies our eternal bliss.

Hallowed be Thy Name—

I pray first that these Thy children and I myself may seek Thy glory, may reverence and love Thee more and more—for "this is eternal life to know Thee and Him whom Thou didst send, Jesus Christ".

Thy Kingdom Come—

Grant that the Lord Jesus may rule in their hearts and possess them with His patience and faith and love.

Thy Will be done in earth as it is in heaven—

Grant them grace to understand something of Thy purpose of infinite love for them, and to give themselves wholly to fulfil it, whatever the cost may be, even as the saints and angels rejoice to fulfil it in heaven. Take away from them all murmuring and doubts, and use them for Thy great glory. Grant me grace to know what Thou wouldst have me to do that I may help them aright and not seek my own will for them, for only in Thy will is their peace.

Give us this day—

Give them all that is needful for them both in body and soul to enable them to do Thy will, e.g. for the body, restoration of health, the right medical treatment, the loving care of friends, food, and shelter; and for the soul, Thy grace and above all the Bread of Life in the Blessed Sacrament. To myself, O Lord, grant love and sympathy, wisdom and capacity to help in whatever way is best.

Forgive us our trespasses—

Forgive me all my sin and blindness that have weakened my love and spoilt my capacity to help: forgive them whatever has been or is amiss in their lives, all that separates them from Thee or stands between Thy grace and their need. Grant to us a true charity towards all, taking from us all bitterness, resentment, or hardness of heart.

Lead us not into temptation—

O Lord, Thou knowest our weakness; let not the trial be too sharp for us lest our faith or our courage fail at such a time.

But deliver us from evil—

Yet in whatever perils we find ourselves, keep us, O Father, steadfast in faith: deliver us from the enemy and his snares, from despair or self-pity, from self-absorption and neglect of Thee, and at the end "suffer us not for any pains of death to fall from Thee" but bring us to Thy peace and the fulness of Thy eternal life in bliss.

It may be useful to add certain practical suggestions if we are to build up our intercessions on these lines.

(1) Insomuch as intercession forms part of our ministry as members of the Body of Christ, we ought to have a scheme and not be content merely with a few haphazard prayers for people we know. And the scheme should be as catholic as possible; that is, it should envisage the needs of the Church as a whole, indeed of the world at large, and not be confined to parochial or local interests. We saw how our Lord in His great prayer prayed first for His own disciples, and then went on to all those who should believe through their preaching, a prayer which included our own selves. Our intercessions must follow that example. They will be first and foremost for the members of the Church. St. Paul says nothing in the eighth chapter of the Romans about the Holy Spirit praying for those outside, but only that "He maketh intercession to God for saints", though we are told elsewhere to pray for all men. Naturally and rightly we begin with those known to us. Then our prayers go out to include our brethren beyond our range, and the Church's missions in foreign parts. They will reach also those not in communion with us, and that will teach us something of our Lord's own yearning that all should be one. Prayer for the members of the Church is so vital because it is also an indirect way of praying for those outside. Just in so far as their fervour is kindled will those others be able to catch a glimpse of the mystery of Christ and be drawn to His allegiance.

(2) Yet at the same time we must beware of the danger of overloading our prayer with lists of names. The little intercession papers which are issued to-day in considerable numbers can prove a real menace to intercession. They distract our attention from God and His love and His plan, and make our prayer a weary recital of

names of people we know nothing about. Some names we must have—the names of those with whom God has brought us into contact. For some we shall pray daily: others will have their place in our weekly scheme. But our main intercession, as we have already said, will consist in trying to unite ourselves with God and enter into His loving purpose for the world, trying to co-operate with Him. Nor do we know how far such prayer may reach. St. Thérèse of Lisieux, commenting on the verse from the Canticle, "Draw me; we will run after thee", cries "O Jesus, there is no need to say: 'Drawing me, draw also the souls that I love' .... A soul taken captive by Thy beauty could not run alone; all the souls it loves are drawn in its train; that is a natural consequence of its attraction to Thee".

(3) If we have a scheme, it is good also to have definite times for intercession. The value of our prayer lies not so much in getting through so many names or subjects as in uniting ourselves with the will of God, or rather in realizing our union with Him. How much time in the day can rightly be given to this all-important work? So long as we are occupied in that work it does not matter a great deal how wide a range is covered by our prayer. Sometimes the Holy Spirit seems to lead us to spend much, perhaps the whole time, over one particular person or subject. We must follow His lead and believe that He will Himself attend to the others for whom we meant to pray.

Moreover to devote a fixed time delivers us from the temptation in seasons of aridity to hurry through our intercessions.

(4) Intercession is a costly business. It means the deliberate linking of ourselves with our Lord's own great intercession on the Cross. St. Paul was well aware of this. He urges the Christians in Rome "to strive together" with him in their prayers for him. It is a strong word that he uses (συναγωνίσασθαι)—"to agonize with". He tells the Colossians that Epaphras is ever striving for them in his prayers. The word carries us back to that midnight scene in the garden where our Lord "being in an agony" prayed yet more earnestly. It means some kind of identification of ourselves with those we pray for—an entering into their sufferings and needs, at least by sympathy. One question we must always be ready to ask, "Is there anything I can do to implement my prayer by word or deed?" It would be vain to pray that such and such a person,

hungry and ragged, should be fed and clothed, if we had the opportunity and wherewithal to meet his need, and made no attempt to carry out the prayer. Our prayer for foreign missions would have little reality if we contributed nothing towards them and took no further interest in them.

However the bulk of our prayer for others concerns matters beyond our control. Indeed it is our very helplessness in the face of so much suffering that throws us upon God. Our consolation and confidence lie in our Lord's redeeming work. But we must be glad if He asks us in our prayer to share something of the pain. As one writer has said, " The fruitful prayer is the prayer with a drop of blood on it " (Le Plus). And we must not shrink from the price. We come to the place of intercession to offer ourselves in union with Christ. It must not surprise or dismay us if sometimes it is a time of darkness and stress, the offering on our knees of our weary bodies as the sacrament of the soul's devotion. But here we begin to touch on the subject of Reparation, of which more will be said later. (See Chapter XVI.)

As our prayer grows more intimate the manner of our inter-cession changes. Specific petitions tend to become fewer, though remembering our Lord's insistence on petition we shall not cease to ask for such things or graces as seem needful. But what grows most is the sense of God's own love of those for whom we pray, His plan for them and for the hallowing of His name. In the prayer of the contemplative the whole process of intercession comes to be as it were telescoped, simplified into one great longing for God's glory, which somehow contains at the same time an immense love for those for whom his prayer is being offered. The difficulty of attending at once both to God and to them has solved itself. What has happened is that Christ Himself has taken possession of his soul and filled him with His own devoted love of others and His own selfless longing for the glory of the Father. More still, so linked with Christ he becomes the more conscious of souls pleading for his prayers, both those known to him and that unknown multi-tude whose sufferings go to swell (in Walter Pater's words) " the great stream of human tears falling through the shadows of the world." The joy of sharing this burden offsets the added pain it brings.

In any case whether we be contemplatives or not, the more

conscious we are of God's purpose of love the more inarticulate our intercessions become. At one time we thought we knew very well what petitions to make for those for whom we prayed. Their needs seemed obvious, such and such were the remedies. God, we knew, was full of mercy and loving-kindness, and we asked for them boldly. Now we are not so sure. Our love of those others has become an overmastering desire for them to know and love God and fulfil His plan for them. Yet that is all mixed up with the desire for the satisfaction of their more mundane needs. The prayer has gone too deep for adequate expression. Is not this something of what St. Paul meant in his letter to the Romans: "We know not how to pray as we ought, but the Spirit himself intercedes for us with groanings that cannot be uttered; but he that searcheth hearts knoweth what is the mind of the Spirit, because he maketh intercession to God on behalf of saints" (Rom. 8. 26)? The whole of that famous passage should be studied in this connection. What a comfort to start with is St. Paul's reminder that we are already in Christ, even the merest beginner, and that His Spirit prays within us, interpreting our puzzled intercession, as we face the "giant agony of the world",

> Desperate tides of the whole great world's anguish
> Forced thro' the channels of a single heart,

and yet catch glimpses of the mystery of God's redeeming love.

Two things, the apostle explains, stand out luminously clear in that mystery.

(1) The end of man, the purpose of his creation, is a share in the glory of God—"adoption", "sonship", "liberty". All creation waits in pain for that. Already we have received the first-fruits of the Spirit and are sustained by hope of that consummation. Our intercessions take their colour from this.

2) God is working out day by day His plan for us all in detail. He has not left the world to itself to work out its own destiny. St. Paul says nothing here about those who are living "without God in the world". What he does say is that "to them who love God all things work together for good [or according to another, perhaps better, reading, "God works all things together for good"] to them who are the called according to his purpose".

All this affords an immense confidence in the work of intercession, though at the same time it makes our former petitions falter on our lips. " Is this or that remedy that seemed so necessary really the best to ask for? " " Can we just leave it all to God? " Deeper than ever grows our love for others as we see them in the circle of God's plan; more insistent than ever our eagerness for God's glory. Well, that is the Holy Spirit within us moulding our wills to His, and the Father understands our incoherent prayers, and grants them according to the abundance of His mercy and wisdom. Nothing else really matters much. In such a setting the things we most feared lose their terror—trouble, persecution, hunger, destitution, sudden death. For nothing can separate us, and those we pray for, from the love of God which is in Christ Jesus our Lord.

PART II

"O soul touched of God, dissevered from sin, in the first estate of grace, ascend by divine grace into the seventh estate of grace, where the soul hath her fullhead of perfection by divine fruition in life of peace. And among you, actives and contemplatives, that to this life may come, hear now some crumbs of the clean love, of the noble love, and of the high love of the free souls, and how the Holy Ghost hath his sail in his ship."—(*The Mirror of Simple Souls*, Div. 1, ch. 1.)

CHAPTER IX

LOVE AND THE MYSTICS

"SOLID food", writes the author of the Epistle to the Hebrews, "is for full-grown men, even those who by reason of use have their senses exercised to discern good and evil. Wherefore let us cease to speak of the first principles of Christ, and press on unto perfection" (Heb. 5. 14)—more literally, "let us be carried on to perfection" (full growth, completeness), for he knew that, as the soul advances towards sanctity, God's control of it becomes more and more pronounced. We shall remind ourselves at this stage of what was said at the beginning about the goal of life, and about aiming at perfection. The soul's perfection lies in the attainment of perfect love. St. Paul says that love is the bond of perfection. Charity is the beginning and end of the Christian's quest. All the self-discipline of which we have been thinking is only to prepare the way for this, to exercise the faculties to appreciate the meaning of love and to give oneself unreservedly to it. For that God gives grace to each member of His Church, especially the virtue of charity and the gifts of the Holy Spirit. The experience of the saints is all woven round the theme of love. They astonish sometimes, if not shock us, by the metaphors and analogies they use to express what this experience of love means in their union with God. But what do they mean by love?

The pagan writers of old also wrote movingly of love, and their writings were well known in the Middle Ages. The philosopher used the word ἔρως to signify the tendency of creatures to follow the law of their being, e.g. of a stone to obey the law of gravity. But normally it refers to sexual love. So love figures often in medieval literature. Aucassin in the French story is to such a degree enthralled by his passion for Nicolette that he is incapable of lifting sword to defend himself against his enemies and as in a trance allows himself to be taken captive. A vision appeared to Dante in his youth teaching him that love was lord of life. Only years later after much suffering and long exile did he learn that the love that was lord of life was divine, something much more than sexual love. Still to-day the world sets sexual love as the supreme example of love. Its poetry and its fiction revolve ceaselessly around the theme. Not to have been "in love" is not to have known love. Christianity also holds sexual love in high honour. The saints choose marriage as the closest metaphor of the union of the soul with God. But the love of a man for a woman, beautiful and holy as they knew it could be, is not to them the supreme form of love. The New Testament writers too have quite a different outlook from the world's on this matter. What is the essence of love? The world has always tended to say, in effect, "Love is God", by which it means that sexual love is the dominating passion and should be allowed free play. Hence if a husband ceases to love his wife and falls in love with another woman he must follow his love, i.e. his desire. Thus love is equated with sexual passion. The New Testament lays even more stress on love, but it says, "God is Love". Men can only know what love really is as they come to know God. The difference between the two sayings is abysmal. And the New Testament significantly drops the word ἔρως, with its associations of sexual desire, and uses a word rarely used before—ἀγάπη—to express Christian love. The emphasis in ἀγάπη is not on desire but on self-giving, not on possessing but on sacrificing. So the true model of love is Jesus Christ. "Hereby know we love" says St. John, "because he laid down his life for us" (1 Jn. 3. 16), and again, "Herein is love, not that we loved God, but that he loved us, and sent his Son to be the propitiation for our sins" (4. 10). And the proof that a man has love is not that he is in love with a woman, or even that he is deeply attached to his friends or relations, but that he is generous in self-giving, even to the laying down of his life for them. St. Paul puts the same truth in a still more challenging way. He is speaking of the love of husbands for their wives, and of Christ's love for the Church. But he does not say that Christ loved the Church as a man might love a woman, but that the man should love his wife "as Christ loved the Church, and gave Himself for it". For Christ's love is the perfect love, and man's love for a woman even at its best will be but a feeble copy of it (Eph. 5. 25ff).

However, we must not underrate the element of desire in all true love. It has its place, though some writers have tried to abolish it altogether from the Christian ideal of love. To remember this element is peculiarly important in considering man's love for God

—man who is God's creature, made for Him, and only reaching perfection in Him. We shall speak of this desire later on in the book, and, how it runs through the Bible; (See page 170.) Love may be defined as the will reaching forward to the beloved for the sake of the beloved alone. That involves the stretching forth of the whole personality to be united with, and to give itself wholly to, the beloved. The fact that this satisfies the soul's desire and fills it with joy remains secondary, but it cannot be dissociated from it—all the more because if the beloved be God, such union both entirely satisfies the soul and also enables it to reach its perfection.

But there is a difficulty in speaking of man's love for God. In human experience love demands some measure of likeness, indeed of equality, between lover and beloved. It is the basis of all true lasting friendship. It is because a man and a woman are the natural complement of each other that their love for one another can be so rich—the richest experience known to them on the natural plane. So long as men regard women as little more than chattels, to satisfy their lusts or produce children for them, they cannot know true love, but only passion. A man will sometimes project on to a woman all those feminine qualities which exist subconsciously in himself unrealized, to find too late that she does not possess them, and that he cannot find in her that likeness necessary for perfect love. Again, a mother will read into the artless almost reflex actions of her infant her own love, as it were creating a personality which meets her own marvellous mother's love. But there is little real likeness between the two, until the child develops.

In the early days of the Church for this reason Christians were chary of speaking of their love for God. Keenly aware of the infinite majesty and holiness of the Almighty, they knew there could be naturally no equality of love between man and Him. No one exalts more highly love and the need of love than St. Paul, love in its deepest sense of self-giving. But even he does not often speak of man's love for God, but prefers to use the word *faith* for that self-surrendering trust which is of the essence of love.

Yet, and here is the staggering thing, God Himself has made man in His own image. He sees as it were Himself in His creature, and so there is after all a likeness wholly God-given—and with it is

given to man the power to respond to His infinite love. Thus it is
possible through this stupendous act of God for man to have God
for his friend. The saints are careful to distinguish three grades
of love in men's relations with God. There is first the hireling, the
man who serves God only for reward, for what he can get for himself. Above him is the friend of God, where the likeness has increased
and he can converse with God freely, without thought of reward.
For a man does not love his friend for what he can get out of him;
for the friendship itself is his reward. So St. Teresa takes for granted
this possibility of friendship with God. " No one ", she says, " took
Him for his friend that was not amply rewarded; for mental prayer
is nothing else in my opinion, but being on terms of friendship with
God, frequently conversing in secret with Him who, we know,
loves us ".[1] Lastly, there is the son of God, led by the Spirit of God
and wholly surrendered to His will. For the growth of man's
spiritual life consists in the removal of all that has darkened the
image, and in his being fashioned more and more into the likeness
of the Son of God. " Behold ", says St. John, " what manner of
love the Father hath bestowed upon us that we should be called
children of God: and such we are. . . . Beloved, now are we children
of God, and it is not yet made manifest what we shall be. We know
that if he shall be manifested we shall be like him, for we shall see
him even as he is. And everyone that hath this hope set on him
purifieth himself even as he is pure " (1 Jn. 3. 1ff.).

Hence it is that St. Bernard and other writers after him can
speak of a man loving himself for God's sake only. It is the return
of the circle. A man begins by loving himself for his own sake; for
every man by nature loves himself, seeks the satisfaction of his own
desires, the preservation of his life, and the attainment of his own
advantage. His conversion to God and his entry into the life of
grace bring him up against other ideals. He has to learn to hate
himself for God's sake, to hate all that selfishness that keeps him
from God. Gradually he comes to realize the wonder and beauty
of a soul (his own) made in the image of God, stamped with His
likeness, and loved eternally by God Himself. It is precious in the
eyes of God Himself, so it must be precious to the man, but he is
looking at himself now from an entirely different angle from before.
And he shows this new reverence for himself by no longer seeking
his own natural satisfactions, but by giving himself utterly to God,

[1] *Life*, p. 60.

which has now become his greatest joy. So he will choose death rather than tarnish that soul so precious to God, saving it by losing it. The martyr not only loves God more than his own life, for he surrenders it rather than deny Him, but he also loves himself for God's sake only. He refuses to defile by sin this soul of his made in the image of, and infinitely precious to God, even though death is the penalty of his refusal. The Church honours the martyrs so greatly just because by enduring to the end they showed forth this splendour of Christian charity. Though they "loved not their lives unto the death", they loved them truly because they loved God supremely. Moreover, their love was seldom a matter of ecstatic emotion, but a bare act of the will that held them "faithful unto death", often through many and prolonged agonies.

But charity has a wider reference still, for it includes the second great commandment: "Thou shalt love thy neighbour as thyself." What we have just been saying throws light on that difficult phrase, "love thy neighbour as thyself". Just as a man has to learn to love himself for God's sake, so he has to learn to love his neighbour for God's sake, to see in him a soul made in the image of God and infinitely precious to God.[1] If he himself has come to love God, his own will will be one with God's, one will of love towards that neighbour—ever seeking his true good, his eternal welfare. As it is God's will that he should be happy, so he will seek to bring what happiness he can to him in this world—all, that is, that can help him forward to union with God. Such a love reaches far further than attending to spiritual needs only, for, as in his own case, so in that of his neighbour, he knows the importance of this-world needs, and of those little acts by which real love will always seek to express itself. Most of all will his love go out to the poor and unhappy, like our Lord Himself "seeking those which are lost". It is all much simpler than it sounds. Love is of God, for God is love. Everyone who loves possesses in some degree this divine quality, however let and hindered it may be by sin. The purer it grows the more it resembles God Himself. Now, God's love, as we know, flows out to all His creatures, and by love He watches over them and sustains them. Our love, then, will become like His—indeed it is His, His gift to us—and we shall "love one another with a pure heart fervently", just because we are growing more perfect in love. The saints interpreted "neighbour" in no narrow sense, for they

[1] Cf. Ch. XI, p. 197.

learned from our Lord the lesson of the Good Samaritan. So we find St. Catherine of Genoa devotedly nursing the sick in hospital; St. Francis Xavier, torn with sea-sickness, ministering unweariedly to his fellow-voyagers in their misery; Fr. Damien devoting himself to the lepers at the cost of his own life. The list of such lovers of their neighbours is inexhaustible. But never will their love lead them to any act which in their eyes may imperil their neighbours' union with God.

The Russian thinker, Soloviev, in his illuminating essay, *The Meaning of Love*, puts the matter rather differently. Man by the gift of reason is able to recognize the unity of creation in God. God created the world out of nothing and stamped His image upon it, making it worthy of His love and able to reflect His beauty. This is what man can recognize. Moreover, he sees also that he himself is made in the image of God, incomplete but capable of perfection in God. This means that he possesses " absolute significance ", i.e. that human personality is endowed with eternal values, and each individual exists for his own sake, not as a means to something else, e.g. the good of society or the continuation of the race. An animal, on the other hand, lacks this significance. What matters, for instance, in the lion is not its own preservation, but the preservation of the race. The individual exists for the species. But man is conscious of his own unique worth. He is conscious of his relation to God and to the universe, and yet he is aware of his own difference from them: he is neither God nor some other creature, nor part of one. Soloviev calls this his " egoism ". He exists as it were in his own right as a child of God. The sole reason of his existence is that he may attain his own perfection through union with God and enjoy for ever the vision of God. This involves other things, e.g. the dovetailing of his own personality with other personalities. Totalitarianism would make him but a means to the community's welfare, and thus set at nought his own eternal value. An animal has no such value. We may use a horse for the furtherance of man's welfare, or slay a sheep to feed him, but we may not treat human lives so. That is why slavery contradicts the Christian ideal of man.

But man does not remain thus isolated in his " egoism ". Love comes to him and makes him aware of the " absolute significance " of another individual, and fills him with the desire to give himself to this other, to be united with it, and enable it also to realize its own

potentiality of perfection. Soloviev is considering the love between
man and woman, which he regards as the supreme form of love.
Man and woman are the complements one of another; each is
incomplete without the other and love is the bond which unites
them into one ideal personality, bursting the banks of individualism.
This " breach of personal narrowness " by love enables a man to
live in another rather than himself. We are reminded of a saying often
repeated by the mystics: " the soul lives where it loves rather than
where it breathes ". To see thus the " absolute significance " of
another means also to see the image of God in that other, and so to
love it for God's sake and in God. Obviously that desire for union
with the beloved through self-giving involves a real love for that
one. It leaves no room for the idea that to love another for God's
sake means a cold formal affair, as though one were more or less
indifferent to that other *qua* individual.

Nevertheless the love at first is mainly a matter of feeling, and
the feeling vanishes and leaves sometimes a sense of disillusionment.
What is needed is that the feeling should be realized in action. It
is this realization which marks true love. " The problem of love
consists in justifying in reality that meaning of love which at first
is given only in feeling."[1] If to love means to live in the beloved
more than in oneself, then it means that the lover enters into and
shares the desires and will of that other, seeking to fulfil them rather
than his own as they reach out towards God. In other words it is
not to enjoy a feeling but to give himself to labour—and that
becomes his own will. So our Lord, whose love for God was
perfect, could say truly: " I came not to do mine own will but the
will of Him that sent me."

Moreover love cannot stay content with the union of the two
individuals. Each soul is a centre or focus of the divine All, and
the whole creation, each single creature, is stamped with the impress
of God. True love will be ever pushing forth towards union with
all—with the other members of the human race, with the rest of
creation, in God. The whole creation is permeated with the eternal
love drawing all these diverse centres of love into union with itself,
and with one another. The individual can only reach his perfection
and the final satisfaction of his love in relation with these others in
God. (But the great saints have always preferred to say that God

[1] Op. cit., p. 33.

is their All, and they have first turned from creatures to give themselves to Him. Then, their love, purified and united with the
divine love, can flow out to them again in stronger purer stream.)

Soloviev's attention was fixed chiefly on sexual love. He
scarcely deals with the mystics' love of God, or even with friendship between two of the same sex. The inference is that apart from
sexual love there could be no achievement of perfection. "The
authentic man in the fulness of his ideal personality obviously
cannot be merely male or merely female, but must be the supreme
unity of both." A "spiritual" love, a friendship which stops short
of physical union, would in his opinion be unreal and incomplete.
Soloviev, however, regarded sexual intercourse not as the goal of
life, but as an experience which opened the door to a spiritual
understanding of the universe. It gave, he maintained, just that
liberation from self, which made this possible. But whatever
the nature of love between man and woman the love between
man and God must stand on a different footing. For God is
spirit, and they that worship Him and love Him must do so in
spirit and in truth. God is Love itself, and He has His own ways
of perfecting man's incompleteness. Holy Scripture puts the difference with startling clarity. The union between man and woman
makes the two "one flesh". Our Lord, in repeating the passage
from Genesis, stresses the reality of that union, "So they are no
longer two but one flesh" (Mark 10. 8)—and there is nothing
derogatory there in the word "flesh". It means that the union
remains on the human level. But, says St. Paul, "he that is joined
to the Lord is one spirit" (1 Cor. 6. 17). The human level is transcended, and the personality caught up and spiritualized in the union
with God.

When, therefore, we read what the saints say about love, we
must take into account these things. Theologians teach us that
charity is one of the three theological virtues. In a sense it is more,
for it is the basis and crown of the Christian life: it is God Himself.
The Bible tells us that "God is love", but it nowhere says that God
is faith or hope. Julian of Norwich had a series of visions vouchsafed to her in her sickness. For long she pondered over their meaning. Only after fifteen years did the answer come, but it was
summed up in one word, "Love". "Wouldst thou learn thy

Lord's meaning in this thing? Learn it well—Love was His meaning.
Who shewed it thee? Love. What shewed He thee? Love.
Wherefore shewed it He? For Love."[1]

As we go on to consider contemplative prayer we shall see how
love comes to fill the whole horizon and absorb the lives of the
contemplatives. One after another they turn to the Song of Songs
and make its enraptured language their own. Or their devotion
breaks out into such high-pitched notes as the poetry of Jacopone
da Todi:

> Love, Love, my Jesu, O my heart's Desire!
>   Love, Love, within Thine arms to die were sweet:
> Jesu, my Love, I climb the Bridal Pyre,
>   Love, Love, among the flames my Spouse to meet.[2]

Another thirteenth-century contemplative declares that the
soul filled with love then takes leave of the virtues, for love sets it
free—a statement which so startled his English translator some two
centuries later that he added a special note to explain its meaning.
It is but a daring expansion of St. Augustine's " Love and do what
you like ".[3]

To read such language may startle us, too, unless we remember
two things. First, when contemplatives talk thus of love, they are
thinking primarily of God's love towards man, of God who is love,
not of their love towards God. When St. Paul said that " hope
putteth not to shame, because the love of God hath been shed
abroad in our hearts through the Holy Ghost " (Rom. 5. 5) he was
speaking of God's love. That love (ἀγάπη) " shed abroad in our
hearts " enables us both to love God and to love our neighbour. The
Christian's love is not a different kind of thing from God's love. It
is the divine love, God Himself, dwelling within him and inspiring
him with love. Secondly, they lay enormous emphasis on the place
of the will in love. Most people think of love mainly as a matter of
the emotions, and in these psychological days are apt to dismiss the
transports of the saints as morbid states due to sexual complexes.
Certainly it is wise to speak with some reserve of our love for God.
Even St. John was cautious here and regarded with some distrust

---

[1] *Revelations*, Ch. LXXXVI.
[2] Translated by Mrs. Beck in E. Underhill's *Jacopone da Todi*.
[3] *Mirror of Simple Souls*, Div. 3, ch. 3.

those who spoke too readily about it, though he has no doubt but that love is the beginning and end of the Christian life. His point was that if a man does really love God it must show itself in love for his brethren, who are made in the image of God and beloved of God. So St. Francis de Sales in his great treatise, *The Love of God*, lays down in the preface the supremacy of love: " *Tout est à l'amour, en l'amour, pour l'amour, et d'amour en la sainte Église*," but he begins the treatise itself with a discussion on the will and its paramount importance in the individual's life. No other writer of his time set forth so persuasively the attractiveness of the Christian Faith or the wonder of divine love. It shone out all the more brightly in an age when Calvinism was rampant, and Jansenism was rearing its head, both representing religion as a desperately difficult and gloomy affair. Some of his contemporaries accused him of making it too easy and soft. But if there was any softness in his teaching it was only in appearance. The attraction of love demanded an increasing detachment, a turning from all that could hinder the soul's response. As he said later in his book, we can well be suspicious of the ecstasies in prayer of those who have " no ecstasy in life ", who do not live close to God in self-denial and detachment from worldly pleasures, in interior simplicity and humility and charity. " For what good can it do a soul to be ravished to God by prayer, if in its conversation and life it is ravished by low earthly desires?"[1]

The saint goes on to show how the soul, as its love increases, gives itself more and more generously to fulfil the will of God, whatever it be, till its own will is one with His. It wills with all its powers what God wills, and it cares for nothing else except that. It has reached the state of " holy indifference ". But of that delighted surrender or abandonment to the will of God, and of the process of detachment by which it is reached, we shall speak in the following pages.

<hr>

[1] Op. cit., VII, 7.

CHAPTER X

THE THRESHOLD OF CONTEMPLATION

THERE is an initial difficulty in writing about contemplative prayer, apart from the immense difficulty of the subject itself. For whom is one to write? The question has sometimes been asked whether St. John of the Cross wrote for beginners or for those far advanced in prayer. Moreover a tendency has sprung up in these days to recommend all and sundry to abandon methods of meditation or even of affective prayer, and merely to be still and wait on God. That generally goes on well for a period. Then it fails. The individual is unable to pray at all: he finds himself up against a blank wall, and yet has an almost insuperable reluctance to go back to ordinary methods. The result may be that he gives up all attempts at mental prayer, and henceforth regards the whole subject with the cynicism of the disillusioned.

The great masters of the spiritual life were well aware of this danger, and their books contain many cautions. It is not so much that they write only for proficients and not for beginners. Rather they write for all those who have a drawing towards contemplation, what Fr. Baker calls a " propensity ". Both the *Cloud of Unknowing* and St. John of the Cross express the same thought—and Benedict of Canfield insists that the third part of his book (*Regula Perfectionis*) should only be handed to those who are in a state to profit by it and not misunderstand it.

Yet, in spite of the danger, those masters have felt driven by the desire to make known to others, so far as they can, the richness of contemplative prayer, to warn them of its pitfalls, and to encourage them to persevere. Richard Rolle, for instance, calls himself a " blabberer " for speaking as he does, yet " compelled to say somewhat of these high matters ".[1] But who are these others? A controversy has been raging on the answer to this. Some maintain that contemplation is an extra gift of the Holy Spirit for a chosen few, not necessary for the final perfection of the soul. The fight rages

[1] *Fire of Love*, p. 180. (Methuen & Co., London, 1914.)

mainly round the writings of St. Teresa and St. John of the Cross. But if one studies the history of the Church's teaching on prayer no such sharp division can be found. The Fathers did not hesitate to preach to ordinary congregations on the deepest kind of prayer. St. Bernard of Clairvaux thought it a normal development for all his monks. St. Bonaventure's teaching leads on to contemplation as the crown of the spiritual life. Nearly all the saints, of whose prayer-life we know anything, seem to have reached the state of contemplation. Perhaps it is enough here to say that though contemplation is the normal goal of prayer, it does not follow that all will reach it in this world. Contemplation belongs to the gifts of the Holy Spirit, being closely associated with the gifts of wisdom and understanding. All Christians receive the sevenfold gifts of the Holy Spirit—all seven, not merely some of them—and as the soul advances each gift exercises its full power upon it to enable it to reach perfection. One thing is certain. In the life beyond the grave when the blessed are vouchsafed the Vision of God, there will be no need then for them to prepare a subject for meditation and think out its implications. At the same time the vision of the infinite God will always be something infinitely beyond the most perfect soul's comprehension. Some kind of contemplation would seem to be its prayer there, however it prayed on earth.

At this point it is necessary to define the word "Contemplation". Different writers have used it in different senses. St. Ignatius in his *Spiritual Exercises* bids the retreatant "contemplate" various mysteries of our Lord's life on earth. He means that he should gaze at that mystery, e.g. our Lord on the Cross, as at a picture, absorb the details of it and learn its lessons. Yet even gazing at a picture can be done in different ways. Take for instance such a picture as Perugino's Crucifixion, copies of which are sufficiently familiar in this country. At first sight the spectator busies himself with the details. He marks the central Figure on the Cross, the moulding of the limbs, the expression of the face. Then his eyes turn to the watchers. Our Lady and St. John he recognizes at once, but who are the saints kneeling beside them? Then there is the landscape in the background, the colouring of the whole, and the unity of all. All the time he is contemplating, receiving impressions, rather than criticizing or arguing. Later on he has no need for such detailed examination. The picture has grown familiar. Now he will spend his time, contemplating it indeed, but taking in the whole scene at a glance. What will come home most to him then will be the general impression—its peace, its colour, its unity—the sense of the Cross as an eternal fact, with the saints in perpetual adoration of their crucified Lord. He "stays there at gaze" and the picture gives its message.

It was something of all this that St. Ignatius meant when he used the word. But the "Prayer of Contemplation" in its technical sense means something more than that. An old name for it was "Mystical Theology". What it does mean should grow more clear as we proceed. Chiefly the result is that in this kind of prayer the soul as it looks to God grows passive in His hand.

But the question rises: "How am I to know that I have this 'propensity', this drawing towards contemplative prayer?" Or to put it in another way: "How am I to know that it would be right for me to leave ordinary methods of mental prayer?"

St. John of the Cross gives the answer to the question most clearly, though it is found in much the same form in many books on the subject. There are three signs:

(1) We find ourselves unable to meditate. This comes as a great shock to most. They had looked forward to a period of increasing enlightenment and ease and joy in their meditation—leading gradually to some still more wonderful kind of prayer, so that they would find themselves suddenly lost in ecstasy. For most of us nothing of the sort happens. Instead meditation seems to come almost to a full stop. Scenes from the gospel which once held us thrilled now leave us cold. The mind flogs itself wearily over them with no result: the heart remains cold as ice, and it is only with difficulty that we can repeat acts of devotion. It is an alarming experience when it first comes. What has happened? "Has God forgotten to be gracious?" Or has our whole prayer been a delusion? Perhaps, after all, we are not the sort of people meant for prayer. We are to be the Marthas of the Church. The advice seems to suit us which was once given by an ill-advised minister to Mary Slessor, that remarkable woman who did such heroic missionary work in Calabar. Mary complained one day to him that she could not meditate. "I canna meditate, and Doddridge says it is necessary

for the soul. If I try to meditate my mind just goes a' roads."
" Well, never mind meditation ", her friend said, " go and work,
for that's what God means us to do ".[1] Advice like that has blighted
many a soul's progress, though Mary Slessor's was too great to be
so easily ruined. Moreover, it suggests a false dichotomy between
prayer and work—a dichotomy suggested by Martha herself in the
gospel story, but firmly corrected by our Lord. The curious thing
is that it is mainly when we try to pray that this paralysis seizes
hold of us. At other times our brain will still function normally,
upon the Bible as upon other things. But now, no: it isn't so much
that it " goes a' roads " as it used to do when first we began to
meditate: it won't go any road at all. Of course, this inability does
not of itself denote a call to contemplation. It is a complaint that
all know, beginners as well as others. For one thing sin may be
the cause; for sin stops prayer and, until the sin has been confessed
and done away, it forms a barrier between the soul and God. So
our first task is to examine ourselves carefully, whether any sin
has come recently to get in the way. If there is, penitence and
confession are the immediate need.

Or possibly mind and body are tired, over-strained—a fact
which would produce the same helplessness.

But such obstacles form only temporary inhibitions. The other
inability has become permanent or almost permanent. It goes on
week in and week out.

(2) This lack of ability to meditate is only one symptom. By
itself it would not indicate any progress in prayer: rather the
reverse. In any case inability to pray sounds a paradoxical kind of
improvement. The second sign is equally odd. We can find no
special interest in anything else. All people know how difficult it is
to pray, how uninteresting prayer seems, when the mind is occupied
with some other interest. The housewife may be thinking what
she is to buy for dinner; the priest may be considering his sermon
or be full of the doings of the previous day; the young man may
have his mind set on his coming game. All three may have their
hearts set on less worthy things. In each case prayer becomes very
difficult. But that is not what we mean here. Instead there is only
a blank. Indeed we grow alarmed at our indifference. Things
which absorbed our interests a short while ago seem to have become

[1] W. P. Livingstone, *Mary Slessor of Calabar*, p. 11. (Hodder & Stoughton,
London, 1917.)

more or less insipid—at least at prayer-time and it may be out of
prayer-time too. The trouble sometimes goes further still. We
even seem to have lost our love for our friends; at least we are
conscious of none of those warm feelings we used to have. Our
Lord once said, " Where your treasure is, there will your heart be
also ". It forms an index to our state to ask ourselves from time to
time, " Where is my heart at the moment? " The lover knows
well what the answer to that will be generally. Most of us have
some dominating interests. But there are few people who would
not be humiliated, perhaps astonished, to find to what trivial and
unworthy matters their minds so often turn, on which their hearts
are to some extent fixed. That question, by the way, is a good
method of learning the practice of the Presence of God, and has
been recommended by more than one writer on the spiritual life.
It gives one an opportunity of recollection, of realizing what is
occupying the centre of our consciousness, and recalling us back
to God. We can make some act of adoration or supplication.
" O my God, I am Thine: keep me Thine! " " My God, I love
Thee: knit my heart unto Thee! " or " O Lord Jesus Christ, Son
of God, have mercy upon me a sinner " (this especially when conscious of some unworthy attachment); " O Lord Jesus, meek and
holy (brave and patient, selfless and loving), make my heart like
Thy heart "; or " Glory be to Thee, O God, three Persons in one
God, Father, Son, and Holy Spirit ", etc.

To return to our prayer. No positive distractions come to draw
the heart away. Rather it seems stupefied. Yet this too is no necessary sign of being on the threshold of contemplation. It may be due
to an increased selfishness, and the fear of that alarms us much. Or
as in the former case ill-health may have produced it, a frequent
result of overstrain. There is a further sign.

(3) A strange longing for God lies somewhere at the back o
our consciousness. Our hearts may be cold, our minds be blank,
yet we are dimly aware that we want God, and we don't particularly want anything else. We want to get away and be alone with
God. Our prayer doesn't actually bore us, sterile though it seems.
We are content to be engaged in it. We long to pierce the fog
that seems to enshroud us. If only God " would rend the
heavens and come down "! " O that I knew where I might find
Him! "

This is the surest sign of all. When these three signs come together the soul has reached the threshold of contemplation. Francis Thompson had some dim thought of this when he wrote:

> When thy seeing blindeth thee
> To what thy fellow-mortals see;
> When their sight to thee is sightless;
> Their living, death; their light most lightless;
> Search no more—
> Pass the gates of Luthany, tread the region Elenore!

(The Mistress of Vision.)

We need not fear that longing for God. A Swedish theologian (Prof. Nygren) wrote some years ago a learned work putting forward the theory that the desire for God has nothing to do with true Christian love, with ἀγάπη; that it represents the invasion o Hellenism into our religion. ᾽Αγάπη means self-giving, he maintains, whereas the desire for God belongs to the ἔρως motive of the Greeks, a selfish desire for one's own satisfaction. But the professor proves too much.[1] That desire for God had its roots in the Old Testament saints long before Hellenism existed. "Like as the hart desireth the water-brooks, so longeth my soul after thee, O God." The Psalms are full of it. It is true that the crowning mark of ἀγάπη is self-giving, as our Lord showed in His own life—and bade men to love one another " even as· I have loved you ", and " greater love hath no man than this that a man lay down his life for his friends ". Obviously, too, God's love for man must be in some way different from man's love for God or even for one another. Even so, it seems arguable that traces of what the professor calls the ἔρως motive can be seen in our Lord. Whole nights spent in prayer suggest something more than self-sacrifice, at least some desire for communion with the Father. The cry of dereliction from the Cross re-echoes that. The parables of the Lost Sheep and of the Prodigal again strike a note of desire for the wanderer, apart from the self-sacrifice involved. In the latter parable the note of self-sacrifice on the Father's part is remarkable by its absence.

Moreover, human love must contain the note of desire. Man was not created perfect. He is a finite, pitiful, incomplete thing, made to find his perfection in God. Further still, man was created a social being, needing other human beings in order to be fully

[1] Nygren, *Agape and Eros*. A study of the Christian Idea of Love (Trans. Hebert and Watson, S.P.C.K.).

human himself. And God made them male and female, neither complete alone. 'Αγάπη does deepen the note of self-giving—but it builds on the natural virtue. It does not overthrow it. So our Lord teaches us. For, whereas He emphasizes the utter self-sacrifice demanded by true Christian love, He is also constant in His promises of reward to the faithful—that His servants' desire shall be satisfied. "Blessed are they that hunger and thirst after righteousness, for they shall be filled." The longing for God continues often outside prayer-time, sometimes as a conscious desire, sometimes as a restlessness and distaste for anything else. This state of prayer has been called the Prayer of Simplicity. St. Teresa also calls it the Prayer of Recollection, although she seems to use this title for two rather different states. Indeed there seem to be two phases of this prayer. The first is a glad simple delight in the presence of God, the mind stayed on the one fact, mostly silent, but sometimes expressing itself spontaneously in aspirations. The other phase is a more painful one, arid, in which one is unable to do anything much beyond remaining at one's post. This is the further side of the prayer.

What to do at this stage

This state often causes considerable bewilderment to those who have reached it. Their ordinary technique has failed. Sometimes they are advised to redouble their meditations, or they find books with meditations elaborately worked out, which, they hope, will supply their need, and they study them assiduously. Or, worse still, they take refuge in reading pious books, hoping that the fervour of their authors will atone for their own coldness. (Yet it is sometimes wise in this state to read such a book for a few minutes at the beginning as an aid to recollection.)

(1) We may note in passing that that failure of technique, if the phrase may be allowed, is a necessary part of God's dealing with the soul—and it happens in almost any state of prayer. A strong tendency nearly always exists in us to turn our prayer into magic. That is to say, we try to discover some method which will ensure fervour, which has power to produce the effects we want of itself. For magic demands some formula for tapping supernatural powers, wresting their secret as it were mechanically and avoiding the shock and claims of personal contact with a personal Being. But God is not an impersonal force. He is our Father and we are His children.

In any human family each child has its own peculiar approach
to its father or mother; no one is quite like the others. The wise
parent recognizes this and deals with each accordingly. If the un-
demonstrative child tries to imitate the ebullient affection of its
sister, it at once becomes unreal and spoils, instead of deepening, its
communion with its father. It is something like that with God
and ourselves. Each of us has his own way of approach—an intimate
personal matter. There is no formula of devotion to take its place.
We may get enormous help from the writings of the great masters
on the spiritual life. They can aid us in learning the ways of prayer,
and sometimes some method suggested by them seems exactly to
meet our need for the moment. But sooner or later, as a method,
it fails us, and we are left once more face to face with God, helpless
" and with no language but a cry ". We may have learnt much
in the meantime, but now we have to assimilate what we have
learnt, apparently by losing it all, so that God may have His own
way with us and that personal relationship go on deepening. And
the deeper it gets the more method-less it becomes, as the Flemish
mystic, Ruysbroeck, has so beautifully and forcibly described.
This is why all attempts at classifying the mystical states of prayer
are so unsatisfactory, and why writers differ so much amongst
themselves in their attempts to do so. Just as one seems to have
found the key, the experience of others breaks through his classifications. St. Teresa draws the line sharply between "mystical
theology " and other types of prayer: St. John of the Cross is much
less definite: he would admit the presence of infused contemplation,
i.e. St. Teresa's " mystical theology ", further down the scale. Both
of these classic writers regard " spiritual marriage " as the goal of
prayer. St. Marie de l'Incarnation (the " St. Teresa of Canada ",
as she has been called) seems to experience stages beyond that.

That, however, is beside our present point. It serves to illustrate
the first great truth to cling to in our prayer. We are not great
mystics following, like the Buddhist, a way with clear-cut stages
which will carry us by the force of our own efforts to the desired
goal. Nor are we great saints enjoying the reward of our toils. We
are merely children, sinful, ignorant, blind, yet the children of God,
beloved by Him—and it is as children that we come to Him along
the lines of the nature He has given to us. From first to last it is an
intimate personal relationship, with all the variety and surprises
of such a relationship, and with all the freedom. When our Lord

taught His disciples to pray " Our Father ", it was not as a method
of prayer merely for beginners. It laid down once for all the pattern
of our approach, and we never grow out of it. St. John in his epistle
recalls his readers to this fact, at a time when gnostic speculations
were rife and mysticism had become a cult, with all its dangers of
spiritual pride and of trying to find the magic key that would open
the door into the supernatural.

The Gnostics above all others claimed to possess that key. It was
the way of knowledge (γνῶσις). Christ, they said, had come and
shown the Way. All that men needed was to follow His example,
to know the secret of the Way by which they could free themselves
from the material and rise to the supernatural. Some of them even
taught the passwords by which they could overcome the planets or
demons that stood between them and their destiny. Much of their
teaching sounded then so plausible; it formed one of the greatest
dangers the Church has ever had to face, greater even than the
persecutions which decimated her ranks. It struck at the very root
of that filial relationship of the sons of God. St. John's words therefore came home with peculiar urgency to the men of his day. We
need them still. " Little children ", writes the apostle, " these things
I write unto you that ye sin not "; and again, " Little children, I
write unto you "; and again, " Little children, it is the last hour ";
and again, " Beloved, now are we the children of God and it has not
yet been made manifest what we shall be "; And he ends his epistle,
" Little children, keep yourselves from idols "—from putting anything else in the place of " Our Father, which art in heaven ".

To keep this in mind will save us from one common pitfall that
lies in our path at this stage, preoccupation with our state. The
temptation is strong, especially if we have read books on the subject,
to be continually feeling our spiritual pulse, as it were, wondering
what stage we have reached, re-reading our books to see what
corresponds with our symptoms. Mercifully, for the reasons just
stated, God sees to it that most of us do not run in such grooves,
and we cannot find out clearly, although the wise director may
diagnose our case with some accuracy, and at least save us from
straying. One of the joys of a director is to find a soul come to
contemplative prayer, puzzled it may be, yet quite innocent of all
book-knowledge on the subject and free from such vain speculations. Its path is all the simpler. St. Teresa relates somewhere how

she came across such a soul, who always took the Lord's Prayer for her prayer and yet her prayer was contemplation—and she did not know it. That does not mean to say that the director should never tell his penitent whereabouts he is in his prayer according to the usual classifications. He must use his discretion: it depends on the individual penitent.

(2) If we have learned this lesson we shall keep our freedom. We shall not say to ourselves, "If I have reached this stage, I must not use discursive prayer at all". Or "Whatever happens I must not be idle in my prayer; I must force myself to make acts of devotion, however reluctant I seem". Instead, as children in the presence of our Father, we shall do whatever seems most helpful at the moment. That is the one rule at this time. Whatever serves to deepen that sense of communion with God is what we are to do. Sometimes considerations will come to us and we can meditate in some sort. Let us do so, so long as it helps. More often the Holy Spirit within us will at intervals suggest to us and urge us to make acts of devotion, what Father Baker calls "aspirations". Do not let us hinder His action. But the acts should be short, and probably the same often repeated, perhaps only the Holy Name. The caution to be short is scarcely needed, for there will be no desire to be long.

Sometimes the soul seems content to stay silent in the Presence, and any attempt at uttered prayer only distracts, and disturbs it. Here too we must follow our Guide, who "teaches us to pray as we ought", and remain still. We must not try to force ourselves to make acts. Nor need we then fear the charge of idleness. Most of us will be able to distinguish quite clearly between this stillness before God and mere inertia.

This way of prayer brings a great freedom. It is one aspect of that "glorious liberty of the children of God" about which St. Paul wrote so forcibly. Those who have been under the law, rightly under the law, of fixed forms of prayer and ordered methods rejoice in the emancipation which it brings. It has its own laws, but these have a splendid elasticity. One comes out of school into the largeness of university life. Every undergraduate in his first year knows and rejoices in that sense of enlargement, of comparative absence of restraint, that he finds in the university. Sometimes he abuses it. The freedom from school discipline intoxicates him. But very soon he finds the secret of the other discipline and learns to adapt himself to it, and in doing so ripens all the quicker into manhood.

(3) What about preparation for mental prayer in this state? Is this one of the old laws that is now abrogated? Our inclination is to say to ourselves that, as we are not going to think over a subject in prayer, there is no value in preparing one beforehand. That is true so far as many subjects are concerned or the consideration of points. On the other hand, preparation is still important for most people for several reasons:

(a) Prayer will not always be easy and spontaneous. Often we shall come to it cold and distracted. But at least we can do something to forestall that. We can prepare ourselves carefully for our time with God, and then gladly leave the issue to Him. He knows what we need each day, whether it be the sweetness of His felt presence, or the discipline of aridity or distraction. For the Holy Spirit is our teacher in prayer, and gives us what we need, not always what we expect or should like.

But our preparation will differ from that of previous days. The choosing of a mystery of our Lord's life with just a glance at it will be sufficient. The fact of choosing it beforehand, as in the case of meditation, gives an opportunity to the mind to adjust itself in the meantime, so that, when the prayer begins, it is enough to set ourselves before the mystery chosen. There will be no need to think about it. Awareness of it is enough, and the soul is already prepared for recollection.

(b) What is more, the mystery chosen remains as a focus for our prayer. It may be that in spite of our preparation distractions come and the attention wanders away again and again. Most people find it much easier to recall their attention to a definite fact like one of the mysteries than to something so abstract as the Presence of God. Benedict of Canfield, in insisting on the use of the mystery of the Passion even for the contemplative, supported his plea on the unanswerable argument that St. Francis of Assisi was one of the greatest contemplatives of the Church, and yet it was precisely whilst contemplating Christ on the Cross that he was rapt in ecstasy and received the stigmata on his body. It is because our Lord is true God as well as true Man, and His humility the most perfect revelation of God, that contemplation of His life and Passion can draw the soul upward into the deepest form of prayer. Benedict, of course, is not speaking of a detailed consideration of one of those mysteries, but only of the contemplative gaze, or momentary remembrance. Nor is he alone amongst the Christian mystics in his contention. It has its roots fixed firmly in the medieval writers, e.g. St. Bonaventure. Even the *Cloud of Unknowing* reveals it as not far from the writer's thought. St. Teresa teaches it, and there is enough in the genuine writings of St. John of the Cross, apart from interpolations, to support Benedict.

(*c*) The objection here may suggest itself, " If at this stage prayer remains much the same throughout its course, what is the good of choosing a different mystery in any case? " It is true enough that the prayer scarcely varies at all, and that there is no attempt to consider the mystery, yet the choice has a subtle power to colour our prayer. Our mood, if that is the right word, in front of the Cross will differ from that in front of the Risen Christ. Our aspirations, whether few or many, will take a different hue according to our mood, though they may be identical in form.

It is important, perhaps, to cultivate this variety so long as it is possible. God has given to us the whole content of His revelation in our Blessed Lord to profit withal. Whilst we could meditate we ranged the whole field. And now, though our prayer has grown immeasurably simplified, we need not lose the value of such variety altogether. Some souls, it is true, find themselves drawn almost irresistibly to one particular mystery. But, failing any such strong "propensity", we shall do well to use many. Even those so drawn will do well to use other mysteries sometimes. But, once again, I would emphasize that there is no question here of meditating on them, but only of choosing one for a focus. Yet some souls will find an attribute of God, or the mere thought of His presence, their best means of recollection. No hard and fast line can be drawn.

(*d*) But, out of prayer-time, Bible study should go on—at least the reading and pondering over the New Testament—in so far as the opportunity is available. This remains true even in the most advanced stages of prayer. God has given to us this revelation—in these days of print so much more accessible to us than to our forefathers. He will not supply in visions or inspirations in prayer what we have failed to learn outside prayer through sloth. Moreover the meditation on our Lord's revelation subconsciously aids us during prayer, and tends towards a greater recollection at other times.

(4) When our prayer begins, stillness must be its keynote, stillness of body as well as of mind. We must hold ourselves quietly before God, allow His presence and His peace to surround us. " Be still and know that I am God." Little by little distractions cease and all our being grows quiet before God. Even more than in ordinary meditation must the body be kept from restless movements, the attention not caught by every passing sound or thought. If we come in great distraction, or with the mind obsessed by some thought or incident, as sometimes happens, so that such recollection seems impossible, a decade or two of the rosary, said with the mystery chosen in mind, often serves to regain it.

(5) Perseverance is of the utmost importance. Prayer at this stage often becomes painfully arid. It is a vast mistake to think of our prayer always developing through meditation into increasing light and fervour, until the blaze of contemplation bursts upon the soul. Rather, as we said above, prayer seems to come to a full stop; the mind will not work and the heart will not feel. Yet there we must be, holding ourselves still in the presence of the All-holy, All-glorious God, whom we can neither see nor feel nor think of, but whom we know to be also our Father and Saviour. What matters is to give generously the time allotted for our prayer. We can at least show our love so far as that. As Sister Elizabeth of the Blessed Trinity once put it: " I arouse my faith and am content to relinquish the joy of His presence, to give Him the joy of my love ".

I remember as a novice reading Fr. Baker's *Holy Wisdom* and coming upon the words, " Prayer is the greatest of all mortifications ". They came to me with a shock. Many other things seemed much harder then, but I know now their truth. After all they only echo what older writers had said. So amongst the hermits Abbot Agatho said, " There is no labour so great as praying to God. . . . Prayer hath the travail of a mighty conflict to one's last breath ".[1]

[1] Quoted H. Waddell, *Desert Fathers*, p. 157. (Constable & Co., London, 1936.)

M

Not only does the concentration needed involve a heavy strain on the whole physical and nervous system, especially during these times of aridity, but also the trouble is increased by the seeming uselessness of the prayer. It brings at the time no consolation, no sense that God is answering the soul's desire, nor afterwards is there anything to show for it. Activity offers something much more positive. Even bright thoughts in meditation give some sense of achievement. Much more is this the case with works—some act of charity or some duty performed. But here we have nothing. There is a new lesson to be learned. Generally only after long perseverance in prayer does God grant us glimpses of what its power is both in our own lives and in the world around. Meanwhile we must go on in hope.

However, it is sometimes advisable in times of real tiredness and stress to break off one's prayer, devote oneself for a short spell to some other kind of work, and then return to complete the time. St. Teresa recommends reading a devotional book for a short time, or taking a look at the beauty of Nature. The break seems to relieve the tension, and recollection comes at once. This ought not to become a regular practice, but only an occasional relief. Yet it emphasizes the importance of gauging aright the normal length of one's prayer-time. The novice sometimes, as his prayer grows easier, lengthens the time he spends at it at a stretch too much, with the result that when aridity comes he discovers that he cannot endure so long at once, and he has to retrench. But here, of course, his director should have stood him in good stead.

One result of perseverance at this stage, and a very consoling one, is that, however arid and even painful the prayer-time may be, moments of recollection and fervour come to the soul occasionally at other times. Thus God encourages the soul that seeks Him with its whole heart. It is by way of reward, and a sign that it is following the right path. But it does not mean, as some are tempted to think, that their way of prayer is to have no fixed times. To do that would amount to making consolations, rather than self-giving, the aim of their life.

(6) So much for our conduct during prayer. How must life be ordered during the rest of the day? Perhaps it is well to remind ourselves that the object of life is not to pray well, but to know and

love God and to give ourselves to do His will. Prayer plays an immensely important part in this. As our communion with God deepens in prayer, so will it have its effect on the rest of our occupations. This call to a greater recollection in prayer, therefore, makes corresponding demands for a greater recollection at other times.

Our life must be all of a piece. So, first of all, comes that "Practice of the Presence of God", of which we have already spoken. This is not quite the same thing as keeping the thought of God ever in the forefront of our consciousness. Most of us would find that impossible and an enormous strain. God sometimes gives us work to do which absorbs and is meant to absorb all our attention. Yet, if we have gained some measure of recollection, God will be always at least on the margin of our consciousness, and again comes flooding in when the pressure is released. Moreover, that fact of His presence colours all our action. So might a man be at work in the open air, with the sun shining bright and a magnificent view before him. His work will engross his attention, yet from time to time he will lift his eyes to gaze for a moment at the scene before him with thankful heart, and his awareness of its beauty and of the bright sun will subconsciously permeate and gladden all he does. Some of the saints indeed were gifted with an extraordinary power to be at once both absorbed in God and engrossed in the work on hand. St. Marie de l'Incarnation when managing her brother-in-law's business in Tours in the seventeenth century, carried out her multifarious duties vigorously, attending assiduously to every detail, yet she remained rapt in prayer, vividly conscious of God's presence. That was a special gift of God, the result not of her own painful efforts at recollection but of God's holding her soul passive in His grasp. Presumably in heaven that same capacity will be possessed by all, but here for most of us it cannot be, and we must do the best we can, aiming at an increasing recollection, but not over-straining our capacities.

But this forms only one part of our efforts at recollection. We find many things besides the work in hand demanding our attention. The contemplative's call to prayer carries with it the necessity of a rigorous course of mortification and detachment, of stilling all those desires of body and mind, not only those which call him away from God, but those which do not help his soul on the way to God. Readers of St. John of the Cross will remember the scarifying course of detachment recommended at this stage.[1] The first counsel lays down the guiding principle, "Let him have an habitual desire to imitate Christ in everything that he does, conforming himself to His life; upon which life he must meditate, so that he may know how to imitate it, and behave in all things as Christ would behave". Then there follows, "in order that he may be able to do this well, every pleasure that presents itself to the senses must be renounced and completely rejected for the love of Jesus Christ". By itself that maxim would be Manichaean or Buddhist rather than Christian— and many people take it so. But there is an all-important qualifying clause, "if it be not purely for the honour and glory of God". In the light of that clause all the subsequent restrictions must be read. It means that instead of an oriental effort to crush all desire, all that seems distinctively human, there is a wise asceticism, where all the capacities of the soul are directed towards and trained for the purpose of their existence—the glory of God—where alone they can reach their proper development. Different souls require different treatment. The sight and smell of a rose will come to one as a breath of heaven, drawing him straight to worship: another will be unable to get beyond its sensuous beauty, and to him it will be a hindrance. But for all the path demands a stern ascesis. Our desires are too impregnated with self. They must be set free, purified before they can be trusted. "I will run the way of thy commandments", says the Psalmist, "when thou hast set my heart at liberty". "To set the heart at liberty"—that is the object of the ascesis, not to crush it. Perhaps the best way of learning this lies in putting to oneself these two questions about any particular attraction:

(1) Is it hindering my recollection, my communion with God?

(2) Does it help them?

To answer these questions aright needs a constant watchfulness and quick obedience to the promptings of the Holy Spirit. It may be some form of recreation which hitherto we have enjoyed in all innocence. Now it seems to get in the way. We know it is not necessary to our life; and it absorbs too much of our attention and money; it has become a fetter that prevents the quickness of our response to God's call. Sometimes it takes up time which ought to be given to prayer; sometimes it spoils our prayer. It must go. Or it may be certain friendships which similarly get in the way.

[1] *Ascent of Mount Carmel*, I, 13.

Indeed our love of our friends needs purifying probably as much as anything else, before it can be as selfless and as generous as God meant it to be.

However, it is worth noticing that not even St. John of the Cross with his terrific ascesis attempts to forbid all recreation or pleasure to the contemplative. No soul can remain perpetually taut: it needs some *détente* to help it on its road to God. It is a point which von Hügel frequently stressed. The secret lies in learning, as the saints often say, " to find God in all things and all things in God ". But before we can find God in all things we must, as it were, stand away from them, shake ourselves free from our merely natural attraction for them. The measure of mortification needed depends on the strength of the attraction. Beautiful scenery perhaps most easily suggests the glory of God and would seldom prove a hindrance: favourite interests or choice dishes would call for much more radical treatment.

In learning this detachment we must keep our eyes ever on our objective—God Himself and union with His will. We must have our rules of mortification, etc., but we must never allow ourselves to get tied to them, or to value them for their own sake. From time to time they will need readjustment. It may be just as dangerous to be tied to a particular mortification as to be tied to a creature. There is a grand wisdom in the words of the unknown medieval contemplative, " Silence is not God, nor speaking is not God; fasting is not God, nor eating is not God; onliness [solitude] is not God, nor company is not God; nor yet any of all the other such two contraries. He is hid between them, and may not be found by any work of thy soul, but all only by love of thine heart. He may not be known by reason, He may not be gotten by thought, nor concluded by understanding; but He may be loved and chosen with the true lovely will of thine heart."[1]

What is happening is that God is beginning to call the soul into a more intimate communion with Himself. Subconsciously it begins to feel something of His marvellous beauty. The soul is puzzled and does not understand this. Yet it behoves it to persevere in this path of withdrawal and detachment, in order to be ready for His further claims and fuller revelation of Himself. Only later does

[1] *Epistle of Discretion.*

it realize that having Him it has everything. So the saint can truth-
fully say in adoring love, "My God and my all". St. Thomas
Aquinas expressed the same thought in the vision of our Lord once
vouchsafed to him. Our Lord is said to have appeared to him and
offered to him anything that he chose to ask for. St. Thomas
answered, "I want nothing but Thee, my God", because he knew
that in having God he had all things. A similar story is told of one
of the early Franciscans, Fra John of Penna. [1] The same truth came
home to Julian of Norwich in the "showings" granted to her:
"God of Thy goodness give me Thyself: for Thou art enough
to me, and I may nothing ask that is less that may be full worship
to Thee; and if I ask anything that is less, ever me wanteth—but
only in Thee I have all". And she realized thereby that her wanting
God thus, not only satisfied her soul, but even redounded to His
glory. Thus the Saints found "all things in God." But here we go
on too fast, for that belongs to the further, more completely passive
stage of contemplation, where God seems to absorb more and more
the soul's horizon.

Before we leave this subject of detachment one point must be
stressed. The duties of the work God has given us to do must not
be neglected on the score that they distract us from our prayer.
Prayer and service go hand in hand. The faithful fulfilment of our
duties, however engrossing they may be, forms one of the means
which brings us nearer to God. It is the fulfilling of the Father's
will which our Lord ever kept in the forefront as the one aim of
His life on earth. "I came not to do mine own will, but the will
of Him that sent me." "I work to-day and to-morrow, and the
third day I shall be perfected." To forsake known duties to spend
the time in prayer brings the soul no nearer to God. It is to mistake
the whole meaning of life. It may be, indeed, that God is preparing
the soul for another path. There may come the call to the Religious
Life, or to a more strictly enclosed life, where more time may be
given to prayer and silence. Then the duties change.

Meanwhile, we must go on our way of recollection and detachment, remaining watchful, sensitive to the pressure of the Holy
Spirit guiding us, urging us now to give up this thing, now to take
that step forward.

[1] *Fioretti*, Ch. XLV.

CHAPTER XI

CONTEMPLATION

THOSE who reach the Prayer of Simplicity generally remain in that stage for a considerable period. For most it remains their high-water mark of prayer in this world. The few, though not so few as is often thought, pass through to "Contemplation" in its more restricted sense, or "Mystical Theology", to give it a classification used both in the Middle Ages, e.g. by the author of *Mystical Theology* (a work long attributed to St. Bonaventure), and by Nicholas of Cusa[1], and by St. Teresa. St. Teresa also calls it, in its initial stage, the Prayer of Quiet, and by that name this stage is usually known. Perhaps here more than ever is the caution needed against trying to classify prayer too rigidly into clear-cut stages. It is true that the great contemplatives bear overwhelming witness to the very definite difference in experience between the Prayer of Quiet and any lower form of prayer. Yet it is difficult to draw a hard and fast line between the ending of one stage, and the beginning of another, and to use such phrases as "acquired contemplation" and "infused contemplation" may be misleading. St. John of the Cross maintains that in the more arid form of the Prayer of Simplicity the soul is already entering upon the more passive state, for it is the action of God's presence then which causes the dryness.

What is this experience of Passive Contemplation? The difficulties in the way of making it intelligible to all and sundry are insuperable. Only those who have had some taste of it can grasp what the saints try to say about it. No one has felt this difficulty more acutely than St. Paul, nor expressed it more vividly. Again and again his readers are brought up against that sense of mystery too deep to be expressed, yet so rich and glorious that every attempt must be made to do so. In any case only the initiated will understand, though the mystery is meant for all. "Howbeit we speak wisdom among the perfect: yet a wisdom not of this world, nor of

[1] *Vision of God*, p. 1. (J. M. Dent, London, 1928.)

the rulers of this world. . . . The things of God none knoweth, save
the Spirit of God. But we received not the spirit of the world but
the spirit which is of God: that we might know the things that are
freely given us by God. . . . Now the natural man receiveth not the
things of the Spirit of God: for they are foolishness unto him"
(1 Cor. 2. 6–14). It only echoes what Christ Himself said to His
disciples, "Unto you it is given to know the mysteries of the kingdom of heaven, but to them it is not given" (Matt. 13. 11, cf.
11. 25; 19. 11). The apostle is not writing specifically of prayer, but
of the whole Christian dispensation, yet his words apply equally to
it. And he is writing specifically of mystical experience in prayer
when he tells of one who was "caught up into Paradise and heard
unspeakable words which it is not lawful for a man to utter"
(2 Cor. 12. 4). St. Bonaventure similarly says of such prayer that
it is so sublime that "only he who receives it can know it and only
he can receive it who desires it, nor can he desire it unless he be
fired by the Holy Spirit".[1] So St. Bernard cried in the well-known
hymn:

> The love of Jesus! what it is,
> None but His loved ones know.

(or more correctly translated, "Only he who has experienced it
can believe what it means to love Jesus ").

It would occupy too much space to quote at length the attempts
of the great Christian mystics to describe the experience. The reader
must be referred to such works as Poulain's *Graces of Interior Prayer*,
where numerous quotations are given. A few samples only must
suffice here.

St. Augustine says, "Contemplation is a holy inebriation which
withdraws the soul from the liquid flow of temporal things and has
as its principle the intuition of the eternal light of wisdom".[2]
The Carmelite Congress defines contemplation as "the experimental knowledge of divine things (or realities produced by God
supernaturally in the soul), and it is the state of closest approach
and union between God and the soul which can be attained in this
life" (ibid. 48).

[1] *Itinerarium Mentis*, Ch. VII.

[2] Quoted Farges, *Mystical Phenomena*, p. 53. (Burns, Oates & Washbourne,
London, 1926.)

Blessed Giles, loved companion of St. Francis of Assisi, said with true Franciscan fervour, " The state of contemplation is a heavenly flame and a sweet inspiration of the Holy Spirit, a rapture and an exaltation of the mind, intoxicated by the contemplation of that unspeakable savour of divine sweetness, a gentle rest and sweet delight of the soul which remains exalted and rapt, marvelling at the wonders of heaven, and a burning inward sense of that unspeakable heavenly glory ".[1]

Blessed John Ruysbroeck, the Flemish mystic of the fourteenth century, gives the following characteristic description: " the simple staring with open heart into the divine brightness . . . the wayless passing and the glorious wandering in the supernatural Love, wherein neither end nor beginning nor way nor manner can ever be found ".[2]

St. John of the Cross is more restrained and more exact, " Contemplation is nothing else but a sweet, tender and loving infusion of God, which, if we oppose no obstacle, inflames the soul in the spirit of love ".[3]

Père Garrigou-Lagrange crystallizes many accounts when he says, " Infused contemplation, above reasoning and in the darkness of faith, is a simple loving knowledge of God, which cannot be obtained by our own personal activity with the help of grace, but which needs a special, clearly manifest inspiration and illumination of the Holy Spirit ".[4]

None has described it more truly or more beautifully than our own Julian of Norwich, " When our courteous Lord of His grace showeth Himself to our soul, we have that [which] we desire. And then we see not, for the time, what we should more pray, but all our intent with all our might is set wholly to the beholding of Him, and this is a high unperceivable prayer, as to my sight: for all the cause wherefor we pray, it is oned into the sight and beholding of Him to whom we pray; marvellously enjoying with reverent dread, and with so great sweetness and delight in Him that we can

---

[1] *Fioretti*, Ch. XI.
[2] *Sparkling Stone*, trans. E. Underhill.
[3] *Dark Night*. Book ii, Ch. 18, § 5.
[4] *La Perfection Chrétienneé* p., 234.

pray right nought but as He stirreth us, for the time. And well I wot, the more the soul seeth of God, the more it desireth Him by His grace. . . . I saw and felt that His marvellous and plentiful goodness fulfilleth all our powers; and therewith I saw that His continuant working in all manner of things is done so goodly, so wisely, and so mightily, that it overpasseth all our imagining, and all that we can ween and think; and then we can do no more but behold Him, enjoying, with an high, mighty desire to be all oned unto Him—centred to His dwelling—and enjoy in His loving and delight in His goodness ".[1]

From these and similar accounts, both those of the theologians and the more rapturous utterances of the less learned contemplatives, certain facts emerge which seem common to all those to whom the experience has been vouchsafed. We will call it " Contemplation ", without forgetting that the word has been used to include prayer which has none of these peculiar features.

(1) This prayer of contemplation is God-given. By no amount of time spent in prayer or acts of devotion can the individual attain to it in his own power, even granted that grace helps everyone in the simplest forms of prayer. As we said above, it represents the normal development of the prayer-life, which all the faithful may look to reach one day, though not necessarily in this world. It is not a special extraordinary gift, as, for instance, the gift of prophecy, or the gift of healing—gifts given indeed by God, but outside the run of normal Christian life, not of its essence. The characteristic mark of the prayer is the inflowing power of God and the apparent passivity of the soul. The soul receives the sense, or rather the assurance, of God's presence flooding it and holding it in His grip, itself being helpless either to produce that assurance or to prolong it. " Passive prayer is not only the *silence of the soul* in the presence of God: it is really the *response of God* to the soul. True, it is a language without words—God takes possession of the whole being in His embrace. In these blissful moments it is no longer I that am there; it is He. I no longer see myself, I see only Jesus. I am not destroyed, but His life takes hold of me, dominates me, absorbs me."[2] It is possible to reach by one's own efforts such a pitch of concentration that the mind is held in gaze at the thought or

[1] *Revelations*, Ch. XLII.
[2] Lucie Christine, *Journal*, 261.

image presented to it. It no longer reflects on its different aspects nor does it desire to do so: indeed it cannot. It remains in a state of admiration and delight at the heart of the whole. Such a condition may overtake the philosopher after long pondering over some great truth, or the lover of beauty before the masterpiece of some great painter or a country scene. All he can do is to gaze in silence, allowing its beauty as it were to soak through his being, perhaps breaking the silence only with some exclamation of wonder. So a worshipper may come to a similar state in pondering over one of the mysteries of the Faith or the attributes of God. Writers on prayer call this by different names. It does not matter much what label they give to it. What is important is to recognize that this is not contemplation proper or "infused contemplation". Here the man is aware of a Presence, of Something stirring in the very depths of his soul (in the "fine point" of the soul). It is concerned with no particular thought or mystery: it is something strangely vague and insistent—a whisper, a knocking at the door, a tapping at the window, a sweetness welling up in the depths and invading the soul. It invites the soul to listen. Any attempt to think about it or to make vocal acts of prayer may not indeed be impossible, but it would only distract. Yet the man does make acts of prayer, uttered as it were in the depths of the soul, without words. Translated into words they would be something like " O my God ", " my Love ", " my All ", whispered slowly from time to time and never varying. In its lowest forms this prayer suspends the movements of neither the body nor the mind, as the Prayer of Quiet does. It may accompany a state of mental distraction and physical restlessness. All the soul knows is that it must attend in stillness to this pressure or call. To attempt anything else draws it further and further away. Here is the genuine note of contemplation, and it is for all those who have felt even the least stirrings of it that St. John of the Cross writes. But this state may exist with, or supervene upon, that natural concentration, though sometimes so faint as to be almost imperceptible. On the other hand, as everyone who has ever tried knows from painful experience, no amount of natural concentration can produce that strange mysterious something in the soul, the something which the soul knows to be the finger of God. Such contemplation can never be " acquired ".

The medieval mystics mark the stages of prayer far less clearly than such writers as St. John of the Cross and St. Teresa, but all alike are definite and emphatic about this difference between active and passive prayer. Richard of St. Victor (twelfth century) in *Benjamin Major* gives six degrees of "contemplation" using the word in its wider sense, the lowest being meditation on the creation. In any of these, he declares, contemplation proper (*mentis excessus*) may occur, though seldom except in the last two degrees. It is thus clear to him that the experience is one which strikes across all ordinary categories and which it lies in the will of God to bestow, and not in the efforts of the soul to achieve. Moreover, it produces within the soul a certainty that it is God Himself who is present thus, God from without, and not some trick of its own psychological make-up. Whatever fervours of devotion the soul may have enjoyed previously, this, it knows, stands on a different level, and smites it with astonishment and joy.

(2) One reason for the difference in labelling contemplation probably lies in the fact that it is difficult to say at what point in the experience God's special action—the infused contemplation—begins. Every contemplative is aware of the moment when God seems as it were to take charge of the soul, and reduce it to a passive role, at least for the time. And every contemplative is vividly aware of God then, and has no doubt about the prayer being due to God's pressure upon him. But he also realizes that before then God had been making Himself known in a new way and making ordinary prayer difficult, if not impossible, for him. All that previous stage therefore, that loving helpless waiting upon God, belongs to the contemplative state. This accounts for Fr. Baker's practical ignoring of the Prayer of Quiet. His first stage of perfect contemplation, the "Prayer of Aspirations", seems to cover all that period. He calls it "Active Contemplation", because the soul still can do something in the way of uttering these aspirations, yet, at the same time, they are due to its "being inflamed with divine love", so that they flow "freely, and in a sort naturally". Even the Prayer of Quiet falls short of being completely passive prayer. Only at a later stage, the Prayer of Union, is all possibility of action taken from the soul, and it is, as it were, powerless in the grip of God.

Moreover, the method of prayer, if it may be called a method at all, remains much the same after as before the moment when God seemed to intervene so decisively. The difference lies in the experience then gained of God's presence within, holding the soul.

It affects all subsequent prayer. But the prayer consists in essence (to quote Fr. Baker) of, " certain most purely spiritual operations of the will, longing and thirsting after God, and an union with Him in the supreme point of the spirit, where His most proper dwelling is ".[1]

That " longing and thirsting " echoes all through the writings of the contemplatives. It grows greater as the soul progresses. We spoke of it in the earliest stage (p. 169). The psalmists were full of it. " Like as the hart desireth the water-brooks, so longeth my soul after Thee, O God " (Ps. 42). Again, " My soul is athirst for God, yea even for the living God " (Ps. 63). St. Catherine of Siena writes again and again of the " fire of holy desire ". The author of the Cloud of Unknowing writes, " to help thee to knit the ghostly knot of burning love between thee and thy God " (Ch. 47). That burning desire goes on, the will stretching blindly after God, though the mind can no longer think in prayer, and all sensible fervour has long died away. But it clings to our Lord's promise, " Blessed are they that hunger and thirst after righteousness, for they shall be filled ". Julian of Norwich most beautifully puts it, " Thus I saw Him, and sought Him; and I had Him, I wanted Him".[2]

(3) The action seems to take place within the soul itself. In meditation, even in the Prayer of Simplicity, we set ourselves, as it were, in front of our subject, whether it be one of the mysteries or something else. As the prayer grows we may become more and more recollected, more and more full of fervour. The presence of our Lord may become increasingly real to us. Some may even have visions at such a stage. But always He remains, in a sense, without. He is there, in front of us, and we are beside Him. But in the Prayer of Quiet something else has happened. God seems to have come right into the soul and taken possession of it, filled it with His presence.

> Then thro' the mid complaint of my confession,
>   Then thro' the pang and passion of my prayer,
> Leaps with a start the shock of his possession,
>   Thrills me and touches, and the Lord is there.
>   F. W. H. MYERS, St. Paul.

That is what so astonishes and enraptures the soul. The experience

[1] Holy Wisdom, IV, 2.
[2] Revelations, Ch. X.

is so different from anything it had had before. It is not a mere intensification of its former fervour. The illustration has been used (and some have found it to express something of their own experience) of a girl, accustomed to wait at the door for her lover, watch him as he reaches the garden gate and comes up the path, and then spend some time looking at him and conversing with him. But one day he fails to come at the appointed time. Anxiously she looks up and down the road, again and again glances at her watch lest she has mistaken the time, and then begins to grow resigned to disappointment. Suddenly she is aware of someone who has come behind her and put his hands over her eyes. She knows well who it is, and she is content to remain in his grasp. Her lover had come in by another way, from within.

(4) "His hands over her eyes." Yes, because, and this is another unexpected factor in the prayer, there is usually no clear vision. Rather the reverse. It is the sense of being in the grip of Another, comforting, filling the soul with sweetness and joy, but without any clear apprehension of that Other. Only, the soul knows He is God, and is infinitely content therewith. We shall consider later the meaning of the Dark Night. Here it is enough to say that the prayer itself is a part of the Dark Night, dark, because the brightness of God's presence dazzles the soul; dark again, because its old ways of approach are useless here and it has to accustom itself to a new method, a way that is wayless, as Ruysbroeck insists so strongly. Moreover, the mind seems equally dazzled: it will no longer function as before: it remains stupefied.

(5) The prayer at this stage so much absorbs the soul that it finds itself in a state of almost complete passivity of body as well as of soul. A man in such a state not only remains still while it lasts for fear of losing it, but he experiences the utmost difficulty in making any movement at all. He may not be entirely oblivious to what is going on around him, but it fails to distract him. If someone should call him, he might hear it, but only by a violent effort could he bring himself to answer. A great and holy stillness descends upon him and keeps him prisoner. Most people have known a somewhat similar experience during sleep—the sense of incapacity to move. But in this case there is no chance of confusing it with sleep: he never felt so wideawake in his life, so vividly in touch with reality.

The same powerlessness extends also to the tongue. There is neither the desire nor the capacity to utter prayers. To do so would not only be very difficult but it would distract the soul, and break that sense of peace and communion with which it is filled. All it can do is to remain passive, though perhaps at intervals the heart forms some simple aspiration, e.g. " O my God, my God ", which, however, never finds its way to the lips.

That remarkable Frenchwoman, Lucie Christine, tried to describe in her diary her first experience of this kind of prayer. Her account apart from its naïve charm has a special interest as she knew nothing from books of the ways of contemplation, and at first it astonished and startled her. She was at Mass one autumn morning when she suddenly found herself unable to utter a single word in prayer. "Astonished and having no idea of what was happening within, my poor soul tried to struggle a little, but quickly realized that it was the will that bound it thus, and so submitted to its helplessness. Finding its will fixed on God, powerless to make any act, it no longer tried to do so, and remained in that state of profound repose in God, in which the soul no longer seeks because it has found."[1]

(6) Another characteristic of this prayer is its duration. The minutes, even hours, go by unobserved in the deep repose of contemplation. The concentration does not, it is true, remain at the same pitch. It wanes for a moment or two at intervals, it may be, only to be re-kindled and held again in its intensity. Therein this prayer differs both from the Prayer of Simplicity, which demands a greater measure of effort on the soul's part, or from deeper forms of contemplation, which normally maintain their intensity for a much shorter period. St. Teresa, for instance, declares that a rapture does not usually last more than half an hour. Fr. Baker says on the same subject, "The continuance of it is but very short, as St. Bernard (who, no doubt, could speak from his own experience) observes, for it seldom lasteth above a quarter of an hour".[2]

What is more, after the prayer is finished, often its effects still remain, holding the soul in a state of recollection as it goes about its

[1] *Journal*, p. 18. (Paris, 1920.)
[2] *Holy Wisdom*, IV, 4.

ordinary duties, sometimes rendering it forgetful or unable to concentrate on the work in hand, as though still listening to the Lord with whom it had held such deep communion. On returning to prayer the probability is that the same prayer supervenes. This state may continue for some days. Then more normal conditions ensue, and it may be some time before a similar state occurs.

Fr. Baker has little to say about the difficulty of movement or uttering prayers except when "passive unions" occur. Rather the soul may pour forth frequent, fervent aspirations, short and with little variety, but is by no means rendered dumb. He also reminds us of the old hermits who were raised to ecstasy as they recited the psalter—though it is difficult to know what he means when he speaks of "saying the Divine Office or other vocal prayers aspiratively", if an aspiration is a prayer forced out of the soul by spontaneous fervour.

Fr. Baker, however, as we have already noticed, seems to recognize no prayer between what he calls "Active Contemplation", which is a prayer of aspiration, and "Passive Contemplation" or "Passive Unions". By them he means the more complete and extraordinary absorptions which occur in ecstasy and rapture. This is the more remarkable because he refers more than once to St. Teresa and the Prayer of Quiet. The truth is, a very real discrepancy exists between the old medieval writers and the more modern ones on this point. Fr. Baker follows the former in his teaching. They say little or nothing about a continuous state of aridity either before or after the bestowal of true contemplation. According to them affective prayer goes on steadily mounting in intensity until it blossoms out into contemplation, though they are emphatic that the *mentis excessus* can come only through the gift of God.

But St. John of the Cross does not teach this. The approach to contemplation shows itself in an increased aridity and incapacity of praying. His teaching seems to be corroborated by the experience of men and women of our own day—in spite of the old tradition. Their experience can scarcely be due to the influence of St. John, for most Anglicans, at any rate, are unacquainted with his teaching, indeed have scarcely heard of the saint. Is it that modern life is lived at a greater pressure, the strain on the nervous system is greater, and men are more self-conscious than they used to be? Perhaps no good purpose can be served by pursuing the question further. It is enough to mark the difference. At the same time, we should entirely misrepresent the old tradition if we gave the impression that the saints of old never suffered from this darkness of prayer. It finds frequent and poignant expression in the writings of nearly all of them, but it seems to be with them an experience that overtook them from time to time—whatever stage they had reached—until the final one. Walter Hilton indeed has a good deal to say about the Dark Night through which the soul must pass.

That first taste of contemplation proper, which St. Teresa calls the Prayer of Quiet, yields sooner or later to a more normal state. To most there comes a reaction, a time of great aridity and darkness. The prayer-life through most of its course exhibits a certain rhythm, periods of spiritual exaltation and light followed by periods of painful aridity, or darkness, sometimes lasting only a day or two, sometimes for years. In the present stage prayer usually swings back to a state similar to that described as the Prayer of Simplicity. There is the same inability to meditate, the same apparent coldness of heart, side by side with the same desire for God and contentedness to be with Him. Yet there is one great difference. The soul's recent experience of contemplation has somehow altered its relationship with God. Its activity, such as it is, takes place within the soul where God seems to dwell. There is a sense of union which it never had before. From time to time this is forgotten and the soul seeks God without, like the bride in the Canticle going through the city seeking her beloved. But in vain. And from time to time the voice of the Beloved calls her back into her innermost self to find Him "whom her soul desired". This action within the soul differs from the introversion taught, e.g., by the medieval writers. That was a normal stage in their ascent to God, where a man left considering creatures to look within himself, and meditate on what he found there, and on the presence of God there. But only in contemplation comes that sense of union within the soul, which, having once experienced, it can never forget—though it may be lost through sin and carelessness, or be unfelt in the darkness.

It comes as a shock to many to find that for them this "day of the Lord", this coming of God to them, is "darkness and not light". No writer has explained it more fully and helpfully than

N

St. John of the Cross (mainly in the *Ascent of Mount Carmel* and the *Dark Night*, and recapitulated in both the *Spiritual Canticle* and the *Living Flame*), though he makes no claim to be teaching anything new. The root cause of the " Dark Night " lies in the Being of God Himself. The very nature of God, the All-Perfect, the Almighty, the Eternal, renders it impossible that our human faculties should be able to understand Him fully, when he vouchsafes that closer communion and revelation of Himself in contemplation. The soul is dazzled, blinded by excess of light. There is one thing left for it to do, that is, to cling blindly to the Will of God as revealed to it, leaving itself in His hands to be purified and made more fit for His habitation. As the hymn puts it:

> Breathe on me, Breath of God,
> Until my heart is pure,
> Until with Thee I will one will
> To will and to endure.

That "Breath of God" to the contemplative is a searing flame that works in darkness. Perhaps modern writers, like Dom Chapman in his valuable *Spiritual Letters*, insist too much on this darkness and aridity as the normal prayer of the contemplative. It tends to create an atmosphere of acquiescence in such a state, predisposing one to it beforehand, and paralysing any effort to get out of it. The old contemplatives were in a sense much more impatient about it, and on the whole seemed to suffer much less from it. Nor does it seem to play anything like the same part in the experience of the saints of the Eastern Orthodox Church. St. Bonaventure declares roundly that we ought not to cease from prayer until caught up in God " so that wholly taken out of yourself, wholly caught up into heaven, wholly reformed and transformed into Christ, you cannot restrain your spirit ".[1] No doubt that is meant to point the goal to which our prayer must tend. The saint did not mean that such rapture must happen every time we prayed. But it looks hopefully to the mountain tops.

St. Mechthild of Magdeburg says that earnest prayer " draws the great God down into a little heart, lifts the hungry soul up to God ".[2] Nevertheless, meanwhile the soul must do what it can. In any case its role now in prayer is more or less passive.

[1] *De Perfectione Vitae*, Opera, Vol. XII.
[2] *Offenbarungen*, V. 13.

As the process of purification goes on, the nature of the man's prayer changes in some measure. All subsequent developments are only the deepening of the contemplative experience, once the border has been crossed. The Dark Night still runs its course. But there is a change. The cloud is there, but it seems to grow more luminous. The sense of union with God remains more persistent. But the soul no longer experiences the difficulty of movement in prayer, nor does its recollection, now grown even stronger, hinder it as it goes about its ordinary duties of the day. Perhaps its greatest development comes in its increased realization of the fact of God, the Blessed Trinity. During certain periods one of the most painful experiences is the sense of God's absence. For this desolation is a very different experience from aridity. The soul had forsaken for Him all the things it had once set its heart upon, and had found a delight in His presence that compensated for all. Then suddenly there seemed to be no one there. God had become a void. The soul was left high and dry, or hung between heaven and earth, its old loves gone and nothing in their place. Gradually God makes Himself known again. There is no warmth of devotion, only a knowledge of His presence deep within the soul, and with it a wonderful and abiding peace. It is the mere fact of God, thus realized, that makes everything else of little count. To say that it is the realization in some measure of the Divine transcendence, of His sheer objectivity, does not cover the experience, though it is included in it. It is rather the man's growing realization of God's solid abiding reality, and of his own transitoriness and utter dependence. The psalmist expressed it long ago, "They all wax old as doth a garment, and as a vesture shalt thou change them and they shall be changed. But thou art the same and thy years shall not fail" (Ps. 102). Psalm 22 takes up the same theme from another angle. It starts from the awful sense of dereliction, "My God, my God, why hast thou forsaken me and art so far from my health and from the words of my complaint?" Long before had come the experience which paralysed the man and left him in misery and doubt. Now, whether he himself feels the joy of God's presence, or whether further trials and suffering await him, seems a small thing. What matters is that God is, and is Lord of all. "Thou continuest holy, O thou worship of Israel." Whatever happens to himself, God's glory goes forward, and somehow he himself will be caught up in it eventually. He feels he is stepping close here in our Lord's own footsteps. The grain of wheat falls into the ground

and dies, Christ Himself is crucified and endures the hours or
dereliction, but God's glory is manifested, the Father's will is done.
So the Apocalypse brings as its central message the glory of God the
Blessed Trinity, upholding all, ordering all, redeeming mankind
—unshakeable, eternal, though all creation seems to be vanishing
in fire and destruction. Finally, there is the picture of the New
Jerusalem coming down out of heaven from God. There God is
all in all—and His faithful shall worship Him, and God Himself
shall be their God.

It was surely a similar experience that led Julian of Norwich
to repeat the refrain, " All shall be well, and all shall be well, and
all manner of thing shall be well ",[1] or to rejoice in God's blissful
showing, " See! I am God: see! I am in all thing: see! I do all
thing: see! I lift mine hands never from off my works, nor ever
shall, without end: see! I lead all thing to the end I ordained it to
from without beginning, by the same Might, Wisdom and Love
whereby I made it. How should anything be amiss? "[2] So the
glory and greatness of God the Blessed Trinity begins to be manifested, still in the "cloud of unknowing", only very faintly here compared with the fulness of it later. Most mystics have something to
say about this. "The Divinity", writes Fr. Baker, "is the proper
vast element, wherein the soul should find life, and an infinite life.
But when out of this element the soul is like a whale that has been
stranded in the brook: the great creature has not space enough to
swim or plunge in its waters. Hence it ever desires the ocean,
which, for its depth and wideness, is capable of containing it and
millions of others. Here these huge creatures find no bottom, but
can swim in all fulness, . . . for here they are in their element, and,
as it were, in their own kingdom. Thus does the contemplative
soul, in virtue of her propensity, ever aspire to her centre and
proper element, the simple Divinity."[3] St. Catherine of Siena likewise loved to speak of God as the "Sea Pacific": "How glorious
is the soul who has been able to pass from the stormy ocean to
me, the Sea Pacific, and in that sea . . . to fill the pitcher of her
heart."[4] The same truth shows itself even more markedly in the
life of St. Marie de l'Incarnation, "Wherever I was, whatever I was

[1] *Revelations*, Ch. XIII.

[2] Ibid., Ch. XI.

[3] *Inner Life of Dame Gertrude More*, Ch. XX.

[4] *Dialogue*, p. 193.

doing, I could only see myself plunged and swallowed up in this incomprehensible Being, and I could only see others in the same way. Thus I saw God in all things and all things in God. His infinite Majesty was to me like an immense ocean which had overflowed its borders, covered me, flooded me and engulfed me utterly." The result is a tendency to rest in the large spacious attributes of God rather than in details of the gospel story—God regarded as Truth, Life, Love, Goodness, Peace. St. Marie de l'Incarnation includes almost all in her outburst, " O Eternité, O Beauté, Bonté, Pureté, Netteté, Amour! Mon Centre, mon Principe, mon Fin, mon Béatitude, mon Tout ".[1]

Now the man begins to understand a little of what the saints meant when they spoke of seeing all things in God or that God is all. " Said the Lover to his Beloved; ' Thou art all, and through all, and in all, and with all. ' "[2] He has already learnt, St. Bonaventure says, to see God in all things, to recognize His impress, traces or footprints (vestigia) everywhere, so that the sight of them lifts him godward. That experience continues to be purified and deepened. But now creatures have become, as it were, transparent, held in the grasp of God, sustained by His life, filled with His beauty, loved for His sake. Most of all does he find that true as he turns to his fellow-men; for man was made in the image of God, and God dwells in the " ground " of his soul in a way He cannot dwell in other creatures.[3] The paradox, which had often troubled him, begins to find its solution—to love his neighbour as himself and yet to love him wholly for God's sake. After all a man loves his friend for his virtues and not for his vices, though he might say that some small faults gave a certain piquancy to his attractions. But he loves him for his qualities, whether physical beauty, or mental gifts, or spiritual qualities, for all that goes to make him what he is, a personality distinct from all others. Yet all that is God-given, God-sustained—the very beauty of God shining through him—God's love manifesting itself in him. So the saint does most truly love his fellow-man, yet at the same time loves him in God and for God's sake. And it is of vital importance to realize that to " see all things in God " does not mean to have no love for or

[1] Écrits Spirituels, Vol. I, p. 354. (Desclée-de-Brouwer, Paris, 1929.)
[2] R. Lull, The Book of the Lover and the Beloved, see p. 67.
[3] Cf. Ch. IX, p. 159.

interest in any person or thing except God, as though God were merely one amongst many others. A piece of finely-cut glass, caught by the sun, shines with a rare beauty, flashing forth the colours of the rainbow. The glass itself catches our eye and fills us with delight, yet all the time it is the sun which gives it its glory, the real source of our delight, and we see it only in the sun. Without the sun the glass would be nothing, yet without the glass we should not see the sun's many-coloured splendour. We must not press this simile too far, but it may suggest something of what the saints meant by their phrase. Closely connected with this seems to be the experience which some mystics, for example Julian of Norwich, call " seeing God in a point ", as though wherever they look they see only God—His immensity gathered even in the smallest creature as in the splendour of the Blessed Trinity.

They gain by their experience a new outlook on the world. All created things and beings they see linked up in God, and it gives them a wonderful fellow-feeling with them all, yet a feeling curiously different from that of the nature-mystic or pantheist. The pantheist sees himself and all things as parts of the Divine, with all distinctions blurred. The Catholic sees them all as created and held in the transcendent God, the Blessed Trinity, and ordered in one splendid hierarchy of being for the glory of God. It gives him a scale of values which the other sadly lacks. He sees God in all things and all things in God, and yet more clearly than ever recognizes God as the " wholly other ".

CHAPTER XII

EFFECTS OF CONTEMPLATION

By this time the soul has attained to a certain equilibrium which has been called a state of " Habitual Contemplation ". That does not mean there is no more suffering, nor that aridity has yielded to fervour. The Cloud has become a little more luminous, but the soul itself has grown more accustomed to the darkness. For a time after the first experience of contemplation its condition varied. Sometimes its prayer was contemplative: sometimes it could go back to meditation. But now the latter has become permanently impossible in prayer-time. Almost immediately its prayer begins, recollection comes. However arid that prayer may be, usually the sense of God's presence in the depth of the soul remains, or rather the sense of being in God. That communion with God seems to take place above the level of the senses, and is realized as something immeasurably deeper and richer than the earlier rapturous feelings of devotion. [The German mystics mainly think of the depths, and speak of the experience taking place in the " ground of the soul ". Others think of the heights and speak of the *apex mentis* or " fine point of the soul ". But all alike are referring to the same fundamental experience of union. But the " ground of the soul " conveys a different idea from its " fine point ". The Germans emphasized the fact that God was in every soul by His " immensity ", by the very act of creation, as He was in all created things, and the task of the soul was to seek Him there. It was God already in the soul who was to be sought. When St. Francis de Sales spoke of the " fine point " of the soul he was thinking of the intellect raised to its highest pitch on the natural level. It had gone as far as it could reach, and it was there at its highest point that God entered and bestowed the grace of contemplation, because the intellect at its highest was man's divinest gift and most apt for God.] Days of utter aridity and distraction may come from time to time, but they are generally of short duration, and then the deep recollection returns. But always the contemplative is keenly aware that this cannot be achieved by his own efforts: it cannot be

" acquired ": it is the gift of God and depends solely on His good
pleasure. Nor is the soul disturbed because of its aridity as it used
to be. Perhaps one reason why the medieval saints had less to say
about the Dark Night lay in their simpler faith and more objective
outlook. That they could not feel devotion distressed them, but
it did not make them wonder whether God was there at all.
They knew He was playing with them what St. Catherine called
" the game of love "—and they sought Him the more vigorously.
" Sensible " devotion had to go sooner or later, for God is spirit,
and they who worship Him must worship in spirit and in truth.
Indeed they tended to ignore and even crush the body too much.
The Renaissance brought a different attitude towards things
human, and no one born after it could be insensitive to the new
outlook. But even St. Teresa suspected that those who made too
much ado about aridity lacked humility.

What are the effects of contemplative prayer? Is it merely a
strange psychological phenomenon that happens to an individual,
passes, and leaves him unaffected by it? Or does it produce an
exhaustion of nervous energy, which is apt to sap morals, too, as
so often happens to mediums in Spiritualistic circles. If so the
prayer would rightly be suspect, and all the cautions and fears
expressed by both believers and unbelievers be amply justified.
The experience of the saints reveals quite the contrary to be the
case. Indeed it must be so if their claim is true that contemplation
means a closer communion with God Himself in Christ Jesus.
Closer contact with Love itself must mean deeper love; closer
contact with Supreme Bliss must mean greater joy.

The judgement of Henri Bergson on this point is of special
value as coming from one who was a well-known philosopher,
but stood outside the Christian Faith. " We can but wonder ",
he wrote, " that they [the great mystics] could ever have been
classed with the mentally diseased. True, we live in a condition
of unstable equilibrium; normal health of mind, as, indeed, of body,
is not easily defined. Yet there is an exceptional, deep-rooted
mental healthiness, which is readily recognizable. It is expressed in
the bent for action, the faculty of adapting and re-adapting oneself
to circumstances, in firmness combined with suppleness, in the
prophetic discernment of what is possible and what is not, in the
spirit of simplicity which triumphs over complication, in a word,

in supreme good sense. Is not this exactly what we find in the above-named mystics? And might they not provide us with the very definition of intellectual vigour? . . . There exist morbid states which are imitations of healthy states; the latter are none the less healthy and the former morbid. A lunatic may think he is an emperor (e.g. Napoleon) . . . does this reflect upon Napoleon?"[1] The whole passage in Bergson's book is well worth reading.[2] We may then proceed to consider some of the effects of contemplation.

(1) The first result shows itself in increased love of virtue and in power to resist temptation. "The burning of love truly taken into a soul purges all vices; it voids both too mickle and too little, and plants the beauty of all virtues."[3] Not that temptation grows less. In some ways it grows much stronger. St. Gregory the Great once said, "Commonly he who is most carried away in contemplation is most harried by temptation".[4] Yet, for one thing, the desire for God has already done much to wean the soul from worldly pleasures and bodily satisfactions. As we said before, it was thus that contemplative prayer first began to reveal itself. Moreover, the Holy Spirit makes the soul more quick to respond to His promptings. The man knows, too, that the smallest infidelity thickens the cloud between himself and God and he would undergo much suffering rather than that that should happen. A saint has been defined as "one in whom God has His unrestricted way".[5] Contemplation which leaves the soul passive in the hands of God gives Him, as it were, a fuller opportunity for having His unrestricted way. The Holy Spirit is at work moulding it more easily into the likeness of Christ, carrying on the work of "deification".

The first need is humility. It stands at the beginning, middle, and end of the spiritual life. There is not a teacher of the Way who does not insist on it. Our Lord Himself set the example by

[1] Bergson, *Two Sources*, quoted Maritain, *Redeeming the Time*, p. 90. (Geoffrey Bles, London, 1943.)

[2] Paris edit., pp. 242–51; New York edit., pp. 216–23.

[3] R. Rolle, *Fire of Love*, Ch. XXII.

[4] Quoted Butler, *Western Mysticism*, p. 117. (Constable & Co., London, 2nd edit., 1927.)

[5] Steuart, *The Inward Vision*, p. 95. (Longmans, Green & Co., London, 1932.)

word and deed—who "counted it not a prize to be on an equality
with God, but emptied himself, taking the form of a servant"
(Phil. 2. 6 f.), who washed His disciples' feet, and told them that
unless they were converted and became as little children they
could not enter into the Kingdom of Heaven. Of all virtues
humility is perhaps the most difficult to obtain. It requires a
supernatural simplicity. For humility is just the truth about
ourselves, seeing our selves in their proper context, in our relation
to God.

St. Bernard says that humility is the virtue by which a man
getting a true knowledge of himself holds himself cheap in his
own eyes.[1] "Who am I? and what art Thou?" St. Catherine
once cried to God and the answer came, "I am that which is, and
thou art that which is not." The follower of Christ must at the
very beginning of his course seek this humility. But whatever he
does, he does not get very far of himself. He finds an irresistible
tendency to go back on himself—as it were even in his humblest
moods to look back on himself and mark his humility—and lo!
it has gone. The devil once appeared to St. Macarius and taunted
him with the ineffectiveness of his mortifications. "Whatever
thou dost, I do also and more. Thou dost fast now and then,
I never take food. Thou dost often keep vigil, I never sleep."
"But", he added, "in one thing alone thou dost over-master
me—in thy humility alone." St. Macarius in dismay stretched
out his hands in prayer and the devil vanished.[2] The eager striving
after humility must always have its place. But as the soul grows
more passive in the hand of God in contemplation, God Himself
takes up the work and purges it far more thoroughly.

The prayer itself aids this in two ways:

(a) God's pressure on the soul, although it is dark and neither
mind nor senses can grasp it, makes it realize, as we said above,
more clearly than ever the grandeur of God and its own utter
insignificance—that it is indeed of itself just nothing. Where all
seems dark and confused, its own sins stand out as in the light
with a dreadful distinctness; or rather, worse than the actual sins
is the sense of sinfulness—the knowledge that the whole self has
been perverted and spoils even the best it does. That, seen against

[1] *De Gradibus Humilitatis*, Ch. I.

[2] H. Waddell, *The Desert Fathers*, p. 204. (Constable & Co., London, 1936.)

God's infinite love and majesty, can become sheer agony. "Sometime he can find no special sin . . . but yet him think that sin is a lump, he wot never what, none other thing than himself."[1]

(b) The soul's helplessness in prayer is humiliating. It has no inspiring thoughts, no fervent feelings of devotion. It remains stupefied with a strange contentment, but can do little or nothing itself. Sometimes aridity and distraction come, and again it can do little or nothing to banish them: it can only wait on God's good pleasure, conscious that it has done nothing to merit anything. As Père de Caussade wrote, "Nothing is more sublime than contemplation in books; nothing more beautiful, more grand than passive prayer, looked at speculatively, but in practice nothing is more tormenting and humiliating".[2] Further still, God allows various trials to afflict the man at this stage. It may be sickness—in many cases, a sickness that entirely baffles doctors, yet suddenly cured—sometimes a well-known complaint that lingers for years. St. Teresa suffered continually from violent headache. Or old temptations, long ago conquered, return with devastating violence, or others, which hitherto have troubled him little. It is true that the grace of God supports him secretly in the midst of them and saves him from sin or serious sin, but the experience is immeasurably grievous and humbling. Thus are the servants of God tested, tempted apparently beyond endurance, yet always secretly held in God's hand. Tauler quaintly pictures such temptations as hounds of God hunting His servant that he may learn humility and a deeper longing for God. "The evil spirit creeps in everywhere and hunts men with his solicitations, now with pride, now with covetousness, now with lust, now this way, now that—and he attacks them with all kinds of vices and especially with self-pity and overwhelming depression. If you stand fast, they can do you no harm for you must certainly be hunted if things are to go well with you. Then come the world and men with bitter angry words to hunt you and cast you out from among them. Then come your own sins and perverted desires . . . so must a man pass with resignation through true humility and gentleness to a solid patience outwardly and inwardly, and feel pity for the men who persecute him so cruelly."[3]

[1] *Cloud of Unknowing*, Ch. 69.

[2] *On Prayer*, p. 119. (Burns, Oates & Washbourne, London, 1931.)

[3] *Predigten*, II, p. 187. (Frankfurt, 1826.)

"You must certainly be hunted if things are to go well with you." That is the experience of the saints. It echoes St. James, "Count it all joy when ye fall into manifold temptations". They are the way to true self-knowledge, which brings humility, and humility is the way to truth, to Jesus Christ, says St. Bernard. St. Teresa had her own way of putting it: "I am not troubled when I see a soul in very great temptations, because if she have a love and fear of our Lord, she will gain a great deal. But if I see any persons always going on quiet and without any kind of war I am never secure of them, and therefore I do often prove and try them all I can (since the devil does not), that so they may see what they are."[1]

The writings of the mystics make it clear that a temptation common to most of them lay in the tendency to criticize others. Perhaps it attacks contemplatives most fiercely of all. They have been called to a greater degree of renunciation than most others, just because the things they were called to renounce meant so much to them that they hindered the completeness of their devotion to God. At first they find it hard to believe that others may not be called to the same renunciations, may not indeed need them. Their constant temptation is a sharp scourge to them, and they learn their own powerlessness to overcome it. But when their prayer becomes passive, God, who is Love, gradually fills them with His love, and little by little gives them a clearer understanding of His wonderful purposes and of the values of diversity. There was a hermit, an Englishman, Brother William, living in Italy not far from Siena in St. Catherine's day, a holy man indeed and exercising a strong influence, yet apt to be harsh in his judgements. St. Catherine wrote to warn him against this. She tells him that the man who has cast away self-will, "rejoices in everything; he does not make himself a judge of the servants of God, nor of any rational creature; nay, he rejoices in every condition and every type that he sees, saying: 'Thanks be to Thee, Eternal Father, that Thou hast many mansions in Thy house.' And he rejoices more in the different kinds of men that he sees, than he would do in seeing them all walk in the same way, for so he sees the greatness of God's goodness more manifest".[2]

[1] *Way of Perfection*, p. 235.

[2] *Letters*, ed. V. Scudder, p. 63. (J. M. Dent & Co., London, 1906.)

In essence self-will is a want of true love. It is a hydra-headed monster: the Christian needs the whole armour of Christ to deal with it, but the gift of contemplative prayer is his most effective weapon.

(2) Another effect of this prayer consists in an increasing desire for God, and for suffering. "The desire of the open heart and the shining of the Divine rays, cause a perpetual pain."[1] There come together both the manifestation of God's unspeakable loveliness, and the sense of the man's own unworthiness and inability either to obtain the clearer vision or to do anything worthy of God's acceptation—even to feel any devotion. Nor can he see his way clear to further action. Such inspirations as sometimes came to him before seem to have gone. He falters where he firmly trod. The man begins to realize the value of this purging process and to welcome it in spite of the pain. But beyond that there grows in him the desire to be more perfectly assimilated to the life of Christ crucified—somehow to take part in His work of redemption. It becomes intolerable to him that he should be left in comfort where His Beloved was scorned and crucified. Moreover, he comes to grieve more over those who live around him in contempt of Christ's commandments, and that deepens within him the desire to share in Christ's sufferings for them, if it be possible. In other words he is drawn into the work of reparation.

(3) Yet in spite of the suffering there grows within his soul a deep peace, the "peace of God which passes all understanding". "Not as the world giveth." The world can and often does offer man peace of a limited kind, some assurance of immediate relief from pain or poverty, some expectation of a temporary happiness. God's peace rises from something quite different. It is the assurance of being held in the arms of the eternal God, that none can pluck him from those arms, and therefore that "all manner of thing shall be well". So Julian of Norwich received her vision at a time of general distress when war and rebellion and pestilence were rife, and evil apparently triumphant, and herself at death's door. She saw the whole creation as a small round thing like a hazel-nut in the palm of her hand, and learned three things about it. "The first is that God made it, the second is that God loveth it, the third, that God keepeth it." "It needeth us", she adds,

[1] Ruysbroeck, *Adornment of the Spiritual Marriage*, Ch. XXIII.

"to have knowing of the littleness of creatures and to hold as
nought all thing that is made, for to love and have God that is
unmade. For this is the cause why we be not all in ease of heart
and soul: that we seek here rest in those things that are so little,
wherein is no rest, and know not our God that is All-mighty,
All-wise, All-good. For He is the very Rest."[1] Julian harps again
and again on this theme, that God is our peace and gives peace,
although we may be in pain and trouble. There are in man two parts,
one outward and the other inward. "The outward part is our
deadly flesh-hood, which is now in pain and woe, and shall be, in
this life. . . . The inward part is an high, blissful life, which is all
in peace and in love."[2] Again, "Thus saw I that God is our very
peace and He is our sure Keeper when we are ourselves in unpeace,
and He continually worketh to bring us into endless peace." St.
Bernard sums it up more concisely, "*Tranquillus Deus tranquillat
omnia*".

(4) The man at this stage is aware of love taking possession of
his heart. It is the divine love drawing him up into closer union
with God, and flowing back through him to his neighbours. "What
may make me more to love mine even-Christians than to see in
God that He loveth all that shall be saved as it were all one soul.
. . . For He willeth that we be like Him in wholeness of endless
love to ourself and to our even-Christians."[3]

"It seems to me", wrote Lucie Christine, "that when the
breath of God sets on fire a poor wretch, it cannot stop there, but
passes on through that sorry veil to shine on others".[4]

The first beginnings of contemplative prayer had drawn the
man away from others towards solitude. His apparent indifference
towards them sometimes alarmed him, and his own deliberate
efforts after detachment only widened the gap. But now the love
returns, only on a different level. Somehow it has become purified, deeper he knows, yet not so dependent on superficial attractions, the bodily presence or animated conversations. Moreover it

---

[1] *Revelations*, Ch. V.

[2] Ibid., Ch. XIX.

[3] Ibid., Chs. XXXVII, XL.

[4] *Journal*, p. 61. (Paris, 1920.)

reaches wider than before. It has grown to include so many, whom formerly he ignored or despised or with whom he felt he had "nothing in common". That returning purified love is a test of the reality of the soul's union with God who is Love. St. John made that clear: " He that loveth not his brother whom he hath seen cannot love God whom he hath not seen." (1 Jn. 4. 20.) For man was made in the image of God and is the likest to God of all things on earth. St. Teresa was only echoing that when she wrote: "I think the most certain sign that we keep these commandments (to love God and to love neighbour) is that we have a genuine love for others. We cannot know whether we love God, although there may be strong reasons for thinking so, but there can be no doubt about whether we love our neighbour or no."[1]

(5) With the peace there grows an abiding joy. Like the peace it is "not as the world gives", but welling up from the depths of the soul. At first it may show itself with some people in strange ways, forcing them to utter strange cries or perform strange gestures. We read in the *Fioretti* of Brother Masseo who after his prayer for humility was frequently seized in this way—it is called the *Jubilus*—" Often, when he prayed, the *Jubilus* came to him and he . . . remained thus in contemplation with heart and face lit with joy" (Ch. 32). The early Franciscans seemed specially prone to these outbursts, but they had no monopoly of them, and both men and women have experienced them. St. Marie de l'Incarnation says that the effect upon her was to send her skipping like a child down the street, to her own dismay and the astonishment of passers-by. But the joy itself is independent of such phenomena: it is a joy which continues to flourish not only in spite of trials and sufferings, but because of them. Richard Rolle in his *Form of Perfect Living* gives seven tests of charity in the soul. The last three tests are illuminating on this point. The fifth is when the difficult thing to do becomes easy through love. The sixth, steady endurance through all pain and difficulties. The seventh is " delightability in soul" and the spirit of praise in the midst of tribulation (Ch. X). "The Beloved", wrote Ramon Lull, "filled His lover with gifts of love, and grieved not for his tribulations, for they would but make him love the more deeply; and the greater the Lover's tribulations, the greater was his joy and

[1] *Interior Castle*, 5th Mansions, Ch. III.

delight ",[1] and again, "Pensively the Lover trod those paths which lead to the Beloved. Now he stumbled and fell among the thorns; but they were to him as flowers, and as a bed of love."[2] What is of vital importance to realize is that this joy in suffering, even the desire for more suffering, has nothing in common with morbid psychological conditions such as masochism, or with a cynic's despair of life. It comes from the love that craves for a closer likeness to the Beloved, to the crucified Saviour, and from the knowledge gained by experience of the value of such suffering in purifying the soul, and in aiding it to "fill up that which is lacking in the sufferings of Christ". Ramon Lull puts it in his own picturesque way, "The Beloved clothed Himself in the garment of His lover, that he might be His companion in glory for ever. So the Lover desired to wear crimson garments daily, tha his dress might be like that of his Beloved."[3] The great contemplatives speak with one voice on this readiness, even eagerness, for suffering combined with gladness of heart. But they are only underlining from their own experience what St. Peter wrote, "Forasmuch then as Christ suffered in the flesh, arm ye yourselves also with the same mind; for he that hath suffered in the flesh hath ceased from sin", and again, "Inasmuch as ye are partakers of Christ's sufferings rejoice; that at the revelation of his glory ye may rejoice with exceeding joy" (1 Pet. 4. 1, 13).

All this does not mean that the contemplative is henceforth free from sin. It does not even mean that he is better than others. Contemplative prayer is no guarantee of sanctity, though nearly all the saints whose prayer-life has been recorded seem to have been granted the gift in this life. Some martyrs might be quoted as exceptions. But then, as Fr. Stolz pointed out, their death itself was an ecstasy of devotion. For whereas the contemplative forsakes the world's pleasures and his own will to go out to union with God, the soul sometimes being apparently rapt from the body in ecstasy, the martyr steps right out of life itself for the sake of that union with God.[4] The true contemplatives have always been themselves painfully aware of their sinfulness, and of the

---

[1] *The Book of the Lover and the Beloved*, Sec. 30.

[2] Ibid., Sec. 35.

[3] Op. cit., p. 251.

[4] *The Doctrine of Spiritual Perfection*, p. 213. (Herder, St. Louis, Mo., 1938.)

fact that contemplation was no sign of sanctity. "Because of the showing", said Julian of Norwich, "I am not good but if I love God the better: . . . For truly it was not showed me that God loved me better than the least soul that is in grace. . . . For if I look singularly to myself I am right nought."[1]

Nevertheless such prayer both draws the soul away from the enticements of the world, the flesh, and the devil, by giving it some glimpse, however dim, of the infinite beauty of God, and also makes easier the path of detachment and mortification which remains to be trod. The degree in which one can practise mortification depends largely on the measure of one's love for God. Love makes one more selfless and whole-hearted in giving: it removes the tension of conflicting desires. A delicate mother will spend herself endlessly tending her sick child in tasks which would otherwise leave her prostrate. But so long as love is weak one's life-force is too much distracted by other claims, and collapse follows. St. Catherine of Siena once wrote with astonishing psychological insight to one who too easily gave way to weariness. "You are tired just in so far as your will tires you. Cast off your own self-will; put on the sweet will of God and your tiredness will vanish."[2] St. Francis Xavier wrote in the same strain, at a time when he was undergoing incredible hardships and disappointments and was physically ill: "If all this be undertaken for whom it ought to be undertaken, it brings great refreshment and many and great comforts. I believe that for those who delight in the Cross of·Christ our Lord such labours are rest, and the ending of them, or the fleeing from them, death. . . . What a rest to live dying every day by going against our own will, seeking not our own but the things which are Christ's."[3]

Here already we are looking towards that final union of the will with God's will, which gives the soul such liberty, the liberty of the children of God. It seems to bring with it supernatural emancipation from ordinary limitations. Sometimes it showed itself in extraordinary ways, as in the case of St. Catherine, who lived for months on no other solid food but the Blessed Sacrament.

[1] *Revelations*, Ch. IX.

[2] *Lettere*, ed. Misciatello, Vol. II. p. 309.

[3] Letter quoted Stewart, *S. Francis Xavier*, p. 167. (Headley, London, 1917.)

o

Others too have found the secret, as for instance the author of the *Mirror of Simple Souls*: "This [the contemplative] soul is the eagle that flies high, so right high and yet more high than does any other bird, for she is feathered with fine love. And she beholds above others the beauty of the sun, and the beams and the brightness of the sun, and the heat thereof gives her in food the gum of the cedar. And then says this soul to her caitiff wretched nature: 'Dame Nature', says she, 'I take leave of you: Love is me so nigh that holds me free of him against all without dread'. 'Then', says Love, 'she afraies her not for tribulation, nor stints for consolation'."[1]

We have already spoken of the desire for solitude felt by the contemplative. What place ought solitude and silence to have in the life of prayer? It seems to play an enormously important part in God's training of the soul. The Bible often speaks of God's saints being drawn away from their fellow-men at least for a period to be alone with Him. Sometimes that happens at a time of discouragement and apparent failure. So Moses went away into the wilderness after his abortive attempt to stir the Israelites to action. So Elijah was sent by God to the Mount of Horeb after the vivid, violent contest with the priests of Baal on Mount Carmel. To each of these God revealed Himself in the silence, and filled them with new hope and the power to carry out their mission. More frequently the withdrawal formed the preparation for the life's work. So St. John the Baptist was "in the deserts till the day of his shewing unto Israel". Even our Lord Himself was led by the Spirit into the wilderness before the opening of His ministry. Perhaps St. Paul's visit to Arabia after his conversion fulfilled a similar purpose.

The history of the Church records innumerable instances of men and women similarly led into solitude in this way. The call of the hermits differed somewhat, for it involved a life-long seclusion from their fellows. St. Benedict followed what he thought to be the same call as they, but God called him to community life, his own life immensely enriched by the period of solitude. St. Catherine of Siena for about three years lived in her own home in complete retirement. But then the Holy Spirit made it clear to her that that time was past, and at once she abandoned

[1] Div. 4, ch. 1.

it and embarked upon an amazing course of activity and prayer in the service of Christ.

But it is not only the saints who have felt the need for solitude. Many great thinkers and men of action have also realized its value. The human soul seems to require some space around it, as it were, if it is to grow to its full stature. Most men are afraid of being alone for long, afraid to be left face to face with their own soul and its destiny. So they fill the intervals of their lives with endless small talk or trifling occupations. If it is true that the devil finds mischief for idle hands, it also seems true that God will not force Himself on minds too full of other things to heed Him. Solitude rightly used provides that element of spaciousness, and fosters the creative capacities of the soul. The world makes too much noise. It thrusts itself upon us, absorbs our attention with itself and its temporal ends and satisfactions, and leaves no opportunity for our deeper needs to assert themselves. The African explorer, Sir Henry Stanley, gives an interesting account of his first experience of the loneliness of the African forests. An American journalist, swept along by the hustle of his countrymen, he was suddenly sent to Africa to search for Livingstone. He had brought with him a Bible and a bundle of newspapers. Day by day he journeyed alone with no one to speak to except his native carriers. At night he would read. He relates how deeply the contrast struck him between the grandeur of the Bible and the triviality of the papers. That contrast was enhanced by the mysterious solemnity and silence of the vast forests. It awoke something in his soul. " I flung myself ", he says, " on my knees and poured out my soul utterly in secret prayer to Him from whom I had been so long estranged, to Him who had led me here mysteriously into Africa, there to reveal Himself and His will. I became inspired with fresh desire to serve Him to the uttermost."[1]

It is not of course necessary to go to the African forests nor to the Egyptian deserts to give the soul breathing-space. Nor is it necessary to spend long periods alone. Some people have a greater capacity than others for withdrawing within themselves, a capacity often acquired through painful experiences in childhood. The Providence of God makes use of such experiences to prepare souls for His coming and for the work He has in store for them. Readers

[1] *Autobiography*, p. 253. (Sampson, Low & Marston, London, 1909.)

of Mary Webb's novel *Precious Bane* will remember Prue, who because of her hare-lip was oppressed with loneliness. But she found eventually that it had its compensations, for it opened up a new world to her: " If I hadna had a hare-lip to frighten me away into my lonesome soul . . . I should never have known the glory that came from the other side of silence . . . that lovely thing . . . like a seed from the core of love." The friends of God know better than the novelist the glory that lies on the " other side of silence ".

God is always at hand waiting to make Himself known to us, and silence helps to open the door of the soul to Him, or rather to make us aware of His presence within. Lovers of the country are familiar with the experience of finding themselves alone with some magnificent view stretched before them, far from town or village. Their first impression is one of utter silence and peace. Gradually they become aware of other sounds which seem only to enhance the peace, the rustle of leaves, the twittering of birds, or the lowing of an ox in the distance. That is a parable of what takes place when the soul seeks God in solitude. First comes the cessation of familiar sounds, the awareness of the silence. Gradually the spiritual world begins to make itself heard. " Be still, and know that I am God."

The contemplative has learned this value of solitude, and that is why he loves it. It is no mere cessation of noise nor absence of other people: it is full of God. A visitor to a Cistercian monastery said afterwards of the monk who showed him round, " *Silence* was not merely his habit but his atmosphere. . . . Silence was not his prison but his freedom; he escaped out of talk into it whenever his captors let him go."[1] Alice Meynell's poem " The Beloved " breathes a similar thought:

> My Silence, life returns to thee
>   In all the pauses of her breath;
> Hush back to rest the melody
>   That out of thee awakeneth;
> And thou, wake ever, wake for me.
>
> Darkness and solitude shine for me;
>   For life's fair outward part are rife
> The silver noises; let them be.
>   It is the very soul of life
> Listens for thee, listens for thee.

[1] *La Trappe in England*, p 174. (Burns, Oates & Washbourne, London, 1937.)

It is perhaps scarcely necessary to point to the reverse side of the picture. The perils of solitude are too well known. The desire for it comes often from a selfishness or fear which shrinks from the demands made upon a man by those around him. Whether he shuts himself up within himself in the midst of them, or lives apart, he finds no spiritual life in his desert. His personality dwindles and tends to become dehumanized. If he is left alone too long it leads to queerness and sometimes to insanity. Normally it is not good that man should be alone. But when God " lures a soul into the wilderness " to speak to it there, then his little human personality is enriched with the very fulness of God Himself, Three Persons in one God. Probably only within the fold of the Church can a soul live for long in solitude and grow in stature thereby, for there it has hidden links both with God and other souls in the fellowship of the Body of Christ.

What matters then is that the contemplative should recognize this value in silence and solitude, and secure of them as much as his duties will allow him. Brother Lawrence found them in his monastery kitchen, thronged as he was with his cooking. The practice of recollection enables one increasingly to find his secret. The Religious Life, at any rate in contemplative communities, deliberately orders life so that a great measure of silence may be had. Elsewhere the individual has to create his own opportunities. To go into retreat each year, or to spend a few days in a Religious House from time to time, will provide his soul with precious breathing-spaces. But that can be no substitute for the constant treasuring of the opportunities for solitude and interior silence that come to him from day to day.

CHAPTER XIII

SOME COUNSELS

THE contemplative's conduct now will not differ very greatly from the programme sketched out at the end of Chapter X, when he was at the threshold of contemplation. It is true that God's action has become much more pronounced and his own more passive. Still he must do what he can. But, even though he follow more or less the same path as that suggested above, a subtle change comes into it all.

(1) The time for meditation has now passed finally. A disagreement seems at first sight to exist between St. John of the Cross and St. Teresa on this point. St. John says that those in the "night of sense" are "to devote themselves not at all to reasoning and meditation, since it is not the time for this, but to allow the soul to remain in peace and quietness".[1] St. Teresa says, "Unless His Majesty has begun to suspend our faculties, I cannot understand how we are to stop thinking without doing more harm than good. . . . God gave us faculties for our use; each of them will receive its proper reward. Then do not let us try to charm them to sleep, but permit them to do their work until divinely called to something higher."[2] But the disagreement is only verbal. St. John's whole point about the "night of sense" is that God has then begun to suspend the faculties. Moreover we know that he was no enemy to meditation. He taught his novices to meditate, and in the *Ascent of Mount Carmel* he tells us that he is not dealing with beginners, "whom it is necessary to prepare through these apprehensible and discursive apprehensions".[3] It is worth calling attention to this, as some writers have imagined that the saint desired even beginners to abandon meditation. Nothing could be further from the truth, and he repeats more than once the signs by which it may be known that a soul may safely leave

[1] *Dark Night*, I, 10.
[2] *Interior Castle*, 4th Mansions, Ch. III.
[3] III, 2.

meditation. St. Teresa was even more anxious that there should be no premature attempt made at contemplation before one was called to it. Preparation for prayer, formerly so important, now becomes nothing more elaborate than the choosing of a mystery or subject, without any consideration of it. St. Teresa is in keeping with the main trend of the Christian writers when she says we never get beyond the need of our Lord's humanity. We have spoken above (p. 175) of the choosing of a mystery as a focus for prayer. At this stage still less will there be any question of thinking out points for meditation. A mere glance at the mystery is sufficient. The difference now is that, whereas in the previous stage the thought of the mystery coloured one's prayer, now it is the action of the Holy Spirit that colours it. For instance, to pray in front of the crib at Bethlehem without any conscious thought of the mystery, beyond the simple intention to adore God in it, tends to give the prayer a different complexion from prayer made in front of a crucifix. Christ is the Door through which the soul goes in and out to find pasture in the land of God, and the Door may be the infant Christ, or the crucified Christ, or the ascended Christ. Or it may be, not a mystery of our Lord, but some other truth. The *Cloud of Unknowing* says, " I care not though thou haddest nowadays none other meditations of thine own wretchedness nor of the goodness of God (I mean if thou feel thee thus stirred by grace and by counsel), but such as thou mayest have in this word Sin, and in this word God; or in such other, which as thee list. Not breaking nor expounding these words with curiosity of wit, in beholding after the qualities of these words. . . . I trow it should never be so in this case and in this work. But hold them all whole these words."[1] It is on similar grounds that Benedict of Canfield insists on the constant contemplation of the Passion of our Lord. He argues that in the Passion there is both the humanity and divinity of Christ; that there is no question of meditating on it here or of forming images in the mind. Just because our Lord is both man and God the mind passes through the manhood straight to the divinity, retaining both. So there is at once both the mental image and absence of all images, which cannot be understood any more than the Incarnation can be understood. Benedict adds, " So there is placed before the eyes both picture and absence of all pictures, body and yet spirit, man and yet God, in one simple gaze, together at one and

[1] *Cloud of Unknowing*, Ch. 36.

the same moment, not separately as is usually the case."[1] Blessed Angela of Foligno struggles to express her own experience of that in her *Visions*. "I saw Him in a darkness—in darkness, because that is too great a good to be conceived or understood . . . moreover, when I see that good I have no recollection at the time of the humanity of Christ, nor of the God-man, nor of any image; yet I see everything and nothing. When I am separated from that good I do see the God-man, and He draws my soul with great sweetness and says sometimes, 'Thou art I and I am Thou!' and I see His eyes and His face. . . . But what results from that vision is that good which, as I said, I see in the darkness."[2]

Lucie Christine has an interesting entry in her Journal. She relates that she had had a vision of Christ, clothed in a white robe, and with His gaze fixed upon her. That sounds sufficiently pictorial and material. But she goes on to say, "When the soul sees our Lord in this way, it cannot look at Him. What I say will seem very strange, perhaps, but it is true. The soul finds itself in the presence of our Lord Jesus Christ, as our eyes are in face of the sun. It cannot look at our Lord, but He impresses the sight of Himself on it, in so far as He sees fit to do so, and it is in this way that the soul sees. Nevertheless it is as a real person that it sees Him, not as a picture."[3]

The explanation seems to be in the fact that our Blessed Lord is both God and man, yet only one person, divine. The contemplative, with a mystery placed before his mind, goes straight to the Person, to God, passing, as it were, to the heart of the mystery, and there takes refuge. St. Marie de l'Incarnation says of her prayer, "I thought of Jesus, not in His humanity, for our Lord had taken from me that way of prayer, but in His divinity."[4] The cult of the Sacred Heart has probably owed much of its favour with contemplatives to the fact that it concentrates in one brilliant focus all the aspects of Christ's revelation. Cardinal de Bérulle approached the problem from a slightly different angle, which throws some further light on it. He taught that, because

[1] *Regula Perfectionis*, III, 10.

[2] *Visiones*, ed. Lammertz, Ch. XXIV.

[3] *Journal*, p. 128. (Paris, 1920.)

[4] *Écrits*, I, p. 160.

our Lord was God as well as man, therefore there was a certain eternal character about each aspect of His life on earth. Though the mystery belongs to the past, yet its virtue abides and is always present and works in souls.[1] Each mystery therefore forms what the cardinal called one of the " States of Jesus ". Christian people therefore could live with Jesus in these "states", and some indeed were called to special devotion to one or other of them. So the contemplative choosing the mystery of Bethlehem would be in communion with the infant Jesus. He would not, could not, "meditate" on any details of the mystery, but the Holy Child would Himself give a special character to his prayer. So with Jesus he could enter into the " state " of Jesus in the desert, or Jesus crucified, or Jesus risen and glorified.

At any rate the great majority of Christian mystical writers have insisted both on the value of attending to these mysteries, and yet on the need of not feeding the mind on " images ", but fixing it only on God. St. Mechthild of Magdeburg in one of her finest poems describes a dialogue with the five senses. Her soul is thirsty for God. The senses tell her that is too dangerous: they offer her something more on her own level—the martyrs, the saints, the angels, and last, the Blessed Virgin with the infant Jesus in her arms. She answers that she is a full-grown bride and that she must have God Himself, for she is created for nothing less.

> Der Fisch mag in dem Wasser nicht ertrinken,
> Der Vogel in den Lüften nicht versinken.
> Gott hat es aller Creatur gegeben
> In ihrer eigenen Natur zu leben,
> Wie möcht ich denn der meinen widersteh'n.
> Vor allem muss ich ja zu Gott eingeh'n,
> Der von Natur mein Vater ist,
> Mein Bruder auch, durch Jesus Christ
> Mein Bräutigam durch Minne, und ich sein.

> (*Offenbarungen*, I, 44.)

(The fish cannot drown in the water: the bird cannot fall from the sky. God has made every creature to live in its own element. How, therefore, can I live out of mine? So must I go into God; for He is my Father by nature, my Brother through Jesus Christ, my Bridegroom through Love. And I am His.)

[1] See Taveau, *Cardinal de Bérulle*, p. 149. (Desclée de Brouwer, Paris, 1933.)

Yet it is abundantly clear from her book that both in her visions and her prayers the Incarnate Lord took a predominant place, and the saints are in His company.

But unless one grasps that elementary fact of Christian theology —of the two natures and one Person of the Incarnate Christ—one cannot begin to understand what such contemplatives as St. Mechthild and Benedict of Canfield are trying to explain.[1]

(2) There is one thing which the contemplative must practise— introversion. Indeed it is almost the only immediate preparation which he can make for his prayer. The old writers never weary of insisting upon its importance. But we must be clear what they mean. In these days psychology has laid great stress on the process of self-analysis, the looking inwards on the soul. It has given the name of "introvert" to the man who tends to turn in on himself rather than out on to the world around him. He is inclined to be introspective, absent-minded, selfish, fearful of what others think of him. His introversion has something unhealthy about it: it becomes, if unchecked, a morbid condition. Even apart from that, we have learned to be suspicious of self-introspection and the type of piety which promotes it. And it is undeniable that many devotional writings and some popular hymns are of this character. So when we find writers telling us to turn away from all that is without and seek God in the depths of the soul, we are suspicious. It sounds like only another form of morbid self-centredness. But it is nothing of the kind. Contemplative prayer begins, as we have seen, with that strange sense of the pressure of God upon the soul, dark and impenetrable, and the soul gropes blindly after it. Or rather it waits helplessly for further light. Introversion, therefore, for the contemplative means surrendering to that pressure. It means abandoning the attempt to understand or to feel devotion, or even to use the imagination. Hitherto he has been busy with his reason and senses, watching for God, trying to find Him in His creation, in His revealed word—always looking outwards, moving out to find Him and know Him—thinking, feeling, seeing, hearing. Now he gives up the attempt, for he has learnt that all that for the time only hinders. God is calling him another way— the way that is wayless. So he turns to God within the depths of the soul—for God, he knows, as the German mystics used to say,

[1] Cf. Walter Hilton, *Scale of Perfection*, ed. E. Underhill, II, 30 f.

is the " ground of the soul ", which He created in His own image
and never forsakes. This is his introversion, but it is a turning
inwards to God, not to himself. And in that utter stillness, when
all the capacities of the soul are gathered together for the encounter, God makes Himself known. Never is there less self-
introspection. The deeper this " looking inwards " goes, the more
oblivious of self does the man become. God's presence and God's
greatness and love dominate his whole consciousness. This is the
essence of contemplative prayer.

Incidentally, such introversion (which is not easily achieved),
brings restfulness to the soul, and often to the body too. At any
rate in the earlier stages, and even long after, the beginner at times
finds himself straining fiercely in his prayer trying to reach out to
God, to hold Him as it were in His grasp, to get some clearer
concept of Him, at least to feel a greater devotion. All in vain,
and he sinks back wearied in mind and body. Afterwards, when
this introversion has been learned, all that is abandoned. All his
being is stilled: there is nothing without to distract his senses, for
they are turned inwards to adore God, so darkly dwelling there.
A great restfulness follows whilst Life Himself holds him, and he
finds the truth of Christ's own words, " Come unto me all ye that
labour and are heavy-laden, and I will give you rest " [or refresh
you]. (Matt. 11. 28.)

There is a method of relaxation of the body taught nowadays
in the interests of physical culture. The instructor tells his pupil
to lie flat on his back and relax all his muscles one by one. Then
he tests the limbs to make sure that this has been done. Where
he finds them still tense he bids the pupil " let go ". If he is also a
psychologist he uses this moment of relaxation to suggest quietly
but insistently to him the lessons he wishes him to learn. Such
suggestion is most effective, because in that state the natural
inhibitions and doubts are for the moment most in abeyance.
Now the contemplative in his introversion performs a somewhat similar relaxation of the soul. Hitherto he has been clinging,
like a limpet to the rocks, to the world of phenomena and the
world of ideas with all his senses and his powers of reason and
imagination. His soul has been looking out as it were through
those windows to find God, or clinging to those outward things
because they seem the only world he knows. Now all its powers

are withdrawn from them, gathered together, and relaxed in obedience to that pressure in its depths. The limpet drops into the mysterious sea of the divine love.

But it is of the utmost importance to realize that this is no abdication of the soul to a state of vacancy, throwing itself open to anything that may seize upon it. It is always yielding to a something, or rather Someone, who impinges upon it and draws it to Himself. Moreover that Someone is no stranger, not like the unknown control of the medium, but its Creator Himself, the source and maintenance of all its being. When God's action is strong and holds it in recollection there is nothing for it to do but wait on Him. Short phrases or single words, "aspirations", will break forth from time to time spontaneously, as when St. Francis of Assisi spent the night in prayer saying only "O my God, O my God" the whole night long. Sometimes the mind wanders off seeking something to exercise itself upon, but this is where the warning of the mystics against the use of images is to be heeded. It is enough to give it some short word or phrase to occupy it, without paying attention to its meaning, so as not to divert the soul from that communion with God. So in conversation with a friend one might dangle a string for a kitten to play with, without being in the least distracted from the friend. That is the advice given by St. Teresa.

For the normal prayer of the contemplative does not consist in one unbroken state of absorption, or even of deep recollection. There is a rhythm—periods of such recollection followed by periods when it wanes. The mind tends to wander away and the senses to reassert themselves. Quite insignificant matters attract his attention, or he becomes acutely aware of his body and its posture, or wonders how much longer he has for his prayer. His prayer then becomes mainly an act of the will, holding the soul in the presence of God, rejecting such distractions, and content to be still both in body and in mind. To occupy the mind it will be sufficient to use some short phrase or word, whether uttered or not, such as "Jesus, Jesus" or "O my God, O my God"—"If they be in words, as they be but seldom, then be they but in full few words: yea and in even the fewer the better. Yea, and if it be but a little word of one syllable, methink it better than of two."[1]

[1] *Cloud of Unknowing*, Ch. 37.

The author of the *Cloud* quaintly illustrates this from an out-
break of fire. In such an emergency a man cries out just the
one word, "Fire", and that is heard much more effectively than
anything else. So one little word "rather pierceth the ears of
Almighty God than doth any long psalter unmindfully mumbled
in the teeth"

There must, however, be no attempt to return to meditation,
either by trying to picture scenes, or to follow ideas. The reason
for this is not because the contemplative now considers himself
too far advanced to descend to such things, but simply because
they only distract him still more. For he is ever aware of that
Someone in the depths of his being, for whom his soul longs,
and such considerations draw him away, "since it so is that a
ghostly worker should evermore be in the highest and the sovereign-
est point of the spirit".[1]

Even when most recollected and wrapped in prayer he is not
in a state of complete passivity. Still his will presses itself blindly
and helplessly in a series of acts, so imperceptible as scarcely to be
called acts, towards God, who holds him and fills his being. The
great Christian teachers are emphatic on this point. It sharply
divides them from the Quietists and all those whose aim is to
produce a state of complete passivity through some process of
self-hypnotism, where the mind is made a blank. No one has
expressed this more forcibly than John Ruysbroeck. Such passivity,
he declares, is only a "natural rest". "When a man is bare and
imageless in his senses and empty and idle in his higher powers,
he enters into rest through mere nature. . . . It is a sitting still,
without either outward or inward acts, in vacancy, in order that
rest may be found and may remain untroubled. But in this the
loving man cannot find his rest, for charity and the inward touch
of God's grace will not be still. . . . This rest is wholly contrary
to the supernatural rest, which one possesses in God. . . ." The
"rest in God, which is actively sought with inward longing, and
is found in fruitive inclination and is eternally possessed in the
self-mergence of love, and which, when possessed, is sought none
the less, is exalted above the rest of mere nature as greatly as God
is exalted above all creatures."[2] The same writer also expresses

[1] *Cloud of Unknowing*, Ch. 37.
[2] *Adornment of the Spiritual Marriage*, p. 155. (J. M. Dent, London, 1916.)

finely the longing of the soul to know more clearly this hidden
God, who holds it so close, and whom it cannot see; to love Him
more fervently, and the heart cannot burn; to give itself more
wholly, and the will remains inert. It has to be content to stay
passive and listen to the Divine voice bidding it, " Be still and
know that I am God ". The difficulty is to make that complete
self-abdication which enables God to possess it wholly. " We feed
upon His Immensity, which we cannot devour, and we yearn
after His Infinity, which we cannot attain: and so we cannot
enter into God, nor can God enter into us, for in the untamed
fury of love we are not able to renounce ourselves. . . . In this
storm of love our activity is above reason and wayless."[1]

It is worth calling attention to this because critics often attack
Christian contemplation on the ground that it is a form of self-
hypnotism, and the beginner entering upon this kind of prayer
in these psychological days fears this very thing. But he may
comfort himself with the knowledge that the great masters were
fully aware of this, and were very clear that true contemplation
is a vastly different matter.

In the later stages of contemplation the method of dealing
with distractions grows simpler still. Benedict of Canfield gives
two ways of doing this—by passive and by active annihilation of
the will. He teaches that the contemplative's life consists in faithful adherence to the Will of God. It has nothing to do with
feelings of devotion or psychological states. It is a matter of
obedience to God who is revealing His will to him at every
moment. What he has to do is to still all movements of his own
soul that conflict with that. When he is alone, quiet and recollected in prayer, God's will holds him and directs him. Any
momentary distraction is stilled in that presence. This is called
" passive annihilation ". But there are other occasions when he
is engaged upon his duties, it may be in dealings with others.
Even here the true contemplative must not lose his recollection.
Ideas and distractions are continually coming to him from without.
Yet he should not try forcibly to deal with them himself. He is
still united in his inmost soul with the divine will. What he should
do, therefore, is by a simple act of advertence (*recordatio*), so simple
as scarcely to be an act, to allow that divine will to act through him.

[1] *Sparkling Stone*, p. 210. (J. M. Dent, London, 1916.)

Benedict terms this " the active annihilation ", and it is significant that he ranks it higher than the passive. (Incidentally, Benedict was very anxious that the third part of his book, in which this occurs, should not be read by beginners, but only by those in a state to profit from it. It was not printed until fifteen years after he had written it, and only then at the order of his superiors.)

Furthermore, the contemplative, just because he is seeking God and His will, not some " state " of his own soul, preserves his liberty, the liberty of the child of God in his Father's presence. There are times when his recollection is less intense and he may be moved to utter vocal prayers. They come from the inward inspiration and belong rather to what Fr. Baker calls aspirations, but they may be none the less vocal. Few of the saints were more subject to, or more the victim of, ecstatic experiences than St. Catherine of Siena, yet she frequently, both in and out of ecstasy, uttered long and even voluble prayers. So it was with many others. Fr. Baker writing of those who have attained to " habitual contemplation " says, " Vocal prayer and other corporal exercises used during actual contemplation often help to elevate the soul higher in contemplation than would be possible without them."[1]

At other times aridity prevails—a similar state to the previous one before contemplation definitely supervened. But even if meditation is no longer possible the man can pray. This is not the time to remain empty and dumb waiting for God to act. Here the saints differ sharply from the Quietists in their teaching. The latter bid their disciples remain entirely passive, making no sort of effort themselves. But the saints insist that the soul must do what it can, while it can. For, while the Quietist is mainly bent on producing a certain psychological state, the saints are concerned only with communion with God. Julian of Norwich, after speaking of contemplation, says, " Well I wot, the more the soul seeth of God, the more it desireth Him by His grace ". " But ", she continues, " when we see Him not so, then feel we need and cause to pray, because of failing for enabling of ourself, to Jesus. For when the soul is tempested, troubled, and left to itself by unrest, then it is time to pray, for to make itself pliable and

[1] *Inner Life of Dame Gertrude More*, p. 169. (R. & T. Washbourne, London, 1910.)

obedient to God."[1] However, even so, the prayer will usually only consist of short sentences and phrases, the same repeated over and over again. And it is good to be reminded that here there are no fixed rules. The contemplative is free in his Father's house, and the Holy Spirit will guide him as to the best way to spend his prayer-time. To force himself to follow some suggested form might be as harmful as the forced inactivity of the Quietist. The abbot Isaac told Cassian that the way to perfect contemplation was by the constant repetition of the prayer, " O God, make speed to save me ". That indeed is the kind of act wholly congruous with the contemplative's prayer, but one is not bound to any particular words.

(3) As his prayer grows he will find the note of adoration taking an ever larger place in it. That must be so if contemplation be what the saints claim that it is—a real experimental knowledge of God Himself. The realization, however dimly, of His grandeur, beauty, love, and power must issue in increasing praise, and what is the corollary of that, the desire for utter self-giving. A young Carmelite nun, Sister Elizabeth of the Trinity, was given a precocious understanding of this—and she endeavoured to make her whole life an act of praise. Taking St. Paul's phrase " the praise of glory " (Eph. 1. 12), she defined it thus: (1) " A soul that dwells in God with the pure disinterested love which does not seek self in the sweetness of His love; a soul that loves Him above all His gifts." (2) " A silent soul, a lyre beneath the touch of the Holy Spirit. . . . Because suffering is a chord which emits more exquisite tones, this soul rejoices at giving it forth." (3) " A soul that contemplates God in faith and in simplicity; it reflects His whole being." (4) " One who is always giving thanks." " She sings and adores perpetually and has, so to speak, gone out from self and become absorbed in praise and love in her passion for the glory of God."[2] That note of praise echoes through the lives of all the saints, growing as their own knowledge of God grew, and it finds abundant expression in the writings of the Christian contemplatives, whether from the poems of an ecstatic Franciscan like Jacopone da Todi, or from the soberer works of a St. Thomas Aquinas.

---

[1] *Revelations*, Ch. XLIII.

[2] *The Praise of Glory*, p. 302. (Burns, Oates & Washbourne, London: 5th English ed.)

(4) With that development there comes an increasing devotion to the Blessed Trinity (see Ch. XI, p. 195). The attributes of God, the Heavenly worship, the relations of the Three Persons in one God, these become almost the sole objects of contemplation, and the contemplative finds it difficult to turn his attention to any other. If he begins with one of the mysteries of our Lord's life on earth, he turns inevitably back to the Trinity. But here again nothing must be forced. The Holy Spirit is all this time gently leading the contemplative. To tell him to leave other subjects to concentrate on the Blessed Trinity might be injurious, if the time for it had not come. But it is a real encouragement to him to know that when he finds this happening, he can thankfully accept it and not try to force himself to pray otherwise.

(5) One common and distressful feature of this stage lies in the inability to join in the liturgical services of the Church with either fervour or understanding. For the " cloud of unknowing " enshrouds the man's corporate as well as his private prayer. This is especially grievous to him before the Blessed Sacrament. He strains to recapture the old fervour, or at least to say the psalms and responses with understanding. What is more, the very effort to do so seems to open the way to a thousand distractions. What can he do? The best course is to recognize this night of the senses, to stay quietly recollected in the presence of God, uniting himself with the intention of Holy Church, and be content to be borne upwards on the wings of the saints and angels and his fellow-worshippers. So long as the will stretches thus towards God, it is a true act of worship, acceptable unto God. Natural mysticism tends to ignore every kind of corporate worship in favour of solitary prayer—the alone with the Alone. It is significant that the great Catholic mystics have always recognized the value of the former, especially of the Holy Eucharist, and insisted on its taking precedence of all other forms of devotion. It is at once the covenanted way of approach, and also a special opportunity of realizing their oneness with their " even-Christians ". Frequency of attendance was another matter and depended on various things. But even most of the hermits of the desert met for the week-end services, and often took the Blessed Sacrament back with them to their cells.

All that bears witness to the objectivity of their faith, and

P

their devotion to the Church. It was God Himself they sought, not a psychological state, and it was His will, they knew, that they should worship Him thus. They were, they felt sure, themselves most unworthy members of His Church, but members they were, and therefore glad to join with their fellow-worshippers in the great act of worship. God was there, and Jesus Christ Himself, through His Body the Church, truly represented His perfect sacrifice to the Father. That was what mattered, not their own feelings, and they were content to be somehow caught up in that, eagerly taking their part in the offering.

(6) The contemplative is reduced at this stage to a strange helplessness in his prayer, as we have seen. He cannot think, he cannot feel, and it grieves him to find himself in so cold and passive a role. But there is one thing that he can do: he can throw himself eagerly into his daily duties with adoring love, seeing God in all things and doing all for His glory. " Love cannot be lazy " is a motto which is repeated and handed on by one saint after another all through the ages from the days of St. Augustine. The outside world thinks of the enclosed Religious as occupied almost the whole day in continuous prayer. But such is far from being the case. The day's programme in all well-regulated communities is nicely balanced, that the whole personality may find adequate means of expression and development. There is the work of the soul, worship (*opus Dei*), the work of the mind, study (*opus claustri*) and the work of the hands (*opus manuum*). No Religious needed to go outside the cloister in order to serve his neighbour. The community itself provided plenty of opportunity for that. Those contemplatives who were not called to the Religious Life found that service in other spheres. What astonishes us nowadays in the lives of these is not the length of time they spent in prayer, great as that was, nor the abundance of their visions or ecstasies, absorbing as they sometimes were, but their devotion to the service of others and its effectiveness. Their fame rests mainly on the impact they made on public life. It is enough to call to mind some of the most familiar names amongst the saints. We may take them at random—St. Gregory the Great, St. Columba, St. Francis of Assisi, St. Louis of France. There is our own St. Dunstan, famous for his legendary fight with the devil, but still more famous for the part that he played in guiding

the destinies of the infant nation. And St. Bernard of Clairvaux, by temperament and calling a scholar and mystic, yet ever pushed forward by his own missionary zeal and the Pope's demands to traverse Europe in the cause of the Church.

These, of course, were all men with great gifts and greatly inspired. But a similar spirit animates countless lesser men and women, who as contemplatives find themselves increasingly urged to the service of their brethren. St. Basil, at a time when the solitary life was still regarded as the most perfect form of Religious Life, deliberately preferred community life on the ground that it provided better opportunity of such service. The Carthusian Order combines so far as possible the solitary with the common life—a strictly contemplative order. Yet in its earliest days the Prior Guigo impressed upon its members the importance of writing books, because it was the only way they had, outside their prayer, for ministering to the world at large.

But, whatever intellectual work may be done by the contemplative, he finds a special value in manual work. And that for three reasons (though he might not be aware of them himself). First, it has a curiously humbling, sobering effect to come from the quick flights of mind and soul to deal with heavy inert matter, or even with animals with their limited reasoning powers. The artist sees in a flash the beauty of the scene or person he wishes to paint. Each delicate shade of colour stands out clear in detail and in harmony with the rest. But when he comes to translate the vision on to canvas a thousand difficulties present themselves. The colours will not mix as they should; the lines lack the sweep and boldness of the vision. The picture is never quite as good as he hoped. " *Als ich kann* ", wrote Jan van Eyck on his great masterpiece as though he would say: " This is not what I hoped to do, but it is the best I can manage." Another man may study the theory of gardening, learn all about the properties of plant and soil, but he finds himself in almost a new world when he comes to deal with the plants themselves and watch their slow growth and be faced with difficulties which had never entered his calculations. Yet all that is dealing with God's creation. It brings him near to God and he learns more of God's inscrutable wisdom. To use a favourite phrase of von Hügel, it reminds him of his own " creatureliness ". Secondly, manual work, as von Hügel also points out, gives him a change of occupation, a necessary relaxing of the bow, which might snap if kept always taut. It is part of our " creatureliness " that we are body as well as spirit, and there is a certain rhythm to be observed between the two. Any attempt to crush or ignore the one unduly leads to the impoverishment of the whole personality. Thirdly, most important of all, it provides a simple and obvious way for the contemplative to express at once both his love of God and his love of his neighbour. This applies to all kinds of service, not only manual work, though the latter is often the simplest and most acceptable form of service.

Especially does he feel this in times when his prayer seems most useless and unworthy to offer to God. It brings a curious relief to the soul troubled by its own helplessness in prayer. The realization of being the unprofitable servant, useless to his Master or his neighbour, grieves him sorely. So he looks about for some way of making good. St. Marie de l'Incarnation at one period of her life took charge of her brother-in-law's business. It involved a crowded day in the midst of porters and lorry-drivers besides being responsible for the care of fifty or sixty cart-horses—duties which she carried out with joy and amazing efficiency. Yet she still found time to nurse a number of sick servants, performing for them the most menial offices. Indeed she delighted in this and would not allow others to take her place. An incident in the life of Blessed Angela of Foligno illustrates how closely linked together were the devotion to Christ and this desire for service. One Holy Thursday she said to her companion, " Let us seek Christ. Let us go to the hospital and perhaps we shall find Him amongst those poor and afflicted." They had no money, so they sold some cloth to buy food and drink which they carried to the hospital. And there they most lovingly ministered to those hapless folk, filled with a great delight, for there truly they found Him whom their souls desired. St. Teresa tells us how, urged by this desire for service, she used to fold up the mantles of her nuns—a small act, hardly worth doing or mentioning, yet something to satisfy that desire to serve, which reached out beyond the fulfilment of her ordinary duties. Love seeks such symbols to express itself. God, who is Love ever urges us on thus to express our love, feeble though it be, and at the same time delights to accept such symbols as offered to Him through our fellows. For " whosoever shall give to drink unto one of these little ones a cup of cold water only, in the name of a disciple, verily I say unto you, he shall in no wise lose his reward ". (Matt. 10. 42.)

That desire for service only increases as the contemplative's prayer deepens. The mystics talk a good deal about cessation from all work, and rest in God. Such talk is misleading, for they are referring mainly to activity in prayer, or restlessness of mind at other times. They are conscious that their minds, being with God, maintain them in His peace, and that they are given a share in God who is *semper quietus* yet at the same time *semper agens*. Their words and deeds as well as their prayer partake of something of the divine simplicity. At the same time they recognize that their own vocation to prayer does call them to a degree of silence and separation from the world, and that they are not to go beyond their limits and meddle with matters that do not concern them. The devil, always on the watch to turn even the holiest inspirations to evil, constantly seeks to play upon the desire for service, and to induce them to embark on a sea of restless activities. No; their work is primarily prayer, and it is there that they render the best service of all. Yet the perfect life of union does comprise both prayer and action. John Ruysbroeck calls it the " universal life ". According to him the final stage of the contemplative's development is not to a state of entire passivity. There is a double action of God upon his soul. By His " inward-drawing touch " God draws him into the stillness of pure contemplation: by His " out-pouring touch " He sends him forth in service. Thus " he possesses a universal life, for he is ready alike for contemplation and for action, and is perfect in both of them ".[1]

This then is the goal which a man must keep before him as he is led deeper into contemplation. It demands an utter selflessness, the self at one moment surrendered in prayer and worship, at another poured out in service. It is to enjoy the liberty of the sons of God, " whose service is perfect freedom ". Or, as St. John of the Cross puts it, " He who truly loves is satisfied then when his whole self, all he is, all he can be, all he has, and all he can acquire, is spent in the service of his love, and the greater the service the greater is his pleasure in giving it ".[2]

[1] *Sparkling Stone*, Ch. XIV.
[2] *Living Flame*, Stanza III.

Moreover, this strong inner impulse to service offers an interesting testimony to the contemplative's claim to union with God. For the natural tendency of his type of prayer is towards solitude and inaction. Witness the story of the nature-mystics or oriental pantheists. He knows full well both the force of that tendency and the need of that solitude and quiet. Yet at the same time he is rapt in union with God in Jesus Christ, who Himself " went about doing good ", and said, " My Father worketh even until now, and I work ". This is to share in that Love, who created the world and never withdraws His sustaining hand from His work.

CHAPTER XIV

THE WILL OF GOD

ONE great purpose of the purification of the soul is to purge it of every trace of self-centredness and self-will, and to bring it to a state of simplicity. "Whosoever", said our Lord, "shall not receive the kingdom of God as a little child, he shall in no wise enter therein" (Mk. 10. 15). His words emphasize both the givenness of the Kingdom and the simplicity needed for its reception. The contemplative learns in the process of purification both his own incapacity to win the grace of union for himself, and also the need of purity of heart. "Blessed are the pure in heart, for they shall see God." In the earlier stages of his prayer his tendency was to concentrate on its effects on himself—the thoughts that came into his mind, and the feelings which came to his senses. All that disappears in the Dark Night. A grand objectivity takes the place of it. God stands forth as the one Reality.

Out of that objectivity there grows the realization of the Divine Will—God's purpose both for himself and for the world. The Divine Will means something much more than God's wishes for the individual, more even than His plan for the world. It means rather, if one may put it so, the driving force of His very Being. The one thing that matters is that that should go forward, and the man must learn to give himself to it in utter simplicity. Once again it is to walk in the steps of the Lord Jesus, to be moulded into His likeness. The Fourth Gospel gives the clearest picture of His devotion to the Father's will. That is the ruling motive of His ministry, not, as so many have represented, the service of man. "I am come down from heaven, not to do mine own will, but the will of Him that sent me." (Jn. 6. 38.) But it underlies the synoptists' accounts as well. "Not every one that saith unto me, Lord, Lord, shall enter into the kingdom of heaven; but he that doeth the will of my Father which is in heaven." (Matt. 7. 21.) Christ taught His followers to pray as the very heart of their prayer: "Thy will be done in earth as it is in heaven." Even in the agony of Gethsemane the accomplishment of that will

remains still the dominant, almost the passionate, desire of His
heart, whatever the cost to Himself.

He speaks of that Will as though it moved to its end by a kind of
divine inevitability. The word "must" is frequently on His lips,
even while at the same time He expresses His own freedom and
eagerness to fulfil the Father's will. It runs all through the gospel
from His first recorded saying, "Wist ye not that I *must* be in
my Father's house?" (Luke 2. 49), to, "I *must* go on my way
to-day and to-morrow" (Luke 13. 33) and, "The Son of Man
must suffer many things" (Luke 9. 22), right on to the end, "All
things *must* needs be fulfilled, which are written in the law of
Moses and the prophets concerning me" (Luke 24. 44).

Or again, equally impressive is our Lord's use of the word
τέλος, or its derivatives, all bringing home the sense of a divine
purpose which cannot be frustrated, and which it is His own
particular joy to fulfil—the sense of completion and perfection.
"The things concerning me have an end" (Luke 22. 37), "The
third day I shall be perfected" (Luke 13. 32), "I have glorified
thee on the earth, having accomplished the work which Thou
hast given me to do." (Jn. 17. 4.) And all that is caught up in the
cry from the Cross: "It is finished"—(τετέλεσται)—brought to its
perfect fulfilment.

What is more, our Lord found the Father's will not only in
the central purpose of redemption but also in the small details
and encounters of daily life. He saw it in the apparently chance
meeting with the woman of Samaria at the well, and it was meat
to Him to fulfil it there. "My meat is to do the will of him that
sent me, and to accomplish his work" (Jn. 4. 34). He saw it again
at the Pool of Bethesda (Jn. 5), and in the case of the man born
blind. They were opportunities for "the works of God to be
made manifest". "We must work the works of him that sent
me, while it is day" (Jn. 9. 4).

It is this extension of the divine purpose to the small details of
life which brings special comfort and joy to the disciple. The
philosopher may discover staggering problems in such a belief, as
inconsistent with any real free-will, even when he recognizes the
divine will in the main purposes of life. But the difficulty seems

to lie rather with the imagination than with the intellect. The imagination boggles both at the thought of God the Creator, the All-Great, descending to trivial affairs, and also at such condescension remaining compatible with man's free-will. Nature itself reveals the Creator's infinite care for detail. Look, for instance, under the microscope at the markings on the wings of some minute pond-beetle. Whether they have reached their beauty through the struggle for existence or from the immediate act of God is immaterial. For in either case it comes from Him, and it is thus through His will that they reach their limited perfection. But the human soul, as our Lord reminded us, is infinitely more precious in God's sight. Moreover, the smallest incidents in daily life may have decisive influence upon the soul's future. Will He not therefore take care for them?—and yet allow the will to have its freedom, without which no soul could reach its perfection?

But then what about evil or disease? Are they also the will of God, who made all the world and saw that it was " very good "? A distinction must be made here. (1) On the one hand there is the revealed will of God—the " will signified "—which is all good. It is, for instance, the clearly signified will of God that man should live according to the requirements of his human nature, that he should breathe and eat and sleep and beget children. It is also His will that He should keep the commandments and believe in the Christian Faith. (2) On the other hand there is what has been called the " permissive will " of God. Evil is in the world but God did not create it. It is His will that no man should give way to it. Yet, inasmuch as God the Almighty, the All-Wise, has for His own inscrutable purposes not abolished it, there is a sense in which it is His will—He permits it to be. Our Lord Himself hinted more than once at this permissive will of the Father, e.g. in the Parable of the Wheat and Tares. " An enemy hath done this ", but, " Let both grow together until the harvest."

The contemplative grows increasingly conscious of this will of God impinging upon his consciousness—the more so, as his prayer becomes the blind reaching out of his will towards God, devoid of all feeling or images. The long process of detachment, mortification, and purification results in the simplifying of the self, and the gathering into one of all its forces, hitherto scattered in a multiplicity of interests. That harmonized concentrated self now offers

itself eagerly to God, seeking not the gifts of God and His consolations, but God Himself and closer union with His will. " One
deep calleth to another" and the " abyss" of God answers with
the pressure of His Being on the human spirit. The man comes to
realize that all things are ordered by the divine will, to find that
will in all things that come to him, and so to find God Himself
there. As one writer has daringly put it, " Everything becomes
just God to him ".[1] So whether it be a call to some new work
or walk in life, or a chance encounter with some individual, or the
onset of some painful disease, in all alike he finds the will of God.
Some great contemplatives, such as St. Francis de Sales, use the phrase
" holy indifference" to describe this readiness to accept the will
of God eagerly in all things, and in whatever shape it comes.
St. Francis illustrated this by the picture of a man dying of thirst.
What the man wants and all he cares about is the water to drink.
He is indifferent to the vessel in which the liquid is brought to
him, whether it be a gold cup or a wooden mug. So the individual's desire must be to know what God means him to do in
each case, and then to give himself to that with his whole heart.
But his attitude differs entirely from that of the Moslem. The
latter also tends to take all that comes as proceeding from the will
of God, and his reaction is one of passive submission, but of submission, not to God, but to the event itself. So in face of sickness
or evil he merely lies down under it, as yielding to a greater power.
The Christian, on the other hand, looks always straight to God,
seeking Him and His will in the event. If it is disease he accepts it
willingly, yet as an obstacle which God means him to use all his
power to overcome. Or, face to face with the oppression of the
poor, he sees there something allowed by the permissive will of
God, but at the same time an opportunity to call forth his courage
and love in combating it. But it makes all the difference to know
that he is dealing with a state of affairs that is under the control of
God All-Mighty, and not with a world that has broken loose.
Monsignor Gay has reminded us that in the celestial sphere there is
an infinite number of spirits, ordered in a wonderful hierarchy, all
intent on fulfilling the will of God, which they see with a clear-
ness and carry out with a joy, far surpassing our understanding.
It is the harmony of heaven. Our business here below is, like them,
to find that will, and moment by moment give ourselves to fulfil
it with eager gladness. So we join in that harmony. That is why

[1] Tauler, *Predigten*, 1, p. 158. (Frankfurt-on-Main, 1826.)

Mgr. Gay uses the word *abandon* instead of surrender or resignation. After all, surrender is the word used of a beaten army that lays down its arms in face of a superior force and fights no more. Resignation suggests again the unwilling yielding to something stronger than oneself. Neither word at all suggests the delighted union of wills as between lover and beloved. The soul, he says, " *n'est à Dieu qu'un oui vivant. Chaque soupir qu'elle pousse et chaque pas qu'elle fait, est un amen brûlant qui va se joindre a l'amen céleste et s'y accorde* "[1]—words which only echo those which our Lord Himself taught His disciples to say, " Thy will be done in earth *as it is in Heaven* ".

Thus the contemplative, following in the steps of Christ and moulded gradually into His likeness, experiences that devotion to the will of God which dominated Christ's own life on earth, and that same finding of His will in all the events of daily life. All life is summed up for him in obedience to the will of God. Obedience, perhaps, sounds too dull a word. We have lost its real meaning nowadays, and it carries a savour of humiliation and servitude. But God has made life and the joy of life to depend on that obedience or glad co-operation. A writer of to-day has observed this paradox: if we call it obedience we make the joy too dull (since we have, except at our momentary best and in our transient illuminations, lost the joy of obedience); "God made—let us say the delight of a perfect response to his initiative a part of the working of the web. We could not otherwise become at once perfect servitude and perfect freedom."[2] That joy is an abiding one for the contemplative. But such concentration on the divine will has a curious effect on his ethical standards, for they seem to be swallowed up in it. Formerly he had very clear ideas about right and wrong. Certain qualities were right in themselves, honesty, modesty, purity, and he was prepared to hold to them however weak his faith in God might be. He was prepared to maintain with Tennyson that, " Right is right and to follow right were wisdom in the scorn of consequence ". Now all that has gone. Those virtues seem important only because God wills them. For that reason of course he pursues them all the more eagerly. At the same time he is aware that if he lost his hold on God, all those things would lose their value, too, for him.

[1] *De la Vie et des Vertues Chrétiennes*, III, p. 180. (H. Oudin, Poitiers, 1878.)

[2] Charles Williams, *Forgiveness of Sins*, p. 18. (Geoffrey Bles, London, 1942.)

The question arises: How is he to know exactly in each case how to respond to this will of God coming to him at every moment? Often the way is plain, for God has made it known by His will signified, and no special inspiration is needed to embrace that. The Religious, for instance, has the bulk of his day clearly marked for him. He knows it is the will of God for him to take his part in the Divine Office, to obey his superiors, to carry out his ordinary duties of the day. It only remains for him in the power of the Holy Ghost to see that his soul is indeed *un oui vivant* to that will.

But there are other happenings where the path is not so clear. Frequently life presents a man with a choice of two alternatives both good in themselves. Which is God's will for him? Should he, for instance, accept the offer made to him of a more useful post in another town, or should he for the possible advantage of his family remain where he is? Or, it may be, he has to balance the desire for more prayer and mortification with the claims of others and the consideration of his own health. Besides those decisions which come only seldom in a man's life, there are the daily contacts and opportunities presenting themselves at almost every hour. How is he to discover and fulfil God's will for him in these?

It is the special province of the Holy Spirit with His sevenfold gifts to meet his need here. The gift of counsel shows him by a kind of intuition the path: the gift of ghostly strength gives him the courage and strength to follow it. But it is the gift of wisdom that most of all prepares the contemplative to recognize the Father's will for him. It gives him an inward knowledge of God, an increased tenderness or sensitiveness to that pressure of God upon his soul, drawing him to Him, making him understand His will. It reveals that will to him by means of holy inspirations. To quote Fr. Baker, " The second way by which God doth immediately signify His will to the intellective soul in virtue of prayer is by imprinting a blind, reasonless motion into the superior will, giving it a weight and propension to one side of the doubt rather than to the other ".[1] The lives of the saints are full of examples of such guidance, ever since the day of Pentecost. Sometimes the Holy Spirit showed them His will in clear unmistakable ways, as

[1] *Holy Wisdom*, II, 7.

when St. Paul on his second missionary journey was " forbidden
by the Holy Ghost to speak the word in Asia ", and then, as he
and his companions were planning to go through Bithynia, " the
Spirit of Jesus suffered them not ". Sometimes the inspiration came
contrary to all that seemed reasonable. So Ananias to his amaze-
ment was sent to the persecutor, Saul of Tarsus, apparently against
all sound reason. So again Philip the deacon was told by " an
angel of the Lord " to go down to the road leading from Jerusalem
to Gaza, although it was mere desert. But there he found the
Ethiopian eunuch and a soul to be saved. More often the inspiration comes in some far less striking way, through the attention
being gently though powerfully drawn to some particular action.
The whole progress of the contemplative's spiritual life depends
on his faithful response to these inspirations. Progress indeed at
this stage consists solely in fidelity to the will of God. Benedict
of Canfield in his *Regula Perfectionis* bases all his teaching on this.
He points out that first of all there is for every soul the need of
obedience to the *exterior will* of God, which is shown in the teaching of the Church—the keeping of the commandments, the f
filment of one's duties. Then there is the *interior will* which
is revealed rather by inward inspirations—a sphere which ngs
more particularly to the contemplative. Those still more advanced
depend rather on the *essential will* of God—a yet more subtle
guidance for the soul in closest union with God.

What it comes to mean for the contemplative is that outside
the ordinary obvious duties of his state, that is the *exterior will* of
God, the " will signified ", which he gives himself to fulfil, with
his whole heart, " in earth as it is in heaven ", he depends wholly
upon the *interior will* made known to him through holy
inspirations. Such guidance brings to him a wonderful sense of
comfort and of God's abiding, controlling presence in his soul.
A still further comfort lies in the knowledge that to be inspired
by God does not necessarily mean to feel inspired by Him. The
Holy Spirit often prefers to work hiddenly, and it is better so.
But the contemplative is content to leave himself in His hands,
and to follow where He points the way, though his heart be cold.
Indeed he comes to wait more and more upon His guidance, and
his own experience goes to corroborate that of the saints, that the
Spirit, as our Lord promised, does indeed lead him into all truth.
To have learned this is to have entered into the liberty of the sons

of God. For " as many as are led by the spirit of God, these are
the sons of God " (Rom. 8. 14). We are reminded of the distinction that the old masters loved to draw between the " hireling
servants ", and the " friends ", and the " sons " of God. The characteristic mark of the " sons " is precisely this dependence on the Holy
Spirit. " Ye have an anointing of the Holy One ", wrote St.
John, " ye know all things " (1 Jn. 2. 20). But if they shrink from
undertaking anything without that leading of the Holy Spirit,
they must on the other hand be very faithful and courageous in
following that leading when it comes, however costly to themselves or however contrary at first sight to common sense.

But terrible danger lies in the way. The history of the Church
is littered with the disasters of men and women who thought
themselves led by the Spirit, and, puffed up with pride, wandered
into trackless deserts of heresy and schism or moral decay, and
were lost there with those they had beguiled. That early Quakeress,
Jane Holmes, was neither the first nor the last who developed " a
wild airy spirit which was exalted above the Cross, which kicked
against reproof, and would not come to judgement ".[1] Not all
indeed who have gone astray have fallen through pride. How
pitiably deluded was the poor Protestant German girl who persuaded her companions to crucify her in imitation of our Lord's
Passion! No wonder the masters of the spiritual life have always
insisted on the paramount importance of humility, and of the long
process of detachment and mortification of self as the necessary
preparation for the contemplative life. The undetached, unmorti-
fied will only mistake its own selfish desires or fevered aims for
the will of God. Such a one " receiveth not the things of the
Spirit . . . and he cannot know them, because they are spiritually
judged " (1 Cor. 2. 14). Mohammed claimed to be guided directly
by God, and he solved more than one awkward political tangle or
outburst of passion by a special inspiration bidding him to add
another wife to his harem. The erring Christian would not be so
crudely deceived, perhaps, but in history he has done grievous
things in the name of special inspirations.

But the Catholic has certain means whereby he may test these
inspirations, "whether they be of God". (1) They will not clash with
the exterior will of God, the will signified, for example in the

[1] Braithwaite, *Beginnings of Quakerism*, p. 72. (Macmillan, London, 1912.)

teaching of Holy Church, or with the duties of his state in life as a Christian. No "holy inspiration" for instance would tell him that he had advanced beyond the need of the Blessed Sacrament or of joining in the Church's public worship. Nor would he be led by the Holy Spirit to leave his wife and children to starve in order to give himself to prayer. St. Jeanne Chantal was, it is true, led to leave her children to become a Religious, nor is she alone in that, but in each case the children were well provided for, and the call was exceptional. (2) The Catholic is never a mere solitary, alone with the Alone. He is one of God's Family, a member of the Body of Christ, and has the experience and help of others, especially of his director, to guide him. If he is truly led by the Spirit he will seek that help in humility and trust. Often he will find that inspirations that have come to him persistently in spite of his own doubts are recognized and confirmed, sometimes to his astonishment, by his director and others—eventually, if not at first—and it brings not only reassurance with regard to the inspiration, but a deepened sense of fellowship in the bond of the Spirit. For the Holy Spirit, to accomplish His purpose even in a single soul, works in countless ways, moving other souls and preparing events, so that, when that soul goes forward in obedience to His prompting, it finds the way made ready. There are often fearsome lions in the way but, as it goes boldly and trustingly on, it discovers them to be chained. St. Francis of Assisi driven by the Spirit came to Rome to get the papal sanction for his new Brotherhood. He did not realize how heavily the dice were loaded against so desperate a venture, yet the way was prepared: friends were at hand and the Pope had had his own message from the Spirit. St. Jeanne Chantal in leaving her children did not depend solely on her own sense of the Holy Spirit's call to her. She was corroborated and even urged to follow that call by her saintly director, St. Francis de Sales. (3) There are, however, innumerable occasions where inspirations come on lesser matters, which do not concern some great change in life; it may be to some small act of charity to a neighbour; it may be to some special act of devotion, or some way of dealing with an occurrence of the moment. The contemplative depends on inspirations for anything that lies outside the line of his daily duties. The temptation may come to him frequently to act on his own initiative. If he yields to it he finds himself led along a path of increasing activity, which is not his path and only results in self-will. On the other hand he

knows that it is in ordinary ways and in ordinary events that the
Holy Spirit most often gives His guidance. There is a sacramental
character about such things for him, and he learns to find God's
will there. De Caussade has stressed the importance of the present
moment, where the will of God presents itself to the soul as an
infinite sea. The business of the soul is to recognize God's will in
it and give himself to it with his whole heart. And for that he
possesses the gifts of the Holy Spirit. This is the safe and true
way. Self-deception and self-will overtake those who look for
God's inspirations only or mainly through special messages, or
who wait in silence for them, as though God revealed Himself
only in abnormal ways. That opens the way for the subconscious
to play strange tricks on the soul, which encourage self-will.
Indeed any "inspiration" which ministers to self-gratification
must be held suspect. True inspirations have certain common
characteristics. (a) Usually they come unexpectedly, often suggesting something that challenges the individual's own inclinations,
or at least that it requires courage to follow. At once sweet and bitter,
they draw the soul with the joy of God's perfect will manifested,
and yet cause it to shrink at first from the sacrifice entailed. The
call of the Religious Life comes to some with great delight as the
goal of all their longing, the answer to strange questionings and
to a growing weariness of the world, but at the same time they
are smitten with anguish at the thought of withdrawing from
people and things they love in that world.

(b) There is a gentle persistence about them. If they are not
obeyed at once they obtrude themselves on the soul again and
again until they are recognized as coming from God, and still it
not obeyed they return, gently urging it to follow. Only when
they have been recognized and definitely refused do they cease—
and the man has missed his chance. For there does seem to be a
point when God leaves him to go his own way. The author of
the *Mirror of Simple Souls* stresses this need of being watchful and
never refusing "what love sendeth". "Love sent thrones and
Cherubim and Seraphim to summon you and you always refused.
So said Love, ' I left you in your waywardness to your own knowledge '." (Div. 9.)

(c) They bring peace to the soul. If at first their unexpectedness
and their costliness cause it perturbation, this is followed by a sense

of peace, which is a mark of the Spirit's presence. St. Ignatius, when pointing this out, says also that the promptings of the evil spirit on the other hand bring at first a feeling of self-gratification and peace, which yields to dismay and restlessness, or to a discontented critical attitude.[1] False inspirations also sometimes rob the soul of peace by suggesting all kinds of scruples and worries, generally about quite insignificant matters. Scrupulosity lies in wait for some people at a certain stage of their spiritual journey. It distracts and delays them with trifles. St. Francis de Sales gives excellent advice to such. He tells them to do "whatever seems best without worrying. Men do not weigh the current coin; it would take too much time to be perpetually testing our pence and farthings."[2]

(d) True inspirations tend to make the man more humble and obedient, distrustful of himself, knowing his own blindness and sin, his almost infinite capacity for self-deception and self-seeking. For he is aware how closely the Scripture fits himself: " Every imagination of the thoughts of his heart was only evil continually " (Gen. 6. 5). Humility must always be the result of any real contact of a human soul with God, the All-Holy; and obedience comes more easily to the man who sees, behind the inspiration, God the Almighty working all things according to His will. So he is ready to take advice and follow the direction of his superiors in simple trust. St. Marie de l'Incarnation at one period of her life was filled with an almost irresistible attraction towards bodily mortifications, and she embarked on a scarifying programme. She felt strongly that this came from the inspiration of the Holy Spirit, but it was only as her director recognized the inspiration and gave his permission that she followed the attraction. What is more, so soon as she entered the convent at Tours and became a novice, she at once dropped all such extraordinary practices in obedience to authority, to fall in line with the other novices.

As the disciple climbs higher up the mount of contemplation and his will becomes more closely united with the Father's will, the process is immensely simplified. God makes him aware of His will at each moment in a way more immediate than by special inspirations. He grows even more humble and obedient, yet he

[1] *Spiritual Exercises, On the Discernment of Spirits*, 2nd week.
[2] *Love of God*, VIII, 14.

no longer needs to apply tests to know whether he is being guided
by God. When God willed that the wise men from the East
should be brought to Christ, a star appeared to guide them to
Bethlehem. The guidance came along the line of their own
studies, and only they in all probability would have recognized its
meaning. To follow it must have entailed great sacrifices and great
labours and much searching of heart. But follow it they did and,
when they saw it again as they left Jerusalem, they " rejoiced with
exceeding great joy ". It brought them to their Saviour. They
presented their gifts and adored Him. But Simeon needed no star
nor vision of angels. A long life of discipline and prayer and
" waiting for the consolation of Israel " had so attuned his soul to
heavenly things, that he was quick to recognize in the infant child
brought to the temple the Saviour of the world.

CHAPTER XV

THE DARK NIGHT

WRITERS on the spiritual life have in recent years made great play with the simile of the Dark Night, and given it undue prominence, catching up the phrase from St. John of the Cross. Some have applied it indiscriminately to the bouts of aridity which occur in the most ordinary states of prayer. Others, like Dom Chapman, have given the impression that aridity is the normal state of the contemplative, without sufficiently explaining what that aridity means. But when one turns to the earlier Christian mystics one finds far less about the Dark Night. Few of them use the phrase at all, though all are familiar with the experience. Certainly they give no indication that blank aridity is the normal state of the contemplative unti' ʰ· ·ʳitual marriage is bestowed. It is true that those familiar ˅...ᵤ ᵤₑ teaching of the pseudo-Dionysius, as for instance John Tauler and his school, talk most about that night; but even then it does not figure so largely with them as with St. John of the Cross. The explanation of the discrepancy lies partly in the fact that the contemplative in his journey to God meets with two sets of experiences. One concerns his communion with God, who is pure Spirit, the Light Eternal. That light dazzles his human senses and intellect and leaves them in the dark. The other set concerns rather his relations with the world, and that entails a series of renunciations on his own part. Meanwhile from others he often has to endure trials and persecutions of various kinds; and spiritually he is beset with doubts, temptations, and perhaps sickness. St. John calls the whole process, between the beginning of contemplation and the final stages, the Dark Night. The earlier writers deal with both sets, but when they speak of the Dark Night they generally refer to the former only. But they make it quite plain that this is far from being a state of perpetual gloom and aridity. St. Mechthild of Magdeburg describes the three heavens mentioned by St. Paul as being: (1) a heaven made by the devil with his false poisonous sweetness, where he turns himself into an angel of light; (2) a heaven made by the desire of the soul and the beginning of love; here " there is no light "—it is the Dark Night (though she does not use the phrase)—but the soul experiences all the same an " incomprehensible sweetness "; (3) " where the true light is bestowed, and the soul sees and knows that God is all in all."[1] Our own Walter Hilton gives a similar division, passing from the false light of the world, through the night of the senses to the true light of Christ. But he adds that this night " is a good night and a lightly murkness . . . sometimes painful and sometimes it is easy and comfortable ".[2] The unknown French author of the *Mirror of Simple Souls* calls it (in the words of his old English translator) " the right sweet Far Night " where the soul " hath her right name of Naught ". " What is this Far Night? " he asks and he gives the answer: " It is the Trinity himself . . . The Trinity openeth to this soul and showeth her of his glory, of which none but he can speak. . . . And the light of this divine knowing taketh from her the knowing of God's self, and of herself, and of all things."[3] The passage itself makes it evident that he does not mean that God is the darkness, but that He is the immediate cause of it by reason of His light blinding the soul. In the *Cloud of Unknowing* its author states definitely that the cloud itself is not God, but comes between the soul and God. St. John of the Cross is in entire agreement with these older writers, but he is chiefly concerned with the more or less painful purifications to which the soul is subjected during the process. But even he speaks of the " night more lovely than the dawn ", and in one of his most beautiful poems, " Although it is night ", he reveals how full of joy and peace the experience can be.

Differences in the temperament and constitution of souls account for different emphasis on the Dark Night. The more intellectual type are led more by faith than by feeling. They would probably experience a more unvaried aridity. The more affective type, led by love, would know a greater variety—moments of vision and great spiritual delight alternating with longer and more painful periods of darkness. To attempt to classify souls is always a hazardous business, as the psychologist Jung has pointed out, even when we have as clear a scheme for it as he had. But, so far as we may make the venture, St. Bernard of Clairvaux and St. Francis of Assisi belonged mainly to the latter. Both were warm and

[1] *Offenbarungen*, II. 19.   [2] *Scale of Perfection*, II, 24.   [3] Div., 7. 6.

impulsive natures, though St. Francis lacked the other's intellectual ability. Both had abundant experiences of ecstatic joys of communion with God: fervour seems to have been their normal state, yet alternated with rarer periods of darkness and desolation. St. Bonaventure was a more complex soul, capable of much of the spontaneity of St. Francis, but the intellect played a far more prominent part, and there is a sober tinge about his spiritual life. Another Franciscan, Jacopone da Todi, reveals in his poems an alternation of spiritual joy and desolation, even more intense than that of his founder. The English author of the *Cloud of Unknowing* seems to be describing an almost entirely different experience, yet both were contemplatives. St. Jeanne Chantal's prayer was normally of a peculiarly arid kind, though it had its consolations, while Lucie Christine, though a woman of considerable intellectual capacity, harks back to the more affective colourful type, short periods of desolation alternating with visions and ecstasies.

This chapter will attempt to consider, briefly and at the risk of some repetition, first the theological implications of the Dark Night, secondly its main features, and the experiences involved, as it runs its course.

I. THEOLOGICAL

The theological explanation of the Dark Night is based on two assumptions.

(1) God is pure Spirit—Absolute, Eternal, Infinite. Man is a mixture of matter and spirit, " strange compost of heaven and mire "—relative, finite, mortal. Moreover through his own sin he has forfeited such vision of God as he once had. God therefore infinitely transcends man's capacity to know Him by his ordinary faculties. The Athanasian Creed states this boldly: " The Father incomprehensible (Lat. *immensus*[1]), the Son incomprehensible, and the Holy Ghost incomprehensible ". But it is of the utmost importance to realize that the great Christian mystics, in common with other Christian writers, owe their conception of God to the Bible and the teaching of the Church. It is wholly in keeping with the old Hebrew picture of God given in the Old Testament—

---

[1] "Immensus", measureless, cannot be confined in space and therefore omnipresent: not to be confined nor grasped by anything and so passing human understanding. Cf. St. Irenaeus, "The immensity of God and His Substance are things beyond human estimation for no man has ever measured or handled them". (III, 24, 2, quoted Wilberforce, *Doctrine of Incarnation*, 93.)

the God who " hideth Himself ", who " dwelleth in thick clouds
and darkness ", who answers out of the whirlwind, yet dwells
also in everlasting peace. In essence such a God differs enormously
from the Greek deity, who dwells serenely above the clouds,
passionless, indifferent to mankind, motionless. There are, of
course, superficial points of resemblance, and sometimes Christian
writers use the same language as the Greek philosophers, but with
significant difference of meaning. 'Aπάθεια for instance, to the
latter meant absence of feeling, utter indifference: to the former
it meant rather absence of disordered passions, the perfect poise of
character.

(2) Though God be incomprehensible, yet man is made for
union with Him, and it is possible for him to know God in some
way. Moreover that knowledge was in God's purpose for all
men, not only for a chosen few with special faculties. Every man
possesses some capacity for knowing this God who is pure Spirit.
This capacity lies beyond the five senses or the use of the reason,
being more immediate than they. In Christ Jesus the barrier of
sin has been removed and man set free to use this capacity.

There are two ways of approach for the creature man, by
which he may attain some knowledge of God.

(a) The positive way. God is a " cataphatic " God, i.e. reveals
Himself through His acts, through creation, in " multiplicity ",
and it is there that man can get some knowledge of Him and
desire for Him. There is the ladder of creation whereby he may
ascend to God.

(b) The negative way. God is also the " apophatic " God—
the God who is hidden, the " wholly Other ". Although He is
Being itself and the source of all that is, and can be said to be at
least all that He has revealed of Himself in the multiplicity of
creation, yet the Reality so transcends all this that it is truer to
approach Him by the way of negation. St. John of the Cross
says, " All that can be known of God in this life, much though it
be, is not true knowledge, for it is knowledge in part and very
far off, while to know Him essentially is true knowledge."[1] Dogmatic theology too has to use the same way. It has its positive

[1] *Spiritual Canticle*, Stanza VI.

statements to make about God, but, for the rest, it speaks cautiously of Him in negatives as " unbegotten ", " infinite ", " impassible ", " incomprehensible ". Such words do not explain God: they confess that, while He includes all we know of reality, He exists in modes far beyond our own experience—the Wholly-Other, Not-Ourselves, veiled in mystery. All that man can know by his ordinary faculties suggests only limitation and temporality, which are wholly unlike God. So while it is true to say, and Holy Scripture says, that God is Light and Life and Love, it is also true or truer to say that He is not any of these, for our own conceptions of them are too human and finite. They hide as much if not more than they reveal. This *via negativa* is not so absurd as it appears at first sight. Our only experience of life is of that which has a beginning at a certain point in time: it grows through a succession of experiences in time: and fades away into death. Growth, successiveness, decay, are its invariable marks. But the life of God is nothing like that. We say that He is eternal, or we speak of His simultaneity, but we can only guess at what those words mean. Again, God is personal. He has revealed to us that He is three Persons in One—but that utterly transcends any experience we have of personality. To speak of Him therefore under the category of personality can be seriously misleading. Or how does it help us to speak of God as Love? For love means for us the attraction of one person for another who lives an independent life possessing qualities quite independent of himself. But, humanly speaking, we have no sort of experience of the mutual love of the Blessed Trinity, nor of the love of God for His creature, man. For there is nothing good or lovable in man but what God has placed there Himself, and what He loves in man is His own image, in which He created him. To call that love conceals at least as much as it reveals.

Dionysius, therefore, taught that man must pass through this *via negativa* if he was to know God " in spirit and in truth ". The positive way had its value, but that orange would soon be sucked dry, and would not take him far. St. John of the Cross also recognizes the value of the positive way, but it does not go far enough, though God uses it as a means of His revelation of Himself. He says that, to souls that are already adept " God grants the favour of giving, through that which they hear or see or understand, and sometimes without either this or that means, a

knowledge clearly conveyed, wherein it is granted them to understand or to perceive the loftiness and greatness of God; and in this
perception the soul experiences such lofty feelings of God that it
understands clearly that all has yet to be understood ".[1] God,
however, has given man the capacity to know Him, and he must
seek Him in the depths of his soul, where God dwells. It involves
a process of renunciation and detachment, of turning away from
created things and of waiting for the Infinite God to make Himself
known in His own way. It is the return of the creature from the
multiplicity of creation back to the uncreated Simplicity of God,
to Unity. Here is the Cloud of Unknowing in which he must
dwell, till God reveal Himself to him in the darkness, in the inmost
being of his soul. Dionysius, therefore, prays that God will
" guide us to that topmost height of mystic lore, which exceedeth
light and more than exceedeth knowledge, where the simple,
absolute, and unchangeable mysteries of the heavenly Truth lie
hidden in the dazzling obscurity of the secret silence, outshining all
brilliance with the intensity of their darkness ".[2] So he goes on,
" leave the senses and the activities of the intellect and all things
that they can perceive—and all things in this world of nothingness", and then, " thine understanding being laid at rest, strain
(so far as thou mayest) towards a union with Him whom neither
being nor understanding can contain ".[3]

It is, of course, of first importance to remember that all the
Christian mystics held firmly that it was only through the sacrifice
of Jesus Christ on the Cross and His redemption of mankind that
such union with God was possible at all. Not only Dionysius, but
even St. John of the Cross, have been accused of ignoring the work
of Christ. If they did not speak of this as often as some might
expect, it was only because they were writing in a *milieu* and for a
public where this was taken for granted as the very basis of life.

II. FEATURES OF THE DARK NIGHT

The experience of the Dark Night at its fullest seems to include
at least three phases. St. John of the Cross speaks of two parts,
which occur in some degree in each phase: (*a*) the night of the

[1] *Spiritual Canticle*, Stanza VII.

[2] *Mystical Theology*, Ch. I, trans. Rolt.

[3] Ibid.

senses and (*b*) the night of the spirit, of the "higher powers" of
the soul—memory, understanding, will. Each of these, he teaches,
has an active and a passive element. The division is a useful one
and perhaps makes for clarity, though modern psychologists have
abandoned the old faculty psychology and taught us to see the
whole man involved to some extent in each deliberate act or
thought. St. John himself recognizes this in insisting so strongly
that it is desire that must be mortified. The musician, for instance,
cannot indulge his senses of hearing and touch without involving
the "higher powers" of the soul. At one and the same time
thinking, feeling, willing, a man moves forward to satisfy his desire;
and joy, hope, or grief may precede, accompany, or follow his
action. We will, therefore, diverge slightly from St. John's termin-
ology, though not from his teaching.

(1) First comes the *Active Phase*. In a sense it is not first, because
it is itself a response to the pressure of God, which begin
Passive Phase, but too gentle to be recognized as such. And every
action of the soul towards God is due to His prevenient grace.
Through that the soul catches obscurely a glimpse of the inde-
scribable beauty of God, and it turns eagerly towards Him:

> Unveil, O Lord, and on us shine
>   In glory and in grace.
> This gaudy world grows pale before
>   The Beauty of Thy Face.
>   J. H. NEWMAN

St. John of the Cross sets forth magnificently at the beginning of
the *Ascent* this fundamental reason for the Dark Night—the glory
and greatness of God, His Beauty, and His Wisdom. "All the
being of creation compared with the infinite Being of God is
nothing. . . . All the beauty of the creatures, compared with the
infinite beauty of God, is the height of deformity." Now "love
creates a likeness between that which loves and that which is
loved". So the soul that is tied in its affections to created things
becomes like them and cannot know this glorious God. That is
why it must enter upon its *ascesis* of turning away from all these,
and towards the light. This results in a time of darkness, for it has
lost the false light of creatures but is too weak and earthly to bear
the brightness of the true light. It is like a man who has been
long in a dark cave suddenly emerging into sunlight. His eyes
remain dazzled. But his blindness is due not to darkness but to

excess of light. So, years before, Nicholas of Cusa had written, "A man seeking to see a light beyond his seeing knoweth that, so long as he seeth aught, it is not that which he seeketh. Wherefore it behoveth him to go beyond all visible light. . . . The place he entereth must needs lack visible light and is thus, so to speak, darkness to the eye."[1]

The man who sets out on this path must deal first with the appeal to his senses, weaning them from wrong or misleading attachments (see Ch. VI). Only when he begins this, does he realize how warped they were, how much they were tied to things and people for their own sake, and for his own satisfaction therein; how little God entered into his relations with them at all. However good in themselves, they hindered him, instead of leading him to God as they were meant to do. It is indeed of the utmost importance to remember that neither St. John of the Cross nor other masters of the spiritual life preach this turning from creatures on the ground that they are evil. It is because human nature is a fallen nature: its faculties are warped so that men cling to them in wrong ways and fail to find God in them as they should. When the purification is completed, they can use them safely. The old writers had a great sense of what they called " hierarchy " in creation. By that they meant that God created all things in a wonderful order, each grade being subordinated to the one above it, with God Himself supreme over all. Even the angel hosts were subject to the same principle, ordered in their nine choirs, each with its proper place in the whole. The pseudo-Dionysius wrote two books on Hierarchy, one concerning the angels, and the other the Church on earth. Indeed his scheme was so compact that it scarcely left room for the saving work of Christ on the Cross. The Fall had upset this hierarchy in man's soul. His perverted desires put things in their wrong place, valued the creature more than God; to use St. Paul's words, " They exchanged the truth of God for a lie, and worshipped and served the creature rather than the Creator." (Rom. 1. 25.)

What matters, therefore, is not so much the possession of creatures as the desire for them, a desire that is " inordinate " because it is out of order, and no longer stands in its right relations with God, the Creator. The artist tends to be captivated by the

[1] *Vision of God*, Ch. VI, trans. E. Salter.

beauty of line and colour; he yields to its intoxication. Not only does he not find God there, but it leads him away from God. It hides from him the source of all beauty. Only when his desire has been purified can he rightly turn back to creatures, and only then can he see them in their true beauty, or use them rightly. Similarly the scholar with his thirst for knowledge needs to have that purged before he can use it rightly and find the true Wisdom. So the contemplative, when the Wisdom of God is pressing darkly upon his soul, must abandon the attempt to understand exactly what is happening, to grasp, as it were, the Incomprehensible with his mind, and must be content to wait in the darkness for the light to shine.

Life in the world, of course, cannot stand still until the work of purification is done. Man must eat and sleep and work and love. But if he is to come to this hidden knowledge of God in contemplation, he must exercise a strong discipline of his whole being, not only of the senses, but also of his affections and thoughts, even the most spiritual of them. What is at stake here is something more than the purification of the soul from all sinful attachments. It is the gathering together of all its energies for the great encounter with the uncreated God—the gathering together, their re-collection, not their destruction.

In normal life in the world the soul tends to be dissipated. There are so many things good in themselves, to see and hear and touch and taste and smell, that they absorb the soul's energies and leave it with little time or capacity for attending to God, in whom are all things, and who is Himself perfect Life and Love and Goodness and Beauty. This process of turning from them, of re-collection, is a painful one. At first the man feels he has indeed entered into the night, where the old familiar things have gone and there is nothing in their place except that strange yearning for God. Moreover, he must not seek after even spiritual consolations, visions, or anything of the kind to lighten the gloom, for that is only to seek self-satisfaction in another form. Nor is it the time to exercise the reasoning powers to try to think what it means or what is the nature of God. That might give some satisfaction, some sense of action, but it would only hinder God's action.

(2) The next phase of the Dark Night is God's own action on

the soul. And here the soul's role is a passive one. But although
St. John of the Cross places it second he never meant to imply
that it only began when the active night had come to an end.
From one point of view, as we said above, the passive night comes
first. Its beginning is the prevenient act of God which summons
the soul to venture on the active phase. But the saint rightly deals
with it second, because it not only works *pari passu* with the soul's
own efforts, but it goes on beyond and works in ways where the
soul must remain passive. Benedict of Canfield gives a striking
illustration of the overlapping of the active and passive night in
his teaching upon the annihilation of the will. It concerns only
those souls in advanced stages of contemplation. Even here there
is some work to be done by the soul itself. Distractions may come
to the contemplative when praying in quiet and solitude. They
must be dealt with by an act of recollection almost too subtle to be
called an act, which allows the divine action to reassert control.
They are still more likely to come when he is amongst others and
engaged in some activity. There too he must use a similar method.
(See Ch. XIII, p. 222.)

The impact of God upon the soul in contemplation at first robs
it of its power to reason. If the man tries to think over the subject
of his meditation, either his mind remains a blank, or the thoughts
which come only distract him from God. It profits him nothing,
even if he can do it, to visualize scenes or form ideas. He finds
himself in darkness. Moreover his affections are numbed too.
He tries in vain to fan into flame the dead embers of his former
fervour. Nor does it help him to repeat acts of devotion. His
prayer becomes painfully arid.

As the night grows darker his state becomes more painful.
Moreover the trouble extends over his whole life outside his times
of prayer. Sometimes a terrible indifference even to those he
loves best seems to overtake him. Old interests lose their savour.
Sometimes his mind seems strangely bound, making him forgetful
or unable to concentrate on work needing much thought. All that
is because subconsciously his attention is still half given to the
pressure of God's love on his soul—where God is making Himself
known to him in a new way.

But other trials follow. Prayer may be arid but not necessarily painful. Aridity may exist on the surface whilst a deep peace and sense of union rule in the depths. Desolation is a far more shattering experience. For then God Himself seems to have vanished with everything else. With God the Dark Night is not too dark. " With thee ", St. Peter cried to our Lord, " I am ready to go both to prison and to death." (Luke 22. 33.) But it was without His Lord that his trial came. Our Lord Himself faced the awful experience. " My God, my God, why hast thou forsaken me? " (Matt. 27. 46.) Something of that sense of desolation, of being abandoned by God, seems to be a necessary ingredient in the purification of the saints, at some stage or other in their life. Some apparently had to endure it only momentarily: for others, as for St. Francis de Sales, it was a prolonged torture, like a taste of hell. It is scarcely surprising that some of them in their agony should have thought that perhaps it was God's will that they should be for ever deprived of His presence, and therefore said that they were willing to be damned eternally if it were His will. The Quietists used such cries of pain to buttress an extravagant doctrine of Pure Love, which made a virtue of being indifferent to one's own salvation. The answer to that aberration is that one of the most certain truths of the Faith is that God would have all men to be saved and come to the knowledge of the truth, for God " so loved the world that he gave his only begotten Son that whosoever believeth on him should not perish, but have eternal life " (Jn. 3. 16). To be indifferent to one's own salvation means therefore the failure to will eagerly the will of God. Poor John Bunyan, Calvinist in creed and outside the sacramental fellowship and experience of the Church, was nevertheless nearer the truth in his agonizing search for assurance of salvation. He found his comfort eventually, not in those words of our Lord, but oddly enough in the message given to the prophet Jeremiah, " I have loved thee with an everlasting love " (Jer. 31. 3).

Sometimes here old long-mastered temptations or quite new ones assail the contemplative with almost irresistible fury and persistence; bewildering doubts about the very fundamentals of his Faith, such as came to St. Francis de Sales; puzzling scruples, such as vexed St. Ignatius Loyola; foul sensual temptations, perhaps the commonest form of the trial. The modern contemplative has to face such temptations in their modern dress. For the devil is always up to date and quick to employ the most insinuating method of attack. In the recent war the enemy always seemed to win success by some new surprise—at first it was the Panzer divisions. No sooner had the British learned to deal with that than they had to face the menace of air-borne invasion on a large scale; then came flying bombs and rockets. The devil is like that, always, as it were, one ahead, and in dealing with the contemplative he prefers infiltration and out-flanking to frontal assaults. To-day, for instance, doubts creep into the mind of the Religious, not only about the Faith, but perhaps still more about the value of the life of prayer and detachment: "If Christ redeemed human nature and the world, why should we not enjoy to the full the good innocent things? Look at so and so and so and so, how good they are, and what good they do, yet apparently they have their fill of such things." Will the soul at the end be greeted with the laughter of the angels and saints, because he has unnecessarily cut himself off from lawful pleasures and thereby impoverished his personality and his contribution to the common welfare? In the old days men recognized that if one was to give oneself to God the road lay through such mortification and prayer, though they might say that that was not the road for them. Nowadays all that is questioned, not only by the worldlings, but often by good people too. Or again when St. Martin gave half his new cloak to the beggar he felt sure that that was what our Lord desired him to do, and he was rewarded with a vision of Christ wearing it. The man who follows his example to-day may not only receive no such vision, but is left with an uneasy feeling that he has been weak and senti-mental, and perhaps debauched the beggar: for other views prevail about indiscriminate almsgiving. In the Dark Night such tempta-tions loom large and arguments carry little weight. But it is a comfort to look at the example of our Lord and His saints and to hold grimly to their track. At the same time, faced with such wiles of the evil one, the contemplative learns to understand why Christ so urgently warns His followers to watch and pray lest they enter into temptation or are caught off their guard. Though often these temptations have to be endured in the midst of desola-tion, God's chosen are not deprived of His presence and His grace to overcome. St. Catherine of Siena, once vexed almost beyond endurance by lustful thoughts, cried, when peace at last was restored to her soul, "Where wast Thou then, O Lord?" The answer came, "In thy heart all the time".

The more wholly the soul lives in God the more torturing does it find such experiences. Lucie Christine has well expressed both the anguish and yet the glad acceptance of it in such a trial: " O my Beloved, when you vanish the hours seem centuries to me; it is the cold and silence of death; my whole being seems to be being sacrificed. Well, let it be so, O Jesus, take what is Thine; my soul remains in Thy loved will. . . . Passive prayer *is God's response to the soul*, and when the soul no longer receives that answer, at least by the felt presence of the Beloved, it lives in a desert. Its one need is to offer continually to God its sacrifice which it is undergoing; its one wish (the only one it is aware of), abandonment to His holy will and the desire to serve its love in all the little things, as devotedly as in times of consolation."[1] The object of these trials seems to be twofold. In the first place there are depths of pride and self-will, and to some extent of disordered affections, which the individual cannot deal with himself, but of which he must be purged before he is fit for the closer union with God. Indeed he is not fully aware of them, and would not know how to deal with them. Moreover, so.long as one is oneself the chief agent in the process, pride has something on which to batten, and real humility lies as far away as ever. Another must take him in hand, strip him of everything, and reveal him to himself in his true nakedness. This is what happens in the Passive Night.

Secondly, God is introducing the man to a new knowledge of the Blessed Trinity, which lies hidden from his ordinary means of apprehension. It is a new country into which he is being led, as it were blindfold, and a traveller " will never reach a new country but by new ways which he knew not ".[2] But left to himself the man would still struggle to find his way according to his natural abilities, trying to see, feel, and reason for himself. All that must go, and he must be left helpless, waiting for another to lead him. Here he is led along the way that is wayless—and the only light that he has comes from within, from that dim pressure of God upon his soul.

(3) The third phase of the Dark Night does not happen to all contemplatives. It seems to be reserved for those who are called to the highest stage of the spiritual life, to the Spiritual Marriage.

[1] *Journal*, p. 130. (Paris, 1920.)
[2] *Dark Night*, II, 16.

Ruysbroeck speaks of those who " are still feeble and have need of milk and of sweet things and not of the strong food of temptation and of the loss of God ".[1] Not that the purification of these weaker souls (and they form the great majority) here stops short. The cleansing fire of God's presence continues, but it works gently, trying none more severely than he can bear. Periods of painful darkness alternate with periods of light and peace. Only beyond this world in Purgatory will the work be accomplished. The stronger souls, however, are subjected to a fiercer, quicker process. Usually a period of some years elapses before this last trial, during which the soul enjoys a deeper absorption in God, and often such mystical experiences as ecstasy and rapture. But the spirit here too " bloweth where it listeth ", and will not fit into any of our nicely calculated schemes. The scholar loves to find categories into which all the facts at his disposal may be neatly placed. One writer some years ago drew up a scheme of the contemplative life in this way and tried to fit into it not only St. Paul but even our Lord Himself—a Procrustean bed which collapsed under the strain. God's workings defy all such efforts. So here. The lives of the saints tend to upset all such calculations. All we can safely say is that the master contemplatives have had to undergo trials which have tortured both body and soul before their purification was complete, and before they reached that intimate union with God which they loved to speak of as Spiritual Marriage. Some of these trials we have already referred to (see p. 203)—desolation, violent temptations, experiences known to every contemplative. Indeed it is not so much the form of the trials which is new, as the exceeding violence of them. Moreover they gain force by their very unexpectedness, coming, as they usually do, after a period of calm and deepening knowledge of God.

These trials come in many forms but they have one characteristic in common. They descend upon the man from sources over which he has no control, and his part is a passive one. It may be his physical powers break down, over-wrought by the strains laid upon them in the impact of God upon the soul, and by its own efforts to answer to His claims. Sometimes some sudden sickness lays hold of the man, which baffles the doctors, but yet may vanish as suddenly as it came. St. Teresa had such an illness as this long before she reached an advanced state of prayer, but to the end she

[1] *Spiritual Marriage*, p. 70. (J. M. Dent, London, 1916.)

suffered from violent pains in the head. St. Bernard of Clairvaux, like many others, seriously impaired by his austerities his already precarious health.

Failure, public and humiliating, has befallen many a contemplative in this phase. The more prominent his influence, the more shattering was the experience. St. Francis of Assisi died young, but he lived long enough to see some of his most cherished aims overthrown by his successor, and a growing rift in the heart of his beloved community. M. Olier in the midst of his work for the revival of the spiritual life in France in the seventeenth century was stricken for two years with a kind of aphasia, which caused him many humiliations in public and put a stop to his activities.

Some have had to endure persecution in the form of calumnies against their moral character. Blessed Henry Suso (according to the story claimed to be given by himself) to his intense grief and astonishment had a small child thrust upon him by a woman who accused him of being its father. The scandal spread far. Henry, though troubled beyond measure, took the child and lovingly tended it, waiting humbly upon God. Eventually the woman herself was brought to repentance and confessed that she had lied. Sometimes the devil with his satellites makes a more direct attack upon the saints. He was wont to appear to them in human shape, as to St. Antony, trying to entice them to some sensual sin or some act of blasphemy or pride. Sometimes he seems to have been allowed to inflict physical suffering, as in the case of the Curé d'Ars. To another he would transform himself into an angel of light, or even assume the form of Christ Himself, as when he appeared gloriously arrayed to St. Martin of Tours. St. Martin put him to flight by asking to see the marks of the Cross on his hands and feet.

What exactly, we may ask, is the significance of this last phase of the Dark Night? Why should it be so necessary? On psychological grounds alone a recrudescence of temptation might be expected. Thwarted desires tend to reappear. The process is familiar in the beginnings of the spiritual life. A period of fierce struggle against disordered passions often follows conversion. After mastery has been achieved temptation weakens, even fades away altogether. But reaction against the long restraint gathers weight, and sooner or later temptation bursts forth with renewed vigour, all the more deadly because unexpected. Some outward misfortune, such as sickness or failure, opens the door more widely to the evil. A reformed drunkard will sometimes lose his craving for alcohol and go on undisturbed for years. Suddenly for no obvious reason his old enemy returns with redoubled force. The man is caught off his guard and succumbs.

But here we are dealing with something far deeper than any natural reaction, though we need not ignore the psychological factor in the experience. God is subjecting the soul to a final, more rigorous purification. Hitherto, in the former phases of the Dark Night, He was weaning the soul from self-satisfaction in its spiritual life, from the use of its own capacities to feel and reason for itself, from delight in the gifts of God rather than in God Himself. So also was it being detached from the world, from its attachments, even innocent attachments to people and things. As we saw, its own efforts in the active phase to effect this did not go deep enough. Only God Himself could bring it about. That took place in the second phase, what St. John of the Cross calls the passive night of the senses.

Yet the purification of the soul is still incomplete. If the soul has been purged from its attachments to the rest of creation, there remains the purifying of its relations with God Himself, in its highest part, called sometimes the " fine point of the soul ". After the second phase the contemplative is left detached, clinging to God alone in faith and hope and love. But even here imperfection lurks. He may give way momentarily, unreflectingly, to impatience or weariness. His union with God must reach a yet more super-natural level. Self is still too prominent. He still tends to think, " By my faith I cling to God; by my hope I look for him; by my love I hold Him ". That egoism, that separateness, must go if the union is to be complete. In this darkest moment of the night, even faith, hope, and love seem to vanish. The darkness purges the soul of the last traces of possessiveness, and leaves it utterly without sense of stay or comfort. Yet is it secretly upheld all the time. Even in the midst of its sorest trials a deep peace subsists within the soul, and it enjoys an almost continual contemplation of God, dark though it be. It is this peace and eager abandonment to the divine will which distinguish this state from a similar one caused by *accidie* or deliberate sin. In spite of the desolation and fury of temptation, the soul looks steadfastly to God and yields not for a moment to the evil solicitations.

But here too it is essential to remember that this purification with all its pain and darkness is effected, not by the withdrawal of God from the soul, but rather by a fuller inpouring of the Holy Spirit. The contemplative now realizes intensely his own inadequacy and unworthiness, yet at the same time grows dimly conscious of that Other at work. Hitherto his faith and hope had depended too much on reasonings, truths he had been taught, memories of past experiences. Though all these fail him now, little by little he becomes aware of a more supernatural faith and hope upholding him and drawing him nearer to God, of a stronger love dwelling in his soul in spite of its apparent deadness. It is the Holy Spirit pouring His gifts upon him, chiefly the gifts of knowledge and understanding, dazzling his own intellectual powers and at the same time teaching him a more intimate knowledge and love of God, whilst the gift of fortitude supports him through all his trials.

Eventually the Dark Night comes to an end. Its object is to purge the soul from every imperfection. It seems to perform on the saints the same purification which is effected in Purgatory, fitting the soul for the immediate vision of God—for the complete union of the human will with the Divine Will. Mystical writers have loved to use the simile of a log of wood in the fire to explain the process. The green log is placed in the fire and there lies passive. The first contact results in a cloud of acrid smoke and crackling and spitting as the fire burns out the damp, while the log is seen a black mass in the glowing embers. Gradually it becomes dry and itself catches fire. Finally it glows white-hot itself, united so closely with the fire as to be scarcely distinguishable from it.

The soul must be " throughly purged ", but it must also learn to desire God for His own sake, not for His gifts nor for the joy of His Presence. That knowledge can only be obtained when the soul is bereft of all such secondaries, and when plunged in the darkness it yields itself unreservedly to God's action upon it. Each soul differs from every other soul, and God treats each according to its own nature. For some the purging process is long and fierce; for others it is short and sharp. Some have to undergo heavy trials visible to all men; in others the same work is accomplished almost entirely within the soul, and their suffering is unknown. But Wisdom knows what she is doing and is " justified in all her works ". She deals with each according to his need. " At the first she will walk with him in crooked ways, and will bring fear and dread upon him, and torment him with her discipline, until she may trust his soul, and try him by her judgements: then will she return the straight way unto him, and will gladden him, and reveal to him her secrets." (Ecclus. 4. 17.)

CHAPTER XVI

REPARATION

THE intensified union with God and the clearer knowledge of His will which goes with it, result, we have seen, in an increasing desire for the salvation of others and in eagerness to minister to them; in other words, to enter into the divine purpose of creation that there might be finite persons to enjoy the bliss of the Blessed Trinity. Even the author of the *Cloud of Unknowing* insists that the life of contemplation must be undertaken for the salvation of mankind. It is one of the surprises that the saints spring upon us, this care for the world, but it follows inevitably from the true understanding of the will of God, who " wills that all men should be saved and come to the knowledge of the truth ". St. Catherine of Siena (and she is not alone in this) was given a piercing vision of the beauty of the human soul, of its preciousness in the sight of God. And she insists that it is through prayer that one comes to realize that beauty. The language of the saints at times seem so absorbed in God, so God-possessive, as though they were God's special favourites, and His love theirs almost exclusively, that their longing to serve and save strikes us with astonishment at first. But then closer knowledge of God teaches them, as it taught St. Augustine, that God cannot be the " private good " of any single soul. He is the " common good " in whom all are to find their bliss and be filled with His love up to and beyond their fullest capacity. Hence they can safely talk of Christ as the bridegroom of their soul, and of their soul as His bride, without danger of spiritual pride, or of selfish indifference to the welfare of their neighbour. They can desire at the same time that He may be equally the bridegroom of every other soul, knowing that that will in no wise alter the uniqueness of their own relation to him. Rather it adds to their joy. In fact, unless it is shared, that joy lacks its fulness. So St. John could write of the wonder of his own fellowship with God, " that ye also may have fellowship with us . . . and these things we write that *our* joy may be fulfilled " (1 Jn. 1. 3 f.). It is in entire keeping with this that St. John of the Cross at the end of his *Spiritual Canticle*, speaking of the bride's desire " to be translated out of the spiritual marriage to which God has been pleased to bring her in this Church Militant, to the glorious marriage of the Church Triumphant ", adds the words, " whereto may the sweetest Jesu be pleased to lead all such as call upon His name, the Spouse of faithful souls ". What a contrast that forms to the Buddhist mystic, absorbed in his self-induced trance, waiting to be swallowed up in Nirvana! He preaches a reverence for life and an abstention from all ill to his neighbour, but that is to facilitate his own spiritual progress. It is worlds away, for instance, from St. Paul's impassioned cry, " I could wish that I myself were anathema from Christ for my brethren's sake, my kinsmen according to the flesh " (Rom. 9. 3).

St. Paul's cry brings us to the problem of election, the problem which he was considering when he uttered it. But it is enough for us here to mark the fact that God has chosen to reveal Himself through special channels. The Jews were the race specially set apart and consecrated to mediate His revelation to the world. They failed in their task, but the true Israel, the Holy Catholic Church, inherited their mission. Why God has chosen this method of selection remains a mystery, and a still greater mystery is why the Jewish race should have been chosen for the purpose. But it lays a glorious, though almost intolerable, burden on the Church. Even within the Church itself the principle of selection is seen at work, not only in the calling and ordaining of priests to minister the Sacraments, but more widely in the bestowal of special gifts to the saints to mediate to their fellow-members. This truth was once vividly brought home to St. Gertrude in a vision, where she was shown Christ's mystical Body, the Church, in the form of His natural body. She was taught then that, just as, when a man eats, the mouth only receives the food and the palate savours it, yet the whole body is benefited thereby, so when individual saints receive special favours all the rest of the Church enjoys the benefit of them.[1]

The tragic history of the chosen people revealed one grim fact: its mission would only be accomplished by suffering. So the prophets portrayed the picture of the Suffering Servant. The picture remained neglected till our Lord came to show its meaning by identifying Himself with the Suffering Servant. No prophet is

[1] Besse, *Les Mystiques Bénédictines*, p. 226. (Paris, 1922.)

needed to proclaim that suffering is " common to the human race ". But here suffering has a peculiar function. It is both vicarious and redemptive. In other words it becomes reparation. We must deal with this aspect of suffering only in the present chapter. The problem of suffering itself is too large a one to occupy us here. But reparation is far too closely knitted with the contemplative vocation for us to leave it on one side. It showed itself perhaps first in its crudest, least conscious form in Moses' request that he might for the sake of his people be blotted out of the book which God had written (Ex. 32. 32).

The word " reparation " has commonly two meanings: (1) It may refer to the restoration of something damaged to its original state. So a broken bridge may be repaired and made as serviceable as before. It is useful to keep in mind this sense of restoring harm done throughout our thoughts on the subject. (2) The word is still more frequently employed to express the making amends for what can never be fully restored. If a man has robbed another of a thousand pounds, or failed to repay the loan of them, either he or another may make full reparation by producing another thousand pounds. But if he has slain that man's son, or wronged his wife, or unjustly ruined his reputation, the damage done is irreparable. Yet never was reparation more urgently needed. All he can do is to show his sorrow for his deed by offering some sort of substitute or compensation for a harm that can never be assessed.

Both these meanings enter into the reparation of the saints. But we shall miss its real significance if we fail to see that primarily with them it is a spontaneous urge, springing from their devotion to Christ crucified rather than from any formulated principle. It is rooted in the fact of the passion which Christ of His great love endured for man, and which every soul *éprise de Jésus* is drawn to desire to suffer too. That would be so even if our Lord Himself had not issued His challenge, " If any man would come after me, let him deny himself and take up his cross and follow me " (Mk. 8. 34). So St. Peter urged his readers to bear manfully the trials which were coming upon them, simply on the ground that Christ too had suffered, and they should be glad to be like Him even in this, " Forasmuch then as Christ suffered in the flesh, arm ye yourselves also with the same mind . . . Inasmuch as ye are partakers of Christ's sufferings, rejoice " (1 Pet. 4. 1, 13). Such

suffering was all part of the imitation of Christ. Yet inevitably it
was linked with the cause of His Passion. The saints realized very
clearly that their sins had been responsible for the agony He had
endured. They therefore welcomed every opportunity which
enabled them by suffering with Him to show their penitence,
and thus to make what amends they could for that for which
they could themselves never atone. From this point of view
suffering was the *wergild* which love bade them pay for the crucify-
ing of their Saviour.

But there was something further besides their own sins. There
was the world's sin—and there was the world's indifference to
Christ's work of love. So they felt themselves constrained to offer
themselves and their own pain in its behalf. Some of them felt
this call to reparation with a peculiar intensity. St. Catherine of
Siena held that even the smallest sin demanded infinite satisfaction,
because committed against an infinite God, and that God required
infinite contrition from every soul both for its own sins and for
those of others. The best way of showing that, and of making
some satisfaction, was by prayer for, and service of, one's neighbour;
for thus one could try to show one's love for God. Not that she
believed that her suffering could atone for sin. Finite pain could
never do that, but it was an attempt to express that perfect contrition which alone could win forgiveness. She made her own life,
so far as she could, an offering and a reparation for the world's sin,
particularly for the sins of scandalous priests and Religious, and for
others who, though members of Christ's Church, were yet regardless of the cost of their redemption. Her prayer for Pope Gregory
shows how fully she realized what such reparation involved:
" O Eternal God, let not Thy vicar yield to the counsels of the
flesh . . . nor let him permit himself to be terrified by any opposition,
and, Immortal God, if Thou art offended by his hesitation and
delays, punish them on my body, which I offer to Thee to be
tormented and destroyed according to Thy will and pleasure."[1]
The Dutch girl, St. Lydwine of Schiedam (1380–1433?) was
another of those who accepted eagerly the call to reparation.
A fall on the ice at the age of 15 reduced her to the role of permanent invalid, and one painful disease after another fastened on
her stricken body. But it was made clear to her that in some
mysterious way she was bearing something of the burden and

[1] *Life* by author of *M. Mori*, p. 185. (Methuen, London, 1907.)

misery of Europe, at that time even more than usual the prey of violence and suffering. The first shock had thrown her into an agony of weeping and depression, but afterwards her *curé* taught her the meaning of vicarious suffering. Then she delightedly accepted the burden, linking her own pain with the suffering of her Saviour on the Cross.[1]

During the Middle Ages this desire to make reparation appears again and again, but it was greatly stimulated later by the spread of the devotion to the Sacred Heart of Jesus. That devotion had a long history, going back to the days of St. Gertrude, St. Bernard, and beyond, but the seventeenth century saw a remarkable increase of it through the teaching of Cardinal Bérulle and Père Eudes. Mainly it was concerned with the Heart of Jesus yearning with love for man, and at first it showed itself in the attempt to answer love by love, the simple effort of the individual soul to give itself in love in response to His infinite love. But the Heart is a pierced heart. So here too the call to suffering sounded. St. Margaret Mary of Paray-le-Monial received in four visions a still further insight into the mystery. They directed her attention to the way in which our Lord's love was still scorned and rejected by the vast majority of the human race. Her devotion therefore took the form of a life to be lived in reparation for all this, expressing the penitence and love which both she herself and others ought to render to the Heart that was broken for them. It introduced an element of suffering deliberately accepted, and more suffering often deliberately undertaken, which was absent from the earlier devotion to the Sacred Heart. But it is important to remember that this reparation sprang from love answering to love rejected: the idea of meeting the claims of justice or of expiation for sins was not emphasized then, as it came to be later.

This persistent call to reparation, though intuitive in the saints, is something much more than an extravagance of devotion, a mysterious summons given to a few special souls. It has a solid enough basis in the teaching of the Church. The core of the Church's Faith lay in the redeeming work of Christ. Our Blessed Lord on the Cross bore the burden of the world's sin and all its load of suffering. By His death on the Cross and His rising again He had redeemed the whole world. The Cross of Christ is the

[1] See Huysmans, *St. Lydwine de Schiedam.*

key to life. His Passion avails for the sins of all men to the end of time. But Christ ascended into heaven, there to suffer no more. Yet in His mystical Body, the Church, He still lives on earth. The life of the Church Militant is not a repetition of His ministry and passion, but it is in a very real sense, as we have already seen, its perpetuation—a continual re-presentation to each succeeding age of that life and passion offered once for all on the Cross, never to be repeated. So St. Paul could truly say to the Colossians, " I rejoice in my sufferings for your sake, and fill up on my part that which is lacking of the sufferings of Christ in my flesh for his body's sake, which is the church " (Col. 1. 24). The truth was caught up and handed on from age to age. The epistle of the Gallican churches about the martyrs of Lyons in the second century spoke nobly of Sanctus's death: " His poor body was a witness to his sufferings, being one entire wound and scar, drawn together and broken out of all human shape. In him Christ suffered and achieved great glory, bringing the adversary to nought, and showing that there is nothing fearful where the Father's love is, nor painful where is Christ's glory."[1] St. Mechthild of Hackeborn (thirteenth century) learned the same truth from a slightly different angle when she heard our Lord say to her: " ' Behold I have ascended triumphant and glorious, and all thy burdens I have taken with me.' And in this word she understood that the necessities and tribulations of all men are present to Him, and that He Himself fighteth gloriously in us and for us."[2] St. Mechthild's devotion was centred in the Sacred Heart. There she was taught that, though Christ is now beyond suffering, yet His friends on earth offer to Him all that they suffer themselves, and that their endurance manifests here below the redemptive work of His Passion.[3] " Bear ye one another's burdens ", said the Apostle, " and so fulfil the law of Christ " (Gal. 6. 2). The greatest burden of all is the burden of sin with its harvest of suffering. Christ bore that burden " in His own body on the Cross ". There is a real sense in which His mystical Body to-day bears that burden. What is important is that its members should recognize this and fulfil their task in union with Him. The saints vividly realized this. Sometimes it shows itself in curious ways. An abbot once wrote to St. Bernard of Clairvaux to say that he had, when saying

[1] Trans. Bindley, p. 30.

[2] *Revelations*, Anon., p 61. (T. Richardson, London, 1875.).

[3] Cf. Besse, *Les Mystiques Bénédictines*, p. 265. (Paris, 1922.)

Mass, inadvertently consecrated a chalice which contained no wine, and asked what he ought to do. St. Bernard enjoined on him and his server a severe penance. But he went on to say that, if the brethren present were aware of what had happened, " I think they also should receive the discipline, that that may be fulfilled which is written, ' Bear ye one another's burden ' ".[1]

There is another element which contributes to the desire for reparation—what is known as the " solidarity of the human race ". Psychologists (e.g. Prof. Jung) have fastened on this and made fearsome use of it. But it finds its proper and deeper expression in the Catholic doctrine of the Communion of Saints. Men have for long realized that a human personality is no self-contained, independent entity, but that it is strangely woven in with other personalities. Even so we know little of the extent to which this interpenetration goes. To speak of a " collective unconscious " is merely to give a name to the unknown, and open the door to wild speculations. Nevertheless we are continually being startled by fresh evidence of inexplicable mental and spiritual bonds between persons. We may label them telepathy, thought-reading, or what we will, but we are still left face to face with a mystery. All this of course is a commonplace to-day. St. Paul was perhaps aware of it when he said, "If one member suffers all the members suffer with it" (I Cor. 12. 26.). It may show itself in what is called crowd psychology, as, for instance, when the people who had followed our Lord from place to place, hung upon His words, and at times almost worshipped Him, at last, moved by some sudden gust of passion, with one voice yelled in fury for His death. It shows itself again in the spirit that spreads through a whole nation or even a continent, as Nazism spread through Germany. Or it can appear in a mysterious sympathy between two persons, as between mother and child, or between twins, when, though far distant from one another, each will fall sick or grow sad in unison with the other.

In the Communion of Saints, the Mystical Body of Christ, this interpenetration is more delicate and more spiritual. It is St. Paul again who first proclaimed the mystery, " Whether one member suffereth all the members suffer with it; or one member is honoured, all the members rejoice with it " (I Cor. 12. 26).

[1] Migne, *P.L.*, CLXXXII, 179.

Faithful communicants, who have been separated by death from
some dearly loved one, know well how real is that communion
with the Church at Rest. In the plague that swept through Siena
in St. Catherine's day, six small nieces of hers died, to whom she
was deeply attached. As she buried one of them she was heard to
murmur, " At least I shall not lose this one ". That cry showed
not only her attitude towards life here, but even more her understanding of the communion of saints. Indeed, wherever Christ is
preached, glimpses of the mystery are vouchsafed. The Quaker
tailor in America, John Woolman (1772) had once a vision of
which he says, " O Lord my God! the amazing horrors of darkness
were gathered around me and covered me all over and I saw no
way to go forth. I felt the depth and extent of the misery of my
fellow-creatures separated from the Divine harmony, and it was
heavier than I could bear, and I was crushed down under it."[1]
George Fox, too, felt that he was born to bear in his own person
the burden and grief of the world's sin. " He bears the iniquity
wherever he comes ", a contemporary said of him.

From the closeness of this communion, this mysterious interpenetration of personalities, it follows that the actions, and perhaps
even more the thoughts and dispositions, of one must have some
effect on others—an effect which it is impossible to calculate.
Just as if one end of an iron rod be heated in the furnace the heat
spreads along the rod, so if one soul be plunged in the fire of God's
love others feel the warmth of it. Or if he be sunk in malice and
rebellion the evil spreads likewise. Thus even on a natural level
the efforts of the saints towards holiness must have some reparative
value. On that level alone their desire for reparation is no senti-
mental extravagance, but sober reason. The closer the links
between the members of a community, the more obvious does
this become. In the seventeenth century two Red Indians (Hurons)
murdered a French settler, and the French demanded compensation.
The tribe paid the fine but made no attempt to punish the murderers,
on the ground that their punishment lay in the shame they would
feel for the sacrifices the rest of the tribe had made for them.[2]
Their action was due, not to any religious idealism, but simply
to their understanding of the natural working of communal
life.

[1] *Journal*, p. 247. (Headley, London, 1903.)
[2] Parkman, *Jesuits in North America*, p. 454. (G. Morang, Toronto, 1898

The saints, however, did not calculate their reparation according to the influence they might have on others. St. Patrick, when confronted by an opponent, sometimes used to " fast against him ". He was not alone in that practice, but it scarcely comes under the head of reparation. It was rather an attempt to win spiritual power to overcome the opposition. And it produced amazing results. Von Hügel tells of a nun who adopted a somewhat similar method. She had heard that an old pupil of hers was living in open sin. She therefore wrote to plead with her. She said that she was scourging herself as an act of reparation for her every day till the blood ran, and would continue to do so until she abandoned her evil course. But that seems an attempt to force the girl's will out of consideration for herself rather than a true act of reparation— a method that might be dangerous to both. Yet here there is certainly an element of expiation undertaken by one for the sin of another. We have already noticed how in the Middle Ages the idea of expiation figured largely in the minds of some saints; how, for instance, St. Lydwine felt that she was suffering for the sins of Europe and offered her pains in union with Christ's Passion as some kind of expiation. It harmonized with the medieval emphasis on justice, and with the legal, almost feudal, theory of the atonement then held. The alarming increase of violence, suffering, and godlessness in those days had given a tremendous impetus to that desire for atonement. It cropped out in the wild extravagances of the Flagellants, who toured the country in bands, scourging one another in procession as they went. It lay behind some of those sudden conversions, when men playing some great part in world affairs, threw up everything to retire to monastery or hermitage. And whenever those periodical eruptions from the volcano of evil have taken place during the centuries, they have been countered with similar efforts in reparation.

Devotion to the Sacred Heart in the seventeenth century gave a new turn to the call to reparation. It attempted to offer to the rejected love of Christ an intensity of love which would in some way meet His demand for love. The pierced Heart of Jesus would be answered by the burning heart of His servant, a heart also pierced by suffering. The expiatory, substitutionary element never entirely died out. Indeed the desire for reparation is too closely bound up with our Lord's redemptive work for that to be possible. And it reappears from time to time in unexpected quarters. General

Gordon, deeply moved by the wrongs committed by his fellow-countrymen upon the natives of Egypt, wrote from Khartoum in 1884: " May our Lord not visit us as a nation for our sins, but may His wrath fall on me, hid in Christ. This is my frequent prayer, and may He spare these people, and give them peace." He refused to escape while it was within his power to do so, and calmly met his death, when the victorious troops of the Mahdi forced their way into the town a few months later.[1]

The Church gives us good reason to believe that the sufferings of the members of Christ's Body, as linked with His redemptive sacrifice on the Cross, possess a special value—that they are something more than a sympathetic sharing of the sufferings of others, or ' Christ Himself. Our Lord Himself suggests it. In His description of the horrors attendant upon the destruction of Jerusalem, " tribulation such as hath not been seen from the beginning of the world until now, no, nor ever shall be ", He went on to say that " except those days had been shortened, no flesh would have been saved ", and then added, " But for the elects' sake those days shall be shortened " (Matt. 24. 21 f.). Moreover there is the mystery of the massacre of the Innocents, set down starkly at the beginning of the gospel without a word of explanation. A recent writer has said of that: " The feast of the Holy Innocents should be one of the most consoling in the Church's year. . . . It is the festival of all *innocent* suffering, as sanctified and rendered atoning by union with Christ Incarnate and Crucified. In virtue of solidarity, not only the suffering of the deliberate martyr atones, but even the suffering of those who are martyrs in deed alone."[2] The innocent suffering of our Blessed Lord Himself, the Lamb without spot or stain, wrought the world's salvation—so great a good out of so heinous a crime. Even His blessed and glorious Mother, who had no sin of her own for which to atone, was drawn into the work, her own soul pierced with the sword, " that the thoughts out of many hearts may be revealed "—strange mysterious prophecy fore-shadowing her share in her Son's work of reparation. And through the Church's history it is they who have lived most close to Christ who have been called most into the fellowship of His sufferings.

The urge to reparation lies embedded in that amazing desire,

---

[1] Butler, *Life of General Gordon*, p. 200.
[2] E. I. Watkin, *Catholic Centre*, p. 194.

even preference, for suffering, which marks the lives of the saints.
St. Paul declares that to know the " fellowship of Christ's sufferings " is one of the three things which it was his one desire to
know, for which he had given up all other things and did count
them but as dung (Phil. 3. 8). The longing to realize more deeply
the meaning of their Saviour's sufferings leads at once to the
longing to share in the purpose for which He endured them.
It is the work of supernatural charity, God's own love for man
taking possession of their souls. A saint, offered in a vision a
jewelled crown and a crown of thorns, chose the latter. But the
purpose underlying the choice of suffering redeems it from morbidity. With the great saints it is never suffering for suffering's
sake. The reproach of masochism has frequently of late been
levelled against this desire for suffering. It behoves us to consider
what justice the reproach may have. Masochism is a perverted
form of the sex-instinct, a man seeking the stimulation of that
instinct through pain inflicted upon him by the beloved, just as
sadism is the perversion which finds that stimulation in the inflic-
tion of pain. It differs *toto caelo* from the desire of the saints to
bear something of the world's burden of suffering, and in particular to share in Christ's Passion for the world. So to share is
indeed to know something of the " fellowship of His sufferings ",
for it is not suffering for suffering's sake (which is barren), nor
merely suffering because our Lord suffered, but it is suffering
which in union with His has value and takes part in His redeeming
work, profitable for others as for oneself. The folly of the Cross
has transformed the meaninglessness of pain. Here lies the secret
of the saints' joy in it. As Eckhart says, " Suffering for thyself, in
whatever way, the suffering hurts thee and is hard to bear. But
suffering for God and God alone, thy suffering hurts thee not nor
does it burden thee, for God bears the load."[1]

In itself, suffering is an evil. It is a privation of that good
which God created and intended for all men. Therefore no man
may desire it for its own sake. That does not mean that all suffering
is necessarily due to sin. Men have argued, perhaps rightly, that
the very fact of the creation of a finite world involves pain. As
one of them has expressed it, " We cannot say that *all* suffering is
the consequence of sin. It may be true that part of the pain in
which the whole creation groans and travails together is an

[1] *Works*, I, p. 37, trans. C. de B. Evans. (T. Watkins, London, 1924.)

inevitable accompaniment of creation as such; that to make a world at all, a world that should be *other* than God, involved a self-limitation of the Infinite of which pain, and pain of which He could not and would not escape the burden for Himself, is a necessary aspect."[1] N. Berdyaev put it a little differently when he maintained that suffering was due to freedom. At any rate the fact remains that suffering is woven inextricably with the world as it is. Every religion has to come to grips with it somehow or other. Hedonism tries to ignore it. Christian Science pretentiously denies its existence. Buddhism accepts it as the very principle of life and finds the only solution in the disintegration of personality, release from the wheel of life. Only Christianity fairly faces it and claims victory over it through the redeeming work of Christ. Christ won the victory, not by avoiding pain, but by enduring its full force and breaking its power. Through Him suffering, which was the most useless, most inexplicable fact in the universe, was transformed into a weapon of triumph. Ever since His resurrection His chosen ones have understood something of His secret, of the mystery of the Cross. No wonder they have loved to share in it. In Christ crucified they have seen the barren tree of pain blossom abundantly and bring forth fruit for the healing of nations, and they have eagerly accepted the call to share in the mystery. Therein lies the essence of reparation. St. Mechthild of Hackeborn in one of her moments of vision asked our Lord how one may make reparation for the agony He had endured; but she desired that it should be at the same time an act of praise and thanksgiving.

But there is something further. If it be granted that suffering linked with our Lord's Passion benefits others, it is small wonder that it came to be prized above any other work for them. In all the active works I undertake self enters in so largely. It is I who think and plan and carry into execution. The more successful the result seems, the more difficult it is not to take some of the glory for myself, filching something from the glory due to God. The offering is smirched with self. But here in suffering it is so little my work. I am conscious only of pain and failure, a cold heart and distracted mind, blindly uniting myself with my crucified Saviour and offering Him to the Father. For the moment at any rate I am intensely aware that I am nothing and have nothing but just the pain. "Nothing in my hand I bring." Less here than

[1] Burnaby, *Amor Dei*, 306. (Hodder & Stoughton, London, 1938.)

anywhere does self enter in to spoil the prayer. Its role has become almost entirely passive—and God does all. The suffering soul can no longer live according to his own desiring and scheming, but it can live in God, carried along on the flood-tide of the divine will. Perhaps this is something of what St. Peter meant when he wrote, " He that hath suffered in the flesh hath ceased from sin, that ye should no longer live the rest of your time in the flesh to the lusts of men, but to the will of God " (1 Pet. 4. 1, 2). The apostle was speaking of the redemptive value of our Lord's suffering and of His glad acceptance of it for the world, and he urged his readers to follow that example, " Arm yourselves with the same mind ".

St. Paul corroborates this when he insists that the glory of God, the life of Jesus, shines most clearly through us when we are most weak. Indeed God seems to delight in reducing His servants to impotence, in order that there might be least hindrance to His power working through them, that " no flesh should glory in His presence ". " We have this treasure in earthen vessels, in order that the exceeding greatness of the power might be God's, not ours . . . for always we who are alive are being handed over to death for Jesus' sake, in order that the life of Jesus may be made manifest in our mortal flesh." (2 Cor. 4. 7, 11.)

This is hard doctrine for most of us. We like to feel that we are really " doing something ", " being useful ". Here we learn that merely to suffer " for Jesus' sake "—to " bear about in our bodies the dying of Jesus "—is to do most of all. It is one of the secrets which the saints were ever proclaiming and it inspired all their reparation.

But if reparation thus depends on Christ's work, and that work is perpetuated in His mystical Body, the Church, then it cannot be reserved only for a few elect souls whom we call " Saints ". The privilege of taking part in it must belong to every member of that Body. Some indeed are called to a deeper partici-pation in it than others, as some are called to more prayer than others. But all have some part to play in the mystery. The problem is, How can we play it? We read of the labours of the saints, the nights they spent in prayer, and their heroic endurance of pain. We know that we could not face such things ourselves,

nor indeed are most of us called to it, for God has placed us in
different circumstances. Our temptation then is to think that there
is nothing for us to do in that way. But we come back to the fact
of our membership in the Body of Christ, and realize that we too
are therefore bound up in this mystery of reparation. What can
we do?

(1) We can pray according to the capacity given to us. It may
not be much now, but it can grow. The Religious, before joining
in the Divine Office, prays silently each time, offering the service
to God in union with the same intention with which Christ Himself offered on earth His praise to the Father. Christ's prayer was
gathered up supremely on the Cross, offered in pain for the
redemption of the world. Each prayer of ours therefore offered
in union with that, partakes of that redemptive character. It
includes reparation both for our own sin and for the world's,
and its shortcomings are made good through His perfect work.
Inasmuch as true prayer means the uniting of our wills with His,
there can be no greater way of reparation, and it lies at the root of,
and inspires, whatever other forms reparation may take. It is
significant that those who have been called to dedicate their lives
most to prayer as contemplatives have most felt the call to reparation, and experienced the effectiveness of prayer. It was so, we
have seen, with St. Catherine of Siena. So it was with the two
Carmelite nuns who both died in their early twenties at the
beginning of this century, girls who had lived such sheltered lives
that one might have expected them to have grown up almost
untouched by the world's " giant agony ". They were St. Thérèse
of Lisieux, and Sister Elizabeth of the Blessed Trinity. The latter
once wrote, " The happy people in this world are those with
enough self-contempt and self-forgetfulness to choose the cross for
their lot."[1] Indeed the cross lays its mark upon such prayer as we
are considering. Another Frenchwoman (Lucie Christine) con-
fesses that often, when she was making her communion or praying
as an act of reparation, trouble and unspeakable anguish descended
on her soul, although at the same time our Lord made her realize
the closeness of her union with Him.[2]

The value of prayer as reparation was made clear in one of the

[1] *The Praise of Glory*, p. 193. (Burns, Oates & Washbourne, fifth English ed.)
[2] *Journal*, p. 130. (Paris, 1920.)

visions granted to St. Margaret Mary, when she heard our Lord ask of her that she should spend the hour between 11 p.m. and midnight every Thursday prostrate, in union with His agony in Gethsemane, for those who still rejected Him. That vision led to the devotion known as the Holy Hour, a devotion which has been widely adopted far beyond the cloister, and can indeed be practised in some form or other by anyone—in the privacy of a bedroom if not in church. And if Thursday night is impossible, a more suitable hour can be found. Different individuals will employ the time in different ways, according to their own methods of prayer. One will find the rosary most useful; another will spend it in wordless prayer; a third with acts and affections. One useful way at any rate for beginners is to give part of the hour to adoration, adoring God Incarnate in the mystery of Gethsemane; part to thanksgiving for so great love and condescension; part to acts of penitence for their own sin and the world's; and the rest to intercession. But whatever the method, the *leitmotiv* underlying it is union with our blessed Lord in His agony. If pain and weariness come during the hour, they will be accepted gladly as a means of entering more deeply into that.

(2) Life brings to most of us day by day its own trials, sickness, disappointments, pains of body or mind, the crossing of our wills, the disturbance of our comfort. Even vagaries of the weather impose their hardships. All such can form a valuable means for our own personal discipline. In fact we know that they are the best forms of such discipline. But we can use them also as acts of reparation. Once again it gives us the opportunity of turning the apparently meaningless, vexatious things into an instrument of priceless value for serving others. In so far as we grasp this we catch again a glimpse of the joy the saints found in their suffering. There is nothing morbid, for instance, when seized with pain in accepting it gladly and uniting it with our Lord's own perfect sacrifice for others, specially for those who may be suffering in the same way, yet without the light that shines on it from the Cross to comfort and uphold them. Something similar may be done when attacked by some dire temptation. But we must remember that to accept it gladly does not mean that we must not at the same time seek to resist and overcome with all our force either temptation or sickness. Such things God allows to come to us sometimes as a challenge to our courage and trust. There is much

truth in the words which Browning put into the mouth of the
Pope, though perhaps they contain a note of over-confidence in
man's own strength—

> Why comes temptation but for man to meet
> And master and make crouch beneath his foot,
> And so be pedestaled in triumph? Pray
> " Lead us into no such temptations, Lord! "
> Yea, but, O Thou, whose servants are the bold,
> Lead such temptations by the head and hair
> Reluctant dragons up to who dares fight,
> That so he may do battle and have praise!

(*The Ring and the Book*, Bk. X.)

Richard Rolle says more simply, " God suffers the devil for to
tempt good men for their profit that they may be the higher
crowned when they have through His help overcome so cruel an
enemy."[1] But the individual helps not only himself by his victory,
but other members of the Body of Christ.

Thus all the little pains and vexations of daily life, as well as
the great agonies, can be ut'lized in this work of reparation. It
opens up a vast field of service within the range of the weakest
Christian. It was characteristic of St. Thérèse of Lisieux that she
should thus employ the little things as well as the great. She was
told to take a short walk each day. She was ill at the time and
the walk meant considerable pain to her. Yet she took it with
unfailing regularity. One of the Sisters urged her to desist, because
of the pain. " Yes ", she answered, " it is painful: but do you
know what enables me to do it? I do it for a missionary. I think
that away in a far country one of them is perhaps exhausted in his
labours, and to lessen his weariness I offer mine to God."[2] Yet a
word of warning must be sounded. Reparation can only be of
value if it is offered in a spirit of simplicity and humility. It means,
it is true, the offering of ourselves, to be linked with our Lord in
His offering of Himself on the Cross, for the redemption of the
world. But that is the ordinary vocation of His followers—to
take up their cross. They must die with Him if they are to rise
with Him—as St. Paul made so clear. But if we begin to talk
about ourselves as " victim souls " or the like, there is a danger of
sentimentality and exaggeration. It is much safer to accept our

[1] " Form of Perfect Living ", p. 19, *Selected Works*. (Longmans, London, 1930.)
[2] *Histoire d'une âme*, Ch. XXII.

pain and offer it for others as just a small act of love, and at the same time to accept it as after all only what we deserve. St. Philip Neri was fully aware of this danger when his Oratory began to grow and men began to praise the devotion of its members. There was a refreshing sanity about his remark: " There is no need to boast: we are nothing: no one of the congregation has shed his blood for the Faith yet."

(3) There is yet another way. Those who have most heeded the call to reparation have felt the urge to something further than merely accepting what comes. They have sought deliberately additional forms of suffering. To most people the idea of self-inflicted pain seems definitely wrong. Here more than ever they think there seems justification for the charge of masochism or morbidity. Besides there is no evidence that Christ Himself, our perfect exemplar, ever inflicted pain upon Himself, but contented Himself with what was thrust upon Him. Nor in the first ages of the Church is there record of any such practices, though St. Paul did say that he buffeted his body and brought it into subjection (1 Cor 9. 27). The truth is that in those days the simple profession of Christianity usually brought in its train more than enough of pain and hardship—persecution, ridicule, possible loss of goods, and even of life itself. There was no need to seek out more ways of sharing in the Saviour's Passion. Later on the scene shifted, and Christians normally had none of those things to fear. Yet still sin abounded and the world went its way regardless of Christ's love. The desire for reparation grew. The practice of undergoing special penances spread. And the Church has always recognized their value.

It is not always easy to distinguish exactly what is meant by the self-inflicted pain to which the objection is raised. Our Lord Himself fasted and made it clear that His disciples should fast, and the Church has always stressed its importance. That was a form of pain voluntarily taken upon Himself, and there are many who would prefer the pain of the rod to the pain of hunger. Furthermore He spent whole nights in prayer, again voluntarily laying an extra burden on the body. How far could that be called self-inflicted pain? At any rate His followers in later years found other ways of entering into His sufferings. We need not enumerate them here, nor attempt to justify, e.g., St. Simeon Stylites' bizarre existence on a pillar, nor the practice of standing for hours in ice-cold water. A whole book could well be written on the "follies of the saints". Less extravagant practices have had their place in the lives of saints and of countless others in the story of the Church, such as the use of the discipline, the wearing of a hair shirt, or praying with arms outstretched crosswise. It would be presumptuous in the face of such compelling witness throughout the ages to condemn or even discourage them as too dangerous. Christianity itself is an explosive thing and it would never have spread far if men had shrunk from the dangers it involves.

Nevertheless the dangers are real; all the more as such devices must depend largely for their use upon the *attrait* or judgement of the individual. We spoke just now (p. 271) of masochism, distinguishing it sharply from the saints' call to reparation and suffering. Yet it is possible sometimes to discern in the desire for mortifications (especially amongst women) the tendency to take a perverse pleasure in physical pain. The voluntary undertaking of pain would then become a kind of self-indulgence and defeat its own aim.

A much greater danger lies in a pandering to self-will bringing self-righteousness in its train. The individual begins to take upon himself practices about which he has heard, subconsciously choosing those which bring him a measure of self-satisfaction. Not only will he cling obstinately to them at wrong times, but he comes to despise others who follow a different course.

All this points to the importance of the Director. It is his ...nce to guide souls in these difficult questions, to distinguish the voice of the Holy Spirit within them from the promptings of self-will, and to judge how far any particular soul may rightly and safely use this or that method of following the call to reparation. Moreover under wise direction the individual is delivered by his obedience from just that danger of self-will, whilst he is assured of the genuineness of the inspiration that had come to him. What really matters in this question, as in most others connected with the following of Christ, is the motive that lies behind the action. It is this which the Director will examine most carefully. Where the aim seems mainly suffering for suffering's sake, as though there were value in the mere fact of suffering, or where the soul would be entering upon a spiritual rivalry through pride or thinking that the pain undergone could itself atone for sin, then no good could emerge from such practices and they should be discountenanced. Nor must the desire to make reparation for others be adulterated with that subtle self-seeking which looks for a kind of boomerang effect of the act as a means of gaining merit for oneself. It must mean the attempt to enter more deeply into Christ's suffering for their sin, and to bear something of the shame and pain that they ought to feel. And they are to get all the benefit.

The saints threw themselves into the work of reparation with a whole-heartedness and simplicity which left little room for that extreme self-consciousness which plagues our own generation. For the most part they were as free from morbidity over it as a young man breaking the ice for his morning cold bath. Sometimes in fact it was for them literally a cold bath, if a prolonged one. It is a healthy and right thing to desire to realize more intensely the pain, pain of body as well as of soul, which our Lord endured for ourselves and for all. After all, His Passion on the Cross was something much more than a beautiful idyll of unselfishness, lived out under the blue sky of Palestine nearly two thousand years ago. It was the horrible, sickening torture of a human body, undergone for us. Moreover, the Cross stretches out its arms over the centuries and we live in the shadow of it and share its reality. " I am crucified with Christ ", cried St. Paul, so completely had the truth come home to him. Anything that brings that home more vividly to us too is to be welcomed. Body and soul help one another. A little physical pain, voluntarily borne or even self-given, with the right motive, can powerfully aid the soul in its realization of part at least of our Lord's agony. One caveat should be entered here. Whatever practices are undertaken they should not be such as to injure the health and incapacitate the body from doing its work. That does not mean that one must not fast because it results in a slight headache, nor use the discipline because it makes the back a little sore. The body itself as a rule responds and adapts itself to treatment, and is all the better for it.

(4) We should, however, miss the real significance of reparation were we to identify it with suffering. For one thing it might tempt us to think that the essence of our redemption lay in the amount of pain endured by our Lord on the Cross. " O Saviour of the world ", we rightly cry, " who by Thy cross and precious blood hast redeemed us, save us and help us." The Church knows

what it means when it prays so. We know that the essential thing
was the perfect obedience of our Lord to the Father's will. " Lo,
I come to do thy will, O God." Man's sin, and sin only, made
the suffering necessary. It is right that we sinners should keep the
Cross before our eyes. Yet even in Gethsemane our Lord's cry
is still, " Thy will be done ". And He summed up His own work
of reparation in the words: " For their sakes I sanctify (consecrate)
myself that they themselves also may be sanctified (consecrated) in
truth " (Jn. 17. 19). That is not only His own self-dedication but
that also of His followers to the work. It means the glad giving
of the whole self in purity and love to God to be united with
Him in His loving purpose of redemption. It thus includes the
whole of life, its joyous as well as its painful aspects. In other
words the best reparation we can make is to live day by day for
" the praise of His glory". The more perfectly we do that, the more
nearly do we fulfil the purpose of our creation and enter into the
joy of our Lord, the more completely do we through grace repair
the havoc wrought by sin in ourselves. And although we look,
and must look, in all that simply to God, " for their sakes " will
be twined about it like a golden thread, and the Father will accept
it so for the sake of His beloved Son.

Reparation thus can only be a symbol of love. However much
we believe in the treasury of grace and the merits of the saints,
we shall be far from thinking that we ourselves can make reparation for our own sins, let alone for others' sins as well. " We are
unprofitable servants; we have done but that which it was our
duty to do." (Luke 17. 10.) We know that our Lord Jesus Christ
Himself made the " one full perfect and sufficient sacrifice, oblation,
and satisfaction for the sins of the whole world", and there is
nothing to add to that. But we may seek to be united more
closely with Him in that perfect work and to help others to realize
the same. That cannot be done without suffering. What we can
do is to learn more clearly the meaning of suffering and how to
use it aright. That admits us into the secret of the sons of God,
to some understanding of that amazing joy which the saints found
in suffering—a joy that was free from all trace of morbidity because
they were looking beyond the pain to their Risen and Ascended
Lord, who " for the joy that was set before him, endured the
cross, despising shame, and hath sat down at the right hand of the
throne of God " (Heb. 12. 2).

CHAPTER XVII

THE FINAL STAGES

THE Dark Night of the Soul, as we saw, is far from being a period of unrelieved gloom and suffering. The Cloud of Unknowing grows a little more luminous. Even though darkness may reign as the senses are concerned, within there burns a deeper and more constant desire for God, usually too a deeper peace and joy and a greater recollection, whilst the work of purification goes on. Very many in this state are granted flashes of light when the darkness is riven, or moments of more rapt communion. The saints speak of a " Prayer of Union ", when the soul is more deeply absorbed in God. Deeper still is the absorption in ecstasy and rapture. All these are normally of short duration; St. Teresa gives half an hour as the limit for the " Prayer of Union ".[1] Visions are granted to many at this stage. It is interesting to notice how carefully some of the recipients distinguish between visions seen with the bodily eyes, those seen with the imagination, and what they call" intellectual " visions. St. Teresa with her customary lucidity distinguishes them most clearly. Blessed Angela speaks of some she saw with the " eyes of the body " and others with the " eyes of the mind ". Sometimes the soul hears God speaking deep within in " locutions ", and it knows at once the difference between that and any words that come to it in any other way. Lucie Christine only echoes the teaching of the great masters when she says of such locutions that they " always effect what they say ", and that the abiding result is an " increase of peace and love ". So Blessed Angela in a time of spiritual anguish and desolation received the message, " When you think you are most forsaken, then are you most near to and dear to God "—and a great peace at once filled her soul.

In the olden days men valued very highly such phenomena, and they were welcomed eagerly. Biographers accepted them at

[1] *Interior Castle*, 5th Mansions.

their face value and recorded them at length. They concentrated
their attention upon them and in some cases gave them a central
place in their stories, making their heroes fit into a conventional
pattern of sanctity. Our modern psychological outlook has made
us much more reserved in our estimate of them: indeed we tend to
explain them all away. But no amount of psychological knowledge
or scientific outlook can ever prevent their being used by God as
a means of revealing His will to His children. The human soul
does possess the capacity for some such visionary experiences.
They may proceed from natural causes, but there is no reason to
doubt that God makes use of that capacity from time to time for
His own purposes, as He uses man's more ordinary endowments.
Not only is the Old Testament full of such divine visitations, but
they are also to be found in the New, and the outpouring of the
Holy Spirit at Pentecost seems to have increased for the Christian
his capacity in this direction. We need not then be surprised that
men of old valued them highly. But what is much more surprising and at the same time reassuring is that the great masters
of prayer, who lived in those uncritical days, should even then
have regarded them with a discriminating eye. St. Teresa certainly
sets great store by all such " revelations ", but she always recognizes
their relative unimportance, and distinguishes sharply between the
good and the bad. St. John of the Cross is much more sweeping
in his attitude towards them. Not that he was sceptical, but that
he regarded them as at best but temporary helps, which were
much more likely to be hindrances. They made their appeal
through the senses, but in contemplation God was communicating
Himself in a new and better way. Besides God had once for all
revealed all that was necessary through the coming of the Lord
Jesus. Visions and locutions therefore were unnecessary. Ecstasies
happened because the contemplative's soul and body were not yet
attuned to the shock of the divine inrush. In time they would
adapt themselves and ecstasies cease. Visions play a much greater
part in the life of St. Catherine of Siena, but there is a similar
robustness in her attitude towards them, and in her quick rejection
of all that was unhealthy and rang false.

In these matters as in all else the Christian contemplative looks
to our Blessed Lord Himself as the perfect exemplar. He enjoyed
always the vision of God, His communion with the Father, unbroken
and undimmed, in a degree far beyond the capacity of fallen man,

for God " giveth not the spirit by measure unto him " (Jn. 3. 34).
Yet the Gospels give no hint of any ecstatic experiences in His life
on earth. Neither the Transfiguration nor the agony in Gethsemane
seems to have corresponded to the phenomenon of ecstasy. The
vision of God is the fulfilment of man's whole being, the purpose
of his creation. It must therefore involve the perfect harmony of
body and soul, not such a disorganization of them as ecstasy seems
to involve. The unclouded vision of God is not his portion whilst
he is still on earth, but the closer he grows towards it, as in the
highest forms of prayer, the more accustomed does his body
become to the shock of the encounter.

We cannot discuss here these physical and psychical reactions
of contemplation. It is enough both to point out the fact and
frequency of their occurrence, and at the same time to say that,
as the saints themselves recognized, they are non-essentials, by-
products of that union of God with the soul, which no words
could describe. In these phenomena, as in the Dark Night, the
experience of the mystics shows a great variety. This is due partly
to the difference in their emotional make-up, some being tempera-
mentally far more prone to such things and far more influenced
by them than others. Another cause lies in the difference of *milieu*
and upbringing, partly intellectual, partly emotional. Different
groups produced different types of mysticism. And the more
receptive a man was by temperament, the more readily would
he correspond to type. We have already marked the difference
between the Franciscan and German schools in their experience of
the Dark Night. So the Carmelite, modelled on St. John of the
Cross, would tend towards a much more sober experience of these
phenomena than say a Franciscan such as Jacopone da Todi. But
underneath all the variety of expression there lies the same fundamental experience. [The tendency to be moulded subconsciously
by one's spiritual environment reveals itself, of course, in other
ways too. Take for instance the phenomena of sudden conversion.
Since the Reformation certain sects have attached enormous
importance to them, and there they occur with an almost monotonous frequency. John Wesley's preaching offers an interesting
illustration of this. His early sermons, though they had great
effect on souls, led to no extraordinary exterior manifestations.
Then during one sermon a kind of frenzy seized one or two of his
hearers. It alarmed Wesley at first. Soon he came to regard it as

an important sign of true conversion—with the result that the same phenomenon became increasingly common.]

Some souls are called to go turther. We have spoken of the last and more terrible phase of the Dark Night, which forms the final purification for the Spiritual Espousals and Marriage. The cost is stupendous and few souls can pay it. " To be espoused to the King of Heaven", says St. Teresa, " requires more courage than you can imagine."[1] When the purification is over, the soul is ready for the closest union with God possible to man on earth, in light and love and peace. Throughout the centuries those who have been vouchsafed this experience, have employed the metaphor of marriage in the effort to give some indication of its richness. Some of them have pressed the analogy to an extent which seems almost indecent to the outsider, though they have strenuously insisted that their words must not be understood literally. They are speaking of something quite other than human love. But, after all, what closer analogy could they use than marriage to express such a union? For marriage is the richest and completest union of persons known to man. Those psychologists are far wide of the mark who attribute these descriptions to repressed sex desires. The contemplative possesses something of the nature of the poet or artist. Like them he has his vision, a vision far transcending theirs and therefore still less capable of being put into words. So, like them, he is driven to the use of symbols, symbols which have some real analogy to his experience, but can only point to it and suggest what he is incapable of describing. Only they are not self-chosen symbols; they have been forged in the heat of the experience, and have been the means by which the man himself has been helped to realize what has been taking place in his soul. St. Catherine of Siena was made aware that she had been granted the state called Spiritual Marriage in a vision where a ring was bestowed upon her by the child Jesus. She never doubted the genuineness of the vision, but she knew at the same time that it was only a symbol of an ineffable happening.

To deal at length with this final stage of contemplative prayer is beyond the scope of this book. The reader is referred to the masters themselves, specially to Bl. John Ruysbroeck (*Adornment of the Spiritual Marriage*), St. Teresa (*Interior Castle, Sixth and*

---

[1] *Interior Castle*, 6th Mansions.

Seventh Mansions, and *Life*), St. John of the Cross (*Spiritual Canticle and Living Flame*). But as we read their attempts to describe their experience, four characteristics of the Spiritual Marriage stand out very clearly. It will be sufficient briefly to call attention to them here.

(1) It means for them the flooding of a great light into the dim contemplation of the Dark Night. They see clearly and realize vividly what before had been dimly revealed. So the new experience is not something entirely different, cancelling the old. Rather is it the confirmation, the reassurance that it was in truth God Himself who had been holding them and making Himself known to them in the dark, that it really was excess of light which had been blinding them. But clearly it has for them a unique character. It is not just one more vision or rapture, like others they may have received. It introduces them into a new and permanent state of a decisively deepened intimacy with God.

(2) They speak of it as a transforming union. The phrase goes back to a still more daring expression of the Greek Fathers, " deification ". It brings to them the conviction that the soul, at last purged from its stains, is transformed into the likeness of the Lord Jesus, and united so closely with God in Him that it is as it were swallowed up in God, whilst still retaining its own identity. The attempt to describe this leads them sometimes into strange contradictory statements, because indeed they are dealing with something which transcends logic. No wonder critics have accused them sometimes of pantheism and produced quotations which seem to justify their plaint. None of them perhaps has more boldly stated the paradox than Bl. John Ruysbroeck, who loved to speak of the union with God " without means ", or of the " wayless wandering in the super-essential Love ". He was trying to express just that mystery of a union between the infinite God and finite man, where the impossible thing has been made possible through the unimaginable condescension of God. But neither he nor any other saint seeks for the absorption of himself in the divine. What they want is union, the closest union attainable, but for that there must always be the two, the self and God. Ruysbroeck himself at times uses language which seems to imply absorption, so eager is he for the closest union, but he always inserts some saving clause. The very use of the metaphor of

marriage would seem to safeguard the Christian contemplatives from any doctrine of absorption. They use it because it has scriptural authority, and because it deals with the most intimate union of two personalities known to man. But its whole meaning would be lost if actual absorption took place, so that lover could no longer contemplate the Beloved, nor the Beloved the lover, both being merged into one. Even so exact a theologian as St. John of the Cross in speaking of Spiritual Marriage does not hesitate to say that then " the soul is made divine and becomes God by participation, in so far as may be in this life ". A little further on he says that there " is effected such union of the two natures and such communication of the divine nature to the human, that, while neither of them changes its being, each of them appears to be God ".[1] He insists both on the deification of the soul and on the retention of its own distinctness in the union.

It is natural that, so united, the contemplative should be occupied more and more wholly with the Blessed Trinity. All that turning towards Him which we noticed in habitual contemplation finds now its justification and its fruition.

(3) The soul has gained a poise which it never had before. As St. Catherine of Siena put it, God no longer plays the " game of love " with it. By that she meant that those periods of desola-tion and distress alternating with the periods of ecstasy and i , no longer take place. They were, on one side, natural reactions of the soul to the strain imposed upon it by the supernatural visitations; on another side, God's discipline of it to fit it for the closer union. Already the contemplative had reached some measure of equilibrium before the last phase of the Dark Night descended upon him. But now the work of purification is nearly done and the Dark Night is passed. It is true that many who have reached this last stage have known days of desolation and spiritual distress, e.g. St. Marie de l'Incarnation and Lucie Christine, but they were of short dura-tion and the depths of the soul remained in peace and certainty. Their union with the eternal and unchanging God has been consummated, and " the sense of stability is the keynote of the super-essential beatitude, the bliss of God in which His children participate " (Ruysbroeck).

[1] *Spiritual Canticle*, 2nd redaction, Stanza XXII.

(4) Suffering takes on a new colour in the brighter light. The end of the " game of love " by no means brings an end to suffering of mind or body. Here again this only develops what the contemplative had begun to feel in the Dark Night. Then he had come to recognize the place of suffering, and even to welcome it as a necessary element in his own purification and as a sharing in the misfortunes of his fellow-creatures.

But now the emphasis is thrown more than ever on his union with Christ crucified, and the desire to be united with Him in His sufferings, or rather the realization that that union is a fact. It is again the result of the union of his will with the divine will, so as to delight in Christ's way of redemption—the heart filled with the divine love that yearns for the redemption of souls eagerly follows Christ's way to that. In other words the contemplative is drawn increasingly into that work of reparation, which forms the subject of the previous chapter. Moreover intense suffering is caused at this stage by the increased desire for death—not the worldling's weariness of life here, but the longing for the unveiled vision of God. The closeness of union now granted to the soul only makes it realize its lack the more vehemently. Some of those who have experienced this speak of it as " the martyrdom of love ". " Dost thou not know, Beloved ", cried St. Marie de l'Incarnation in her anguish, " that it is an intolerable martyrdom to souls who love Thee to be separated from Thee, and thus separated to see Thee slighted by hapless subjects, who care nothing for Thee, nor for Thy love? . . . O God! what bliss to be set free from the body, which sets so great a barrier to love's perfect union! "[1] Yet she would have wholly agreed with the words which were received by St. Catherine of Siena in ecstasy—" Such souls, though they desire to come and be with me, they are contented to remain, if I desire them to remain, with their pain, for the greater praise and glory of my Name and the salvation of souls. So that in nothing are they in discord with my will, but they run their course with ecstatic desire, clothed in Christ crucified and . . . glorying in His shame and pains. Inasmuch as they appear to be suffering, they are rejoicing. . . . Were it possible for them to have virtue without toil they would not want it. They would rather delight in the cross with Christ, acquiring it with pain, than in any other way obtain Eternal Life."

[1] *Écrits*, I, p. 223.

Both St. Teresa and St. Francis Xavier echo the same desire in their cry for more sufferings. But it is no morbid pleasure in suffering for its own sake. And all great lovers of Christ have known something of this mystery of their union with Him. Dom Besse speaks of pain as the characteristic sign of the true contemplative.[1] It first found expression in St. Paul: " I am crucified with Christ, nevertheless I live, yet not I, but Christ liveth in me " (Gal. 2. 20); and again, " God forbid that I should glory save in the cross of our Lord Jesus Christ, by whom the world is crucified unto me and I unto the world " (Gal. 6. 14). The New Testament everywhere proclaims the need of suffering, of taking up the cross, but only in such passages as those just quoted, does the joy of it break out. " It must needs be ", said John Tauler, " that the friends of God have their bodies full of pain and their souls full of God "[2]; and again, " Suffering is the gift of God to His friends "[3]; or " Suffering reveals what is in a man as fire reveals a silver-plate penny to be only copper."[4] The lives of the saints are eloquent commentaries on such sayings.

(5) Far over-topping such suffering is the state of abiding peace and exultant joy. Peace not pain is the ruling note here, and no amount of pain can shake that peace or take away that joy. The soul that has reached this stage " is imprisoned and fettered and holden in a country of entire peace, for she is there in full sufficiency. There she shippeth and saileth and floateth and swimmeth, and is filled of divine peace without the moving of her inwardness and without the work of her outward doing. . . . Nothing may grieve her, nor nothing encumber. . . . For she hath naught of herself, she hath all given freely without any ' for-why ' in Him that is all."[5] No useful purpose would be achieved in trying to speak of such experiences at second-hand. Only they can do that effectively who speak out of the fire of that divine love, which makes them glow with its own radiance.

Moreover the mere description would sound little more than a repetition of much that has been already said. The spiritual life

[1] *Les Mystiques Bénédictines*, p. 203. (Paris, 1922.)

[2] *Predigten*, I, p. 259.

[3] Ibid., II, p. 212.

[4] Ibid., I, p. 298.

[5] *Mirror of Simple Souls*, Div. 9. Ch. 8.

has often been spoken of as a spiral way. As one climbs a spiral staircase, one sees at each turn the same view, only each time from a higher standpoint. So, as the pilgrim climbs the spiral to the heavenly Jerusalem, he seems to meet with similar experiences, but each time in an intenser form and in a wider context. That is why the beginner, if he possess humility, can safely read and profit by the writings of the great masters, when they speak of the heights, for their words help him to see and understand more clearly what he sees from his present level. That too is why the Bible ever remains the supreme guide and comfort for beginner and saint alike. The neophyte may at one period seem to find other spiritual books more helpful or at least more interesting, and he regards a little impatiently the familiar scriptures. By and by those others lose their attraction, and he turns back a little wearily to the Word of God, to find there the food his soul was seeking. The great classics of the prayer life will regain their value for him later, but never again will they usurp the Bible's rightful place. Finally that is why most of the ordinary pious books so soon become insipid. They have little or nothing to tell or suggest of the heights above, and cannot show their own limited view in any wider context.

So the spiral way begins with desire for God, the noughting of self, the virtues of humility and charity in particular set before us, with God's own desire for us and His presence in our hearts; and it ends with the same. So it comes to the " over-abundant love and the worthiness of God in Himself; in beholding of the which all nature quaketh, all clerks be fools, and all saints and angels be blind ".[1]

[1] *Cloud of Unknowing*, Ch. 13. (Ed. E. Underhill.)

T

BIBLIOGRAPHY

To compile a satisfactory bibliography is an almost hopeless task. So many bibliographies seem designed to show how many books the author has read rather than to guide the reader—jungles of books with no way through. The following is an attempt to make a selection of the most useful and (with some exceptions) of the most accessible books for the benefit of the ordinary reader rather than of the scholar. Such a selection must be somewhat arbitrary in its omissions and inclusions. The classification of the Mystics according to countries is more convenient than accurate. Those who wish to study Christian mysticism more widely are referred to the excellent bibliography at the end of Miss E. Underhill's *Mysticism*.

GENERAL

F. P. Harton, *The Elements of the Spiritual Life*.

* ..ges, *The Ordinary Ways of the Spiritual Life*.
  The above two books are very useful outlines of Ascetical Theology.

V. P. A. Rodriguez, S.J., *Christian Perfection*. A much used seventeenth-century manual, recently reprinted in two vols.

K. E. Kirk, *The Vision of God* (Bampton Lectures).

P. Pourrat, *La Spiritualité Chrétienne*, trans. *Christian Spirituality*. A valuable history of the Church's ascetical teaching.

A. L. Lilley, *Prayer in Christian Theology*.

J. Tissot (ed.), *The Interior Life*. Starts from the fundamental principle of life, the Glory of God, to be achieved by following the Will of God. Something of an astringent, but valuable.

St. Ignatius, *Spiritual Exercises* (ed. by Fr. Longridge, S.S.J.E.).

St. Francis de Sales, *Introduction to the Devout Life*. A well-known classic and easily obtainable.

M. Letourneau, *La méthode d'Oraison mentale du Seminaire de S. Sulpice* (Paris, 1903).

V. Lehodey, O.C.R., *The Ways of Mental Prayer*.

E. Leen, C.S.Sp., *Progress through Mental Prayer*.

Bede Frost, *The Art of Mental Prayer*.

L. Scupoli, *The Spiritual Combat*. Used and recommended by St. Francis de Sales.

L. Lallemant, S.J., *Spiritual Teaching*.

P. R. Garrigou-Lagrange, O.P., *The Three Ways of the Spiritual Life*.

C. Butler, O.S.B., *Ways of Christian Life*.

E. Herman, *Creative Prayer*. Suggestive and stimulating.

PART I

INTERCESSION

E. L. Strong, O.M.C., *Christ's Method of Prayer*. A useful booklet on the use of the Lord's Prayer in intercession.

F. W. Faber, Chapter on Intercession in *All for Jesus*.

S. Harton, *Intercession*.

D. Jenks, S.S.M., *Study in Intercession*.

L. Hodgson, Chapter on Intercession in *Concerning Prayer*.

PSYCHOLOGY

R. H. Thouless, *Introduction to the Psychology of Religion*.

—— *Social Psychology*

W. McDougall, *Social Psychology*.

A. Adler, *Social Interest—a Challenge to Mankind*.

C. G. Jung, *Modern Man in Search of a Soul*.

—— *Analytical Psychology*.

—— *The Integration of Personality*.

     The above two books for deeper study.

R. Allers, *Psychology and Character*.

J. Lindworsky, *The Psychology of Asceticism*.

J. A. Hadfield, *Psychology and Morals*.

W. Brown, *Psychological Methods of Healing*.

PART II

Re Chapter IX.—LOVE AND THE MYSTICS

St. Bernard of Clairvaux, *On the Love of God*.

St. Francis de Sales, *The Love of God*.

M. Muller, *St. Francis de Sales*. An invaluable exposition of the saint's teaching.

P. R. Garrigou-Lagrange, O.P., *L'Amour de Dieu et la Croix de Jesus*.

Aelred Graham, O.S.B., *The Love of God*.

J. Burnaby, *Amor Dei*.

J. Moffatt, *Love in the New Testament*.

V. Soloviev, *The Meaning of Love*.

A. GENERAL

E. Underhill, *Mysticism*. A useful introduction to the whole subject, rich in quotations from the Mystics, and containing an excellent bibliography.

W. R. Inge, *Christian Mysticism*. An interesting historical sketch, but seriously misunderstands its meaning and value.

A. Saudreau, *The Life of Union with God*. Also historical and much more understanding and useful than the former, but with some bad gaps.

—— *Degrees of the Spiritual Life* (2 vols.). On the development of the prayer life, of special value to directors.

F. von Hügel, *The Mystical Element in Religion* (2 vols.).

—— *Essay on the Life of Prayer*.

E. Gilson, *The Spirit of Mediaeval Philosophy*.

E. Herman, *The Meaning and Value of Mysticism*. As reflected in the life of Bl. Angela of Foligno.

L. de Besse, O.S.F.C., *The Science of Prayer*. Dealing with the early stages of contemplative prayer.

P. R. Garrigou-Lagrange, O.P., *La Perfection Chrétienne et La Contemplation*.

A. Gardeil, O.P., *La Structure de l'âme et l'expérience mystique*.

E. I. Watkin, *The Philosophy of Mysticism*.

A. Poulain, S.J., *The Graces of Interior Prayer*. Valuable for quotations and an attempt to describe the stages of the mystical life, but classifies too rigidly.

R. Plus, S.J., *The Ideal of Reparation*.

J. V. Bainvel, S.J., *Devotion to the Sacred Heart*.

A. Stolz, O.S.B., *The Doctrine of Spiritual Perfection*. An important book.

V. N. Lossky, *La Théologie Mystique de l'Église d'Orient*. A book of the greatest value.

A Treasury of Russian Spirituality (ed. by F. Fedotov).

B. SCHOOLS OF MYSTICS

I. The Early Centuries

Cassian, *Conferences*.

St. Macarius Magnus, *Fifty Homilies* (ed. by A. J. Mason).

—— *Christian Perfection*.

Palladius, *Lausiac History* (ed. by C. Butler).

H. Waddell, *The Desert Fathers*. Selections from their lives with a valuable introduction.

P. Pourrat, *Christian Spirituality* (Vol. I).

St. Augustine, *Confessions*.

N. Arseniev, *Mysticism and the Eastern Church*.

Dionysius the Areopagite, *Mystical Theology* (ed. by J. Rolt).

—— *The Divine Names*.

II. Benedictine

C. Butler, *Western Mysticism*. A valuable study of the teaching of St. Augustine, St. Gregory, and St. Bernard, forming an excellent introduction to those saints, and to the Benedictine spirit.

St. Bernard of Clairvaux, *Sermons on the Song of Songs* (trans. by Eales).

E. Gilson, *The Mystical Theology of St. Bernard*.

St. Mechthild of Magdeburg, *Offenbarungen*.

St. Gertrude, *Life and Revelations*.

L. Blosius, *The Book of Spiritual Instruction*.

A. Baker, *Holy Wisdom*.

—— *The Inner Life of Dame Gertrude More*.

J. Chapman, O.S.B., *Spiritual Letters*.

Bishop Hedley, O.S.B., Chapter on Contemplation in *Evolution and Faith* (Sheed & Ward).

III. English

W. Hilton, *Scale of Perfection*.

R. Rolle, *The Fire of Love, The Mending of Life, and The Form of Perfect Life*.

Julian of Norwich, *Revelations of Divine Love*.

Anon., *The Cloud of Unknowing*.

—— *The Epistle of Discretion*.

—— *The Ancren Riwle*.

IV. Italian (mainly Franciscan)

The Little Flowers of St. Francis.

The Mirror of Perfection.

Bl. Angela of Foligno, *Visions and Instructions.*

St. Bonaventura, *Works*, especially *Itinerarium ad Deum, Incendium Amoris, De
    Septem Gradibus.*

Jacopone da Todi, *Laude* (see *Life of J. da Todi*, by E. Underhill).

St. Catherine of Siena, *Dialogue.*

—— *Letters.*

St. Catherine of Genoa, *On Purgatory, Life and Doctrine.* See von Hügel, *Mystical
    Element*, Pt. II, for the best modern account of this mystic.

V. German and Flemish (mainly Dominican)

Hugh of Saint Victor, *The Soul's Betrothal Gift* (trans. by F Sherwood Taylor).

Anon., *De Adhaerendo Deo* (once attributed to Bl. Albert).

Meister Eckhart, *Works* (ed. by F. Pfeiffer, trans. by C. de B. Evans). To be
    read with caution, often violent, flippant and impatient, and sometimes
    heterodox, but exercising a profound influence.

J. Tauler, *The Inner Way.* A selection of his sermons translated by G. R. Hutton.

—— *Predigten* (3 vols., Frankfort, 1826). Very uncritical and containing sermons
    of Eckhart and others of his school.

H. Suso, *Life and Writings.*

—— *Book of the Eternal Wisdom.*

Bl. John Ruysbroeck, *Œuvres* (trad. par les Benedictins de S. Paul de Wisques.
    Vroment & Co.).

—— *The Adornment of the Spiritual Marriage* (trans. by E. Underhill).

—— *The Seven Steps of the Ladder of Spiritual Love* (trans. by F. Sherwood
    Taylor). One of the most forceful and inspiring of all the Christian
    mystics, but not always easy to understand.

Anon., *Theologia Germanica.*

Thomas à Kempis, *The Imitation of Christ.*

Gerlac Petersen, *Fiery Soliloquy of Divine Love.*

VI. Spanish

Bl. Ramon Lull, *The Book of the Lover and the Beloved.*

St. Peter of Alcantara, *The Golden Treatise of Mental Prayer* (Orchard Books).

St. Ignatius Loyola, *Testament* (trans. by E. M. Rix).

St. Teresa, *The Way of Perfection.*

—— *The Interior Castle.*

—— *Life.*

St. John of the Cross, *The Ascent of Mount Carmel* (ed. by E. Allison Peers).

—— *The Dark Night* (ed. by E. Allison Peers).

—— *A Spiritual Canticle* (ed. by E. Allison Peers).

—— *The Living Flame* (ed. by E. Allison Peers).

E. Allison Peers, *Studies in the Spanish Mystics.*

Gabriel of St. Mary Magdalen, O.D.C., *St. John of the Cross* (Thomas Baker).

VII. French

Anon., *The Mirror of Simple Souls.* The work of a late thirteenth-century mystic, containing passages of great beauty and spiritual depth, though sometimes obscure and over-bold in utterance. (Orchard Books.)

Benedict of Canfield, *Regula Perfectionis* (1610). An English Capuchin living in France, where his book had a great influence.

Cardinal de Bérulle, *Œuvres.* For his teaching, see C. Taveau, *Le Cardinal de Bérulle,* and H. Bremond, *L'Histoire Littéraire du Sentiment Religieux en France,* Vol. III.

St. Francis de Sales, *The Love of God.*

St. Jeanne Chantal—see A. Saudreau, *Prayer according to J. J. Chantal.*

J. B. Bossuet, *Les États d'Oraison.*

François Fénelon, *Les Maximes des Saints.*

St. Marie de l'Incarnation, *Écrits Spirituels* (especially vols. I and II).

J. P. de Caussade, S.J., *L'Abandon à la Providence Divine.* Translated in three vols.: *Abandonment to Divine Providence; Ordeals of Souls; The Workings of the Divine Will.*

C. Barbanson, *The Secret Paths of Divine Love* (Orchard Books).

J. N. Grou, S.J., *How to Pray.*

—— *Manual for Interior Souls.*

Bl. John Eudes, *La Vie et Le Royaume.*

St. Thérèse of Lisieux, *Autobiography.*

Lucie Christine, *Journal Spirituel* (ed. by A. Poulain).

N. Philipson, O.P., *Spiritual doctrine of Sister Elizabeth of the Blessed Trinity.*

INDEX